The Letter to My Younger Self

100 Inspiring People on the Moments That Shaped Their Lives

Devised and edited by
Jane Graham

First published in the UK by Blink Publishing
An imprint of Bonnier Books UK
4th Floor, Victoria House, Bloomsbury Square, London, WC1B 4DA
Owned by Bonnier Books
Sveavägen 56, Stockholm, Sweden

facebook.com/blinkpublishing
twitter.com/blinkpublishing

Hardback – 9781788702324
Paperback – 9781788702348
eBook – 9781788702331

A CIP catalogue of this book is available from the British Library.

Designed by Envy Design Ltd
Printed and bound in Great Britain by Clays Ltd, Elcograf S.p.A.

1 3 5 7 9 10 8 6 4 2

First published in Great Britain in 2019 by Blink Publishing.
Paperback edition first published in 2021.

Interviews on pages 79, 91, 100, 154, 172, and 307 by Adrian Lobb
Interview on page 34 by Eamonn Forde
Interview on page 84 by Andrew Burns
Interview on page 238 by Vicky Davidson
Interview on page 335 by Thomas Quinn
All other interviews conducted by Jane Graham.

Blink Publishing is an imprint of Bonnier Books UK
www.bonnierbooks.co.uk

Dedicated to all the people who have ever sold or bought *The Big Issue*

Contents

Chapter 3: Self-belief

Chapter 4: Inspiration

Chapter 5: Family

Chapter 6: Friendship

Chapter 7: Tenacity

Chapter 8: Courage

Chapter 9: Fate

Chapter 10: Ageing

Chapter 11: Hindsight

Chapter 12: Fulfilment

Chapter 13: Love

Bonus Material

Foreword

Back in 2007, I had a brainwave. I'd conducted a lot of interviews as a journalist, and had long been thinking about how I could encourage subjects to talk about their lives in a revealing and honest way. It struck me that the one person we all try not to lie to, the one person who has known us at our worst and best, is ourself. I wondered how very successful people felt, looking back on how they were before the big dream came true; did they think that teenager would be bursting with pride at their subsequent achievements, or were there things they wished they didn't have to tell such a hopeful innocent?

I first pitched the Letter to my Younger Self column 14 years ago, and it originally ran as a single column in the arts section of *The Big Issue*'s Scottish edition. The editor and I quickly realised we'd found a key to unlock even the most guarded of big names. The feature doubled in length, then doubled again, to fill two pages at the front of the UK-wide edition of *The Big Issue*, where it still runs every week.

In the intervening years I have interviewed over 600 people and learned a lot about human nature and the ways we respond to fame, wealth and power. Many subjects have told me that our conversation pulled up long-buried memories, while others said that its intimate focus on home truths and personal values made it feel like therapy. A lot of tears have been shed.

What has been most telling is how fundamentally those formative teenage years shape the way we face our future and weigh up our past. Some interviewees, like Sir Paul McCartney and Archbishop Desmond Tutu, felt warmly towards their uninhibited, excited younger selves, unaware of the curveball life was about to throw at them. Some highly accomplished individuals, such as Sir Ranulph Fiennes and Eddie Izzard, felt their 16-year-old selves still dwelt deep inside them, occasionally flooding them with feelings of melancholy or inadequacy.

John Cleese, Imelda Staunton and Dominic West all struck me for their lack of interest in public glory, caring more about how their family will remember them. Some subjects just turned out to be extraordinarily impressive people – who could fail to fall in love with the funny, gutsy, romantic Olivia Colman, the uniquely spirited and mischievous Werner Herzog or the big-hearted, irrepressible will.i.am (whose words so inspired Mark Carney, the Governor of the Bank of England, that he quoted them in a keynote speech in 2018 – surely the first time will.i.am, *The Big Issue* and a major financial leader have appeared together in a landmark address!)

Some of the stories I've heard have knocked my socks off, from Miriam Margolyes' shocking experience coming out to her mother, to Sir Mo Farah's emotional reunion with his twin brother Hassan, 12 years after they were separated by cruel circumstance in Djibouti. Almost everyone who had lost a parent missed them more than they had anticipated. And Wilko Johnson's description of his marriage remains one of the most affecting evocations of passion and devotion I've ever heard.

Since the first publication of this book in 2019, I've conducted many more fascinating interviews, a handful of which have been added to this paperback edition. So now you can also read about the teenage Jarvis Cocker's meticulous plans for stardom (involving duffel coats, C&A trousers and 'silly socks'); discover what Dolly Parton has always wanted to say to Elvis; and imagine my personal hero Lin-Manuel Miranda leaping to his feet in a busy London restaurant to rap Alexander Hamilton to me (I'm pretty sure it really happened, though it feels like a dream now).

I've often discussed with my friend and fellow journalist Adrian Lobb, who conducted some of these interviews, what a privilege it is to speak to remarkable people like the ones in this collection. Between them they've led nations, won Olympic golds, conquered the highest mountains in the world and literally been to the moon and back. In the end, almost all of them agree that, in the words of F. Scott Fitzgerald, love is 'the beginning and end of everything'. That's why the original edition of this book finished with Wilco Johnson's wise and poignant words about that most crucial human base-note. I hope those words leave as deep an impression on you as they have on me.

Jane Graham
Books Editor, *The Big Issue*
June 2021

Lord John Bird

Co-founder of *The Big Issue*

The advice I would give my younger self is 'Don't get caught.' There I was, aged 16, in an institution – I hated all institutions and the forced company with boys. I hated boys; I hated their lives, their smells, their preoccupations. I loved girls so much that I grieved, not because I'd done wrong, but because I'd put myself out of the way of girls.

I also didn't like boys because they were bullies and cowardly and they would gang up on one another. Or they would hit the smaller boys. There was never any equality between them. I got beaten up at times because I'd stand up against bullying. But eventually I got my own back by becoming stronger or by befriending even bigger boys. Some spectacular revenge attacks were orchestrated by me and another boy who also rejected bullying.

At 16, I was in a reformatory for three to five years for receiving money under false pretences. I had also run away just before my sixteenth birthday and, with another boy, had stolen an Austin-Healey Sprite and smashed it up while travelling at 87 miles per hour. The police said it had been travelling at 102 miles per hour and I believed them, until I met a car enthusiast who said that at 87 miles per hour, the steering wheel shakes uncontrollably and that I should pursue the police for compensation for their exaggeration.

I was sent to Ashford Boys' Prison and it was there, over a few months, that my life changed. The prison officer understood that my reading skills were deficient and gave me a book. He asked me to underline all the words I didn't understand with a pencil; he was astonished by which words I knew and equally astonished by the silly little words, the ones which gave the sentence its meaning, that I didn't know.

I came back to the reformatory with a reading ability that had leaped in a matter of weeks, and all because I'd had the bravery to admit I could not understand what I was reading. I was most fortunate in being brought before Baroness Wootton who'd been giving me sentences since I was 10 for crimes like shoplifting, housebreaking, truancy and stealing bikes. I came back reading ferociously, and I've been reading, rather than pretending to read, ever since. But at 16 I was anticipating at least a few years more of incarceration and the company of boys and their slimy, small-minded ways. What could I do?

I decided to become a painter. Not a painter and decorator – I would draw and paint and keep myself away from the knobheads who wanted to talk about girls as pieces of flesh, fast cars, football and all that macho shit. And I would fight and stand up for the rights of the weak against this murderous little society of bullies. Needless to say, I received more kickings than I gave out, but being a knight in shining armour seemed something worth striving for. I was also inspired by being a devout Catholic – Jesus was everywhere in my life. I was going to be a painter priest like Piero della Francesca, one of the greatest painters who ever lifted a brush.

My advice to the younger John would be not only to not get caught, but to not do wrong in the first place, so he'd have no reason to fear the long arm of the law. Or those horrible, smelly, fart-drenched boys' institutions, where boys wanted to have boasting or wanking competitions.

I'd also tell my younger self to try not to be eaten up by hatred for his fellow man. Don't do wrong and live to regret it. Try and stop fighting people for the sake of it. And keep those brushes moving – you can only become the genius you think you are through application.

The other advice I'd have loved to drop into the ear of my younger self would be that my mother wasn't going to make it long in life. She died when I was in my early twenties and that was the greatest of reversals possibly in the whole of my life. Even now, when people complain to me about how they are burdened with their mums and dads, I recoil. I often say that I wish I still had parents to tell me what a muck-up I've made in my life, or to give me advice that I think is dead wrong.

My disdain for men lifted when I had boys myself. I would have loved to say to my younger self that there's depth in all of us, but you sometimes have to go in deep, even among boys. I would also tell my younger self that it would be women who'd make John Bird into something bigger than the sum total of his mistakes: my three wives who civilised me and my mothers-in-law who treated me evenhandedly. And possibly Anita Roddick, who created the peppermint foot lotion revolution that helped me and her husband Gordon to make *The Big Issue* a reality.

To sum up, I'd tell my younger self, 'You're going places in the company of many. For no man or woman is truly an island.' At the same time, I'd love to say to myself, 'Stop trying to be a guide and an atlas to others.' Only now do I realise that people have to truly embrace their own skills and abilities and not keep waiting for the next 'Mother Teresa of Fulham Broadway' to lead them out of the swamp.

CHAPTER 1:

Ambition

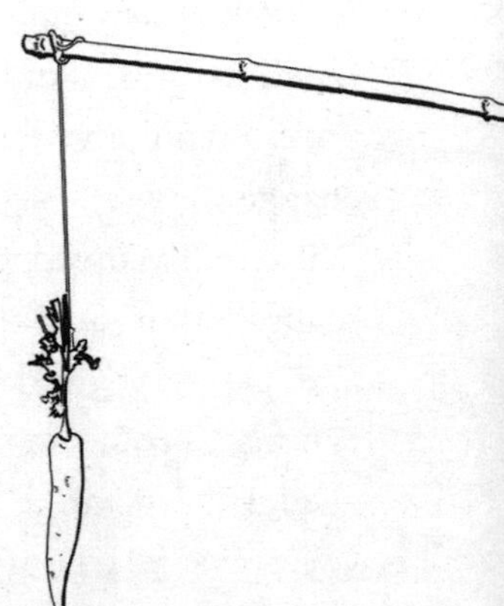

Billie Jean King

Tennis Player

5 February 2018

I always wanted to change the world. I had an epiphany when I was 12, when I noticed that everyone in my sport wore white shoes, white clothes and played with white balls – and that everybody who played was white. I asked myself: 'Where is everyone else?' So I made my promise that day, that I would fight for the rest of my life for equality for everyone. And I knew I could have an opportunity because of tennis. I didn't understand the idea of having a platform, but I knew I would have to be number one if I was going to really change things.

I actually loved piano first, but I wasn't that good and realised that quickly. But God gave my younger brother and me very good hand–eye coordination, and we could run fast. From the second time I picked up a tennis racket, aged 11, I wanted to be the best in the world. So, by 16, I was five years into my mission and was starting to play well in adult tournaments. Wimbledon seemed really far away from Southern California, but after I lost in three sets to Anne Jones, Harold Guiver offered help to get there. I turned it down. I wasn't ready. A year later, at 17, I felt I'd earned it and went back to him. There was no money in tennis then. You played because you loved it. We were amateurs on $14 a day. Professional tennis started in 1968, but we had to fight for equal pay, which is why we created the WTA Tour.

Because my parents had lived through the Great Depression and my dad fought in the Second World War, they taught us to be risk-averse. 'If you don't have it, don't spend it.' My mother sat me down when I was ten and showed me their budget. It was one of the greatest things she ever did, because I had no idea that every time I flipped the light switch it was money, or that every trip in the car cost petrol money. My dad was a firefighter so money was always tight, but I learned how to manage my finances from my parents and I'm so thankful.

I would have loved to march with Martin Luther King Jr, but I was hitting tennis balls all the time. When he gave the 'I Have a Dream' speech in 1963, I was 19 and it was huge. Then JFK was assassinated on my twentieth birthday, then King was assassinated, and then Robert Kennedy. All those people were killed in the '60s and I loved every one of them. I would have done more if I had the chance – or if I had the courage. I became politicised because I noticed things. When we were trying to change tennis, I got really into it. I tried to help Title IX, which was a huge piece of equality legislation in the US, get passed. By the late 1960s I was figuring things out and had the opportunity to help, but

I was still hitting tennis balls. Hopefully each hit of the tennis ball helped amplify my voice a little, but I felt guilty. I wanted to go beyond that. I wanted to change things.

I don't think about tennis much now, but my younger self would have been most proud of winning Wimbledon and being number one in the world more than once. I actually loved doubles more than singles because I grew up playing team sports. My younger brother played professional baseball for the San Francisco Giants. We loved pressure and thrived on it. I always say pressure is a privilege and champions adjust. And I mean champions in life, not solely athletes.

Being a leader can be very lonely. There was real solidarity among the nine of us who set up the WTA Tour, but we were ostracised by our fellow players. That was a rough time. It was not fun. Every day I imagined what would happen if I had lost against Bobby Riggs.[1] He'd followed me around for two years and I always turned him down, but as soon as Margaret Court played him and lost, I knew what I had to do. I knew it would be huge. I knew it would get crazy. It didn't matter where you went, this game was the talk of the town. And I knew how important it was that I win.

I didn't feel comfortable in my own skin until I was 51. It took me forever. So I would tell my younger self, 'You're going to go through a tough time with your sexuality (she would have said, "Huh? What's that?") but everything is going to turn out all right.' My mother used to say: 'To thine own self be true,' but being true to myself was tough. My mother was very homophobic, so that was an interesting time, figuring out how that was going to work. My dad came around faster. My mother had more

1 In the famous Battle of the Sexes in 1973.

trouble and it took time. I was trying to figure out who I was and see different people, but I am not a one-night-stand kind of kid. Things came good when I had a solid relationship. Ilana and I have been together 30 years, and when we got together I finally felt settled.

I am a little confusing – I prefer men's bodies. If we're at a party, I look at men's bodies but at women's faces. It's more about emotion and connection. Right now, I'm a lesbian. I'm queer. The kids say queer now. That used to be the worst thing you can say, but I'm always asking the young ones, and if they say queer, that's all I need to know. It's important to keep up. The young ones are setting the pace. I didn't have as much time as I would have liked to help the LGBTQ community when I was hitting tennis balls. I still hadn't fully figured out who I was, so I was pretty late to the party.

My mom and dad have passed away, but I talk to them every day. I don't know if they're hearing me, but I talk to them. I'll say, 'What do you think about this?' And I usually know what my parents would say. They were very strict and they would always tell me to be honest, have integrity and do the right thing. 'You've got to live with yourself first and have peace of mind.' Oh my god, my parents were like gold.

My life has turned out better than I could have imagined. If somebody had sat me down and said I would be the best in the world for years, have two movies made about me – with Holly Hunter and now Emma Stone playing me – and have a song written about me, actually more than one, do you think I would have believed them? No way.

Every generation has to fight for equality. You have never won. It's shocking that Trump is president and that we are going backwards. That's the way the pendulum goes and it's our fault. But the millennials and kids today are the most positive generations ever about inclusion and they can make it happen, so that is my hope. They are going to nail it. They are going to make such progress. I wish I was that age again, because I would be rockin'! They have a chance to really make this world a better place. Better than we ever dreamed...

Meera Syal

Comedian and Actress

24 September 2012

My world when I was 16 was small and sleepy. I lived in a small town, had a close family and went to a small all-girls grammar school. My main worry was how I'd get on with my O-Levels and whether I'd be picked for the netball team. I went to a good school which encouraged girls to get a good education and make the best of themselves. Boys didn't figure too much, which was great for me – with them out of the equation, I could spend time working out who I was before things got more complicated.

I was quite overweight and shy and I lived in my own head. No boy ever looked at me or ever asked me out, and I didn't expect them to. I wouldn't have asked me out. Boys would, if they talked to me at all, just engage in banter or complain about their girlfriends. I was very aware that I was surrounded by hormones and some of my friends were getting off with each other, but I think I put boy worries away in a box somewhere and just hoped to God that one day someone would see beyond everything else and like me for who I was.

I was relatively happy, but there was real frustration inside me too. I had my own issues. I was only one of three Indian girls at my school. I had ambitions about writing and acting, but I kept them to myself because girls like me didn't do things like that. I was waging an inner clash with myself, between all these artistic dreams I had and the other side of me, which was practical and sensible. That used to tear me up quite a bit actually. I knew there was something inside me that desperately wanted to escape this small world, but I didn't know how to do it. So there was a fear of unfulfilment, rather than being angry at the world.

If I met the teenage Meera now, going on first impressions I'd just see someone rotund and frumpy and might not bother getting to know her any better. But if I got her to open up, I think I'd like her. There's humour and imagination inside her, waiting to get out. I'd tell her not to be so hard on herself – she has so much time. I'd say, 'It won't all happen quickly, but it's not meant to. You have lots of things to get through. But have some faith in yourself.' I'd tell her the idea that having a boyfriend was the thing that made you successful and accepted – what a weird concept that is to me now. The one thing that will attract anyone will be if you like yourself and are happy in your own company. And I'd break it to her gently that she won't marry one of the Osmonds. I actually once thought that really could happen.

The fork in the road for me was the one-woman show I did in my final year at Manchester University. It was a dark comedy monologue about an Indian girl who runs away from home to be an actress. I played about 12 characters, male and female. It was everything I felt, poured into 50 minutes. Ironically, I wasn't even that nervous doing it, because I thought I had nothing to lose. It was my swansong for all the creative dreams I'd ever had, because by then I'd accepted they were never going to happen. I was getting those dreams out of my system before I settled down. No one knew me – so what if I made a fool of myself? And actually, it was that foolhardiness that changed everything. When I did it, and felt the audience's reaction, I realised the magic of theatre. The show picked up a lot of attention and I ended up taking it to Edinburgh where it won a few awards, and then I was spotted by someone at the Royal Court and offered an acting job. I could have carried on with life in academia or I could jump. And I jumped.

I'd reassure my younger self that she will meet kindred spirits, but not until her early thirties. That's when I hooked up with the *Goodness Gracious Me* team. It wasn't easy getting that show on, but the process was so magical. All the secrets we'd each had in our head growing up as the second generation, all the stuff that made us laugh but didn't make anyone around us laugh – suddenly, oh my God, I wasn't the only one. We all just got it, without having to explain it. We approached the show with the same foolhardiness I had approached mine with – we didn't know if anyone else would get it, but we knew we had to do it with truth. But it made a huge impact and won awards and did a big live tour – the nearest I'll ever get to rock'n'roll.

I'd tell my younger self that social networking and forming industry relationships is far more important than she thinks. I used to believe the work would speak for itself. I'd come away from a job having made friends with the make-up girl, and not the director. But the world does work along tribal lines; people tend to use and re-employ their own tribe. I'm still not really in a tribe, and it's probably too late now. Perhaps I should have been savvier when I was younger about cultivating connections, though I'd have done it through gritted teeth. And it wouldn't have come naturally – you can't just say, 'Give me a bloody job.' I'd have become like Alan Partridge, telling the editor to smell my cheese. I still don't know what I'll do after my next job, but I've accepted my career's always going to be like that. I'm difficult to cast. That occasionally disappoints me, after the body of work I've done.

The young me just wouldn't be able to believe that my life would turn out the way it has. Only a tiny part of her would think, 'Oh my God, really? Can I make a living doing what I'd dream of doing?' You become afraid of hoping, but at the same time you have to have a bit of optimism in you in this business.

If I told my 16-year-old self that one day Donny Osmond would be a guest on a show in which I'd play an 85-year-old woman – that would be the point at which the younger me would have fainted. That man on the poster on your wall – you're going to be taking the piss out of him on a sofa, while dressed as an 85-year-old Indian woman. How brilliant.

Alice Cooper

Musician

24 October 2011

At 16, I spent all of my time either training or rehearsing. I was a competitive distance runner in school, and I was also in a little band called The Spiders – the original band that formed Alice Cooper. So I spent all of my time either training or rehearsing. I just didn't have much time for homework. The guys in the bands always had girlfriends who would do our homework for us. Did you ever see the movie *Ferris Bueller's Day Off*? I was Ferris Bueller, the class clown, the class conman.

I know I'd like that kid, the 16-year-old me, if I met him now. He was Mr Personality. I would tell him, 'Always follow your instincts, they're really good.' I had some good ideas when I was a kid, and I followed them through. I looked around and thought, 'No one wants to be the villain of rock.' So I created Alice to be the villain. I didn't want to be like everyone else; I wanted to be totally different. I think that, and the appreciation of really good rock music, and knowing how to play it, will take you a long, long way. We were so different that other bands said we didn't have a chance. Most of them have gone now and I'm still here, 27 albums and 40 world tours later.

My dad was a very strong pastor, but he also loved music – Sinatra and then early rock'n'roll. He never thought it was the devil's music – he said it was just music, why were people trying to turn it into a religious problem? He liked what we were doing and understood our sense of humour, that I was playing Captain Hook. And we never yelled at each other, we were always the best of friends. But what he couldn't condone was the lifestyle – drinking every day, living the rock star life, that wasn't the life he wanted me to live.

I think the teenage me would be surprised at the length of my career. I remember when the original band was all together – I was about 22 and we'd just released 'School's Out' – and someone walked into the room and said, 'Your record just went to number one.' We all looked at each other and started laughing. It was so absurd – that a band that should never even have stayed together could have a number one record. We could not believe it – this little high school band that everybody hated was at number one.

Nevertheless, I was totally convinced I was going to be a rock star. I had no doubts whatsoever. We weren't going to stop until we were. We were very determined. When you're a long-distance runner you never stop. You have this mindset: this race is not over until I've won or crossed the finish line. I also think that had something to do with the way we viewed our music careers. Mick Jagger once said he hoped he wouldn't still be singing 'Satisfaction' when he was 30 – well, he's 67 and still singing it. I took it all in my stride. If someone asks me to host the Grammys, it doesn't faze me at all. I was born to do this. Onstage is where I'm most comfortable.

If I could go back, I'd advise that kid to avoid drinking. I didn't start until I was about 21 and I didn't realise then that I was going to be an alcoholic. For most of my career I was a functioning alcoholic, though I was never a monster. I was a happy drunk, not a destructive, mean, cruel, stupid one. I was just as I am now, except for the fact that alcohol was killing me internally. My wife and I have been married for 35 years. The first five years of it probably involved my heaviest drinking, but it never affected our relationship. When it started to kill me – that's when we went to the hospital. So that was bad, but it's also true that beating alcohol was a very important part of my life. Going through that and winning still teaches me. And now that it's not in my life, there isn't much else to worry about.

I've done about 18 films now. It was a simple move for me to go into acting; I felt I already had so much experience doing what was like a Broadway show, when Alice Cooper went onstage. All I had to learn on film was technique – I had to make smaller moves. But in terms of performing a character, I'd been playing someone other than myself for years already. Alice is a horrible, arrogant bad guy. It's fun to play him – it's almost like therapy, he's so unlike me. The real me is a husband who's been happily married and totally faithful for 35 years. I go to church with my kids and hang out with them. We go to concerts together – say, Snoop Dogg or Marilyn Manson – and we talk about it afterwards. My daughter might say, 'Do they really have to swear that much?' and I say, 'Well no, I don't think you have to do that to be an entertainer.'

I'm glad my dad was alive to see me come back to being a Christian. I think that was a big moment for him. He saw me turn into the prodigal son, who went away and came back. After my alcoholism, my wife and I said we had to really think about what was important and we had to get back to church. Being a rock star is just a profession – it's not more important than your soul, what you believe in. And you have to be accountable to the Lord. After my alcoholism I really realised that being a rock star is just a profession. It's not more important that your soul. But I think that understanding was always in my DNA. There was never anything blasphemous in my show – if anything, I made fun of Satan. And I don't think the Lord minded me making fun of Satan.

Jon Ronson

Author

6 June 2011

I was miserable at 16, living in the suburbs of Cardiff. I was going through a difficult phase. I was unremarkable, I wasn't very popular, I'd put on quite a lot of weight. I didn't enjoy much about school – I did alright, but nothing great. It was probably the worst period for me. I just wandered around the streets of Cardiff, really. I had the odd friend, I suppose. But I met a kid I used to know at school who hadn't done well in his life, and he said he blamed that on being so popular at school. It took him years to get over being the King of Cardiff High. It would be lovely to go back and tell the young me that; all the misery – it's all good.

There was a cinema in Cardiff called Chapter, which showed indie films. I remember going to a double bill of *Zelig* and *The King of Comedy* there. Last week I met Debbie Harry and Chris Stein from Blondie, and I told them that so many of the things that gave me hope when I was a teenager were from

New York – Blondie, Lou Reed, Woody Allen, Martin Scorsese. And around the same time I discovered Kurt Vonnegut, as well as *Private Eye*, *Time Out* and *The Guardian*.

My mum forced me to volunteer at the local radio station. At first it was really boring community stuff, helping people who were having problems with the council. But there were a couple of maverick DJs there who'd get me on the air and I began to get little slots on their shows. So they must have seen something in me, I suppose.

I went up to the Edinburgh Festival on my own when I was about 16. I hung around with comedians like Mark Thomas and Jo Brand, like a sad groupie. I remember Mark giving me a real telling off, saying, 'Look at you, you're just sitting around watching. When are you going to do something yourself?' At the time I just thought he was insulting me. But he was probably giving me extremely good advice, though I didn't take it for at least another five years. But that experience was really important to me, because I was out of miserable Cardiff and actually sucking in life.

The 16-year-old me wouldn't have chosen writing as a career; he'd have assumed that it would be lonely and boring. All he wanted to do was what he did do for the next five years – totally underachieve. I went to London when I was 18 and lived in a squat. I was hedonistic and washed Cardiff right out of myself. My life became amazing from the second my mum dropped me off: I lost the weight, started going out with girls, I became confident, I was popular. My dream came true.

If I met that teenager now, I don't think I'd like him. He was kind of unlikeable, ungainly and awkward. I met up with Tim Booth from the band James recently (we'd actually met back when I was a teenager), and he said, 'You were very uncomfortable in your own skin back then.' That's why, when anyone did take me under their wing, it really was very philanthropic – I wasn't a delight.

But the young Jon would be amazed by all the things I've done. He was a bit of a shallow idiot, so the fact that George Clooney made a film out of one of my books would bowl him over. And if he knew he'd meet Debbie Harry one day – that would have blown his head off. I was on *The Daily Show* last week, and I thought, 'If the daydreaming 16-year-old Jon could see me now...' It would be great to go back and tell him that not fitting in, being picked on, being shoved to the side to observe, to look at the world in a different way – that it will all help when he comes to make a career.

When I first became a father, they passed me the baby and I said, 'What do I do now?' By the time Joel was three or four, I'd got better at it, though my wife often has to be the authoritarian – I'm not good at that part. My son's an interesting, unusual kid. I remember proudly telling someone that when he was younger he was really good at sarcasm, and they looked at me like, 'That's not necessarily great.'

There was no one in the world that I loved more than Clare Grogan when I was 16. I'd love to tell the young Jon that one day he'll get to meet her, and she'll be really nice to him and even give him a peck on the cheek, as it'll be quite obvious that for 20 years, he loved no one more than her.

Melanie C

Musician

19 September 2011

At 16, I was getting ready to leave school, leave the North and go down South, starting the journey to follow my dreams. I was going to performing arts school in London. When I think of my daughter doing that at 16 it freaks me out, but although I was quite daunted to be leaving my friends and family, I was so excited to go onto the next chapter in my life.

I think I found those teenage years tricky, but they are, aren't they? I did a bit of soul-searching. I still have the same close group of friends today as I had then, and we had great times over the years – discovering everything together, getting drunk for the first time together, gossiping about boys. But we all shared a passion – we all loved the arts. We were in plays and dance shows together. I had a couple of boyfriends through school, a long-term boyfriend and a lot of break-ups and heartbreak, and hopefully I learned some lessons pretty early.

I look back and think, 'I must have been so annoying.' I was so ambitious. I really wanted to be a pop star, and I told everyone about it. I was going to London to follow my dream. I don't think there were many people around where I grew up who did that. Most of my friends went on to sixth form and then uni, but I was very driven. I loved Annie Lennox – she's a great vocalist – but it was Madonna who made me want to be a pop star. She was my first experience of a pop star who did a big show, a huge production with dancers. I saw her and thought, 'That's what I want to do.' Her first album was in 1984 when I was about ten, and she was very prevalent all through my teenage years.

I think I almost had a dual personality. At school I could be quiet – I have a shy side, which came out in lessons, and with boys, too. But when it came to drama or the local dance school, that's when I felt happiest and the extrovert in me came out. I'm still nervous when I meet famous people, and I do blush. I remember when the Spice Girls met Stevie Wonder, the ultimate person we could ever meet. My mum had been a huge Stevie fan. We did a gig with him in Italy, and there's a photo with me and Emma, mouths wide open. We were literally speechless.

I feel quite an affection for my younger self. When you're young, there's a great naivety and innocence – I had no doubt that I would do fantastic things and meet fantastic people. I was willing to work hard, but there was no doubt in my mind. And when the Spice Girls got together, though we had very different personalities, we were all absolutely sure that we were going to succeed. Sometimes thinking about what we were like makes me cringe a bit – but hopefully it was quite charming, that self-belief.

Maybe that's one of the qualities it takes to realise your dreams, to be 100 per cent sure it's going to happen. It's something to hang on to, because it gets knocked out of you so quickly. When I auditioned I was 19 and when we released our first single I was 22, and I still felt that. And it did all happen – the first single, the first album, the number ones. And that success went on and on. It wasn't until we broke up that the next phase of our lives started and I realised that, actually, you're not always going to get to number one.

I feel a bit regretful now that I wasn't always in the moment when things were good. Once I went solo I had to be more realistic about the world – and when you've been part of something so extraordinary, that's difficult to come to terms with. All the media interest meant that I was surrounded by other people's opinions of me, and that started to affect me. My way of dealing with it was about controlling the way I ate and exercised. It got to the point where my body couldn't do that anymore and I lost control and felt like I was falling apart. It took me quite a long time to recover.

All my life, I hoped I'd be a mum. But I was single for quite a long time and it never bothered me – I just hoped it was in the future. Then, about four years ago, I felt the old body clock ticking. I'd talked to my boyfriend about it, but it suddenly changed from me saying I'd like to have children one day, to 'I want a baby now'. The day I gave birth to my little girl, as traumatic as it was – that was my ultimate day. That was the best one of my life.

Sir Mo Farah

Athlete

5 December 2016

I wasn't focused when I was 16. I was just chilling out, going to school and seeing my friends. I wasn't taking running seriously. It's hard as a teenager – there are a lot of distractions. I'm not complaining, but I think if I'd listened to my coach more then maybe I could have been more successful. I could have won more medals.

My twin brother Hassan was born first, and he used to always beat me up. He was chatty, much more popular than me, and a lot smarter than me. All the exams that I failed, he passed first time. We had to leave him behind when we moved to England, due to his illness. I was just eight, and we were separated for 12 years. I remember being in London, thinking, 'Tomorrow he'll come', and the same the next day and the next day. I was so excited at the thought that we were going to be a family again, but in the back of my head was a voice saying, 'It might never happen.' I tried to block that thought out, that doubt in my mind, but the years went on and he never came. When we finally met again, in Somalia, it was like nothing had ever changed. It was like looking at myself, looking at him… He was even skinnier than me – not possible! I said, 'I run and you don't, so how can you be skinnier than me?'

I was excited to move to London – I thought it was beautiful. I remember walking into the airport, and the doors opened, and there were escalators – it was fascinating to me. It was a new world, like when I went to Disneyland. And it was where my family was, so it was home. Somalia was different – we never had our father. That's the main reason we came to London – for our family to be as one.

It was difficult to adapt to London at first, but when you're eight, you somehow find a way. You make friends. I was always accepted, I think because I never saw myself as different to anyone else. I had white friends and black friends – I was easy going. I just chose not to hear the occasional comment. I was good at running, so the kids liked me for that. If I hadn't been into running I wouldn't have made friends, met so many people or learned the language as quickly as I did.

My PE teacher took me to the local running club, and I started going twice a week. I ran for Middlesex, then for England. I didn't even know about the Olympics then. Then, once I'd run for England I asked, 'What's the next step?' And they said, 'Great Britain.' So I said, 'Right, I want to run for Great Britain.' Then I said, 'Okay, I've done well, I've won for Great Britain – what's the next step?' 'European.' I started to do my research and learned about Seb Coe, Steve Ovett, Crammy… I watched the Sydney Olympics when I was about

18, Haile Gebrselassie versus Paul Tergat. And that's when I told myself, 'I want to become the Olympic Champion.'

I was always a happy kid, up for laughs and joking around. And I always had that cheeky smile. If I was causing trouble, I could get away with it because of that. I used it on my mum quite a lot. I was a lot closer to my mum than my dad – I'm a mummy's boy, really. When I got to know people I was quite a lad, but with strangers or on camera, I was very shy. I hadn't seen much, you know? But now I've travelled the world, I've met people and learned how to talk to them. I'm not shy now, not anymore.

When I went back to Somalia after 12 years, I ran in the street through the village. And people were like, 'Oh my God, there's a crazy man running!' because no one runs there. If you see someone running, it means someone stole something or someone's running from trouble. When I go back now I get mobbed and all the old ladies come out and say, 'I used to know you when you were a little boy.' And almost everyone I meet seems to be my cousin. It's like, 'Hey cousin, hey cousin,' and I'm like, 'Really? How many cousins do I have?'

I don't have a clue where my determination comes from – maybe you're just born with it. I look at my twin girls, and they're so different – one is so determined and the other is very laid-back. You can't give it to kids, they're born with it. Everyone who's done well at their sport has something special. For me, I know I just really hate losing and I'll work as hard as I can to avoid it. After every race I lose, I go home and analyse it. What did I do wrong? You think of everything. Did I pace myself? Did I work hard enough?

Having faith has kept me on the right path. If I hadn't had that, it would have been different. Feeling what will be will be – that kind of stuff. Some things are out of your control. I was brought up with that and I want to give it to my kids, let them do what they need to do. And be that good person that they can be.

I went training with the Kenyans so I could learn from them, and that's when I realised I could be the best in the world. I thought, 'I could beat these guys.' They didn't know what they were dealing with, did they? They wouldn't have let me in if they had.

Losing in Beijing 2008 is one of the best things that ever happened to me. In our religion, we believe everything bad that happens is probably a good thing. It was like having a bucket of cold water thrown in my face. It was a voice saying, 'Do something.' There was a lot of doubt and I was in tears for a couple of weeks. It could have gone two ways: one would have been for me to say, 'I'm done. I can't do this anymore.' The other was for me to say, 'I'm not going to let this happen again. How can I correct this?' And that's what I did.

I wish I could go back and run the 5,000m in London 2012 again. I'd rewind the whole race and enjoy each step. And I'd pause it when I was going round the side, and just listen to the crowd. It was just incredible. If it wasn't for the crowd, I don't think it would have happened. 100 per cent. That crowd lifts you, gives you that little extra bit of energy, that final push. Do you ever watch football? The last ten minutes of a home match? You can see what happens when the crowd get behind the team. That's what happened to me in London.

Sir Tom Jones

Musician

12 October 2015

I became a man very quickly when I was 16. When my 15-year-old girlfriend Melinda got pregnant, all my aunties and uncles came to my house and had a big discussion about what should be done, while Linda and I sat in the corner, all wrapped up in each other. And my mother noticed us, and said, 'Look, we're all planning their lives, but they're oblivious to what we're saying. You can see these two kids are in love and they'll get married when they're old enough anyway, so what's the point in standing in their way?' So as soon as Linda turned 16, we got married. We moved in to the back room of my mother-in-law's house and everyone chipped in to help. And I had a job, so we didn't really want for anything. It was a happy time – there was nothing negative about it.

I realised years later, looking back on those days, that being a young husband and father didn't hold me back – it just made me more determined to be successful for my wife and son. The only problem was that I was doing shifts in a paper mill, and sometimes that stopped me getting out to sing in pubs and clubs as often as I wanted. But I knew I was only biding my time – I had tremendous drive.

If I met the 16-year-old Tom Woodward, I'd like him very much, because my values haven't changed. Even my taste in music hasn't changed. 'Great Balls of Fire' excites me as much now as ever. 'Rock Around the Clock' – that influence fed me so much, got my blood pumping. Then I heard Elvis Presley and I thought, 'My God, I can sing like that!' We have exactly the same range.

Growing up in Wales, in a large working-class family, was so wonderful. That kind of grounding gives you a sense of wanting to be successful, and you learn the values of working-class life, which I think is an asset. I know people who were born with a silver spoon in their mouth, and they can *see* working-class people, they can go into pubs and mingle with them, but they'll never *be* one of them. I was one of them, and I still am.

I was always ready for success. Sometimes I drive around the streets in Pontypridd now and I think, 'My goodness, I must have had big balls in those days, to think I was going to do it all.' I remember singing in the local pub and they said, 'You're a great singer, Tom,' and I said, 'Yeah, I'll meet Elvis one day.' And they said, 'Yeah yeah yeah.'

The one thing that would really impress the teenage me, the thing I never even dreamt of, was being knighted. Hit records, I was up for that. Hit TV series, I was up for that. Making it in America, I was up for that. But being knighted… I've always been a royalist, and I was knighted by one of the greatest monarchs ever known, so that's a big deal to me.

I've never said I came from nothing. To be honest with you, I saw a special that Rod Stewart did in LA and he said, 'I came from nothing.' And I thought, 'You didn't come from nothing. I saw your mother and father in the documentary and they were hard-working people.' To say you come from nothing... I don't agree with that. We all come from something.

I was never anti-establishment. I was only rebelling against what was happening at the time. I knew 'Rock Around the Clock' was going to wipe the slate clean of all that crap, and it did. It killed all other music. Later on, I appreciated singers like Frank Sinatra and Al Jolson. I know a lot of Americans frown on him because he blacked up, but to us he was just a white man who loved the way black people sang so much that he even blacked up. It wasn't a derogatory thing, it was celebrating black people.

I was ready for most aspects of the music industry, but when I met the producer Joe Meek, that threw me off a bit because he was a homosexual. I thought, 'Wait a minute, is the London scene, the people who run British show business – are there a lot of homosexuals involved here? Because if there are, I'm going back to Cardiff.' So when I signed with Decca and Peter Sullivan became my manager, and he said, 'Tell the boys to pack their gear up, I want to talk to you myself', I said, 'You're not one of these queer fellows are you?' And he said, 'What are you on about?' I became paranoid, you see. I genuinely wondered whether being homosexual was required to make a hit record. But then I got into it and realised it just so happened that the first guy to record me had been homosexual. Once I got over the shock of that and realised it wasn't true and most people were normal. Well, I shouldn't put it like that. Homosexuals are normal – it's not that they're not normal. It's just that they are what they are.

The women, the sex – that's all been talked about so much, but that's not the essence of me and it's not what makes me tick. 'It's Not Unusual' was a hit before anyone saw me. It was the power of my voice. The media always bring up the women, they say, 'And how did that affect your wife?' With everyone famous, not just me, they always bring sex into it. It's part of life, of course, but what's important is how you are different and unique. I don't regret anything. All in all, no matter what happened, my marriage is still solid and my son still loves me. I haven't done anything bad in my life.

I still live in LA, but I get my British fix and come home a lot. When I went through immigration last time, one fella said to me, 'You've had your green card since 1976! Why haven't you become an American citizen?' I said, 'Read the name on my passport.' He said, 'Sir Tom Jones. Ah, the Queen wouldn't like it, right?' And I said, 'Exactly.'

I'd love to go back and spend a day with my mum and dad and tell them how much I love them. Maybe I'd go back to 44 Laura Street in Treforest and be a little boy again. There's a song Jerry Lee Lewis recorded, and I sang it onstage, called 'The Things That Matter Most to Me'. It goes, 'I wish I could go back and relive yesterday, and for a while be my mam's little boy again.' And that's true. Just to relive that for a day would be lovely.

CHAPTER 2:

Creativity

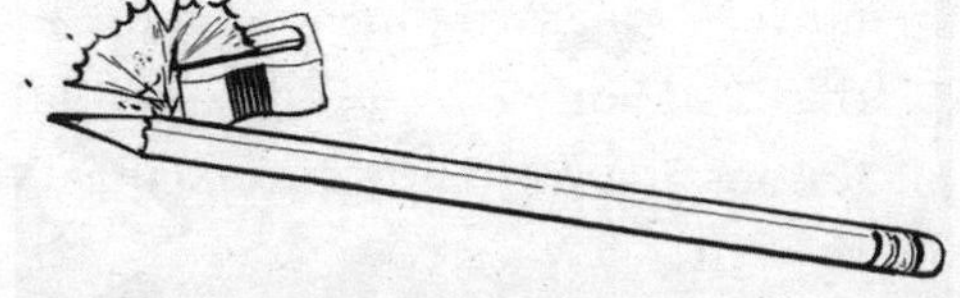

Lynda La Plante

Author

9 February 2009

At 16, I'd just left Liverpool to go to RADA. I didn't really know what I wanted to do. I'd only been to the theatre once – I'd never seen Bernard Shaw or Ibsen. My drama teacher at school had recommended it to me, but I didn't have a burning ambition to act, really. The fantasy I had that I was going to the premier drama school in the world evaporated when I got there, because I found it very stressful. I was too young – I was only just 16. I'd lied to them and said I was 18, to get in. And it was stressful because there were so many mature students – 30- and 40-year-olds – and I found it very difficult to fit in.

I don't know what I expected from RADA; I'd done ballet from the age of six, so when they tried to teach me how to move – 'One two three, bend the knee' – I thought, 'Bleugh, this is so boring.' And I'd done a lot of speech and elocution lessons at a very early age, so that wasn't new to me. I didn't find the teachers encouraging. I overheard one of them saying, 'We need plain-looking girls for maids' and the other one said, 'You can have Lynda.' So I went through quite a loop there. It was an extraordinary time.

I'd reassure my younger self that although RADA might not be for me, my experience there might be part of why my writing is successful. Being a trained actor means you have the confidence to talk to anyone and do proper research, like going into prisons and talking to criminals. When you're a writer, no matter how famous, you still have to make a pitch for a commission, and acting comes in very useful then!

I think the 16-year-old me has still got some growing up to do – I was very naive and unworldly. I had no experience of life at all. I remember a young actor – Ian McShane, no less – asking me if I knew what 'gay' meant. I said of course I did, and he said 'No, *sexually*?' And I didn't, so he went into great detail telling me that my best friend at RADA was homosexual and what that meant he did. I didn't even know that lesbians existed. I was shocked.

It took me a long time to find my identity as an actor. I had no guides or mentors, I didn't know about agents, how to dress or how to put make-up on. It took me a long time to be my own person and make the best of myself. I did farce for a while, until someone told me that though my timing was great, I should leave farce if I ever wanted to play Hedda Gabler. So I left and became a leading lady in repertory. I played Ophelia and Desdemona, and I did get to play Hedda Gabler.

I walked out early from RADA, but I didn't start writing until I was nearly 30. I'd always been in work as an actor and had got decent parts, but there comes a point when if you're not famous and not in your early twenties, you know it's going to be a very hard life. I was working on *The Gentle Touch* with Jill Gascoine, and the script was so bad that I asked if I could have a go at writing. My ideas were rejected but someone wrote 'This is brilliant' across my manuscript, and in 1983 that became *Widows*.

I wasn't burning to write, but I found it easy when I started. I had dyslexia, but the typewriter made it possible for me to write physically, and once I'd started, I never stopped. I still wonder what would have happened if I'd written earlier and hadn't got stuck in one genre; if I wrote a costume drama now, I don't think it would be commissioned. I'd very much like to write lots of different things, but I have to make a living and people want crime from me and nothing else.

On *Widows* I had a superb teacher in Rosie Lambert who ran Thames TV. She was a brilliant editor and taught me how to edit. I even find myself now, when I'm encouraging young writers in my production company, going back to the things she taught me. Simple things, like pointing out that the leading man doesn't come in until page 48. The other great thing about Rosie was that she encouraged me to let the women get away with it. She always wanted the women to win.

I never missed acting. I was born in the wrong era, really – I was a Lillie Langtry-type and loved musical theatre. I might have been a huge star in the 1880s, but I wasn't skinny or pretty, and I had lanky hair. When I left RADA, a teacher told me I wouldn't come into my own as an actor until I was in my mid-forties. Telling that to a young girl, it was very depressing to hear.

I always think I could have written everything better. Writing can be solitary, but once you finish a script, there are so many hands reaching out and grabbing it. I physically enjoy the process of writing and I'm very fortunate in that I don't get rejected a lot, and that encourages me to keep writing. I remember when we got the Emmy for *Prime Suspect*, I didn't believe it was true. Granada TV took the award off me and said it didn't really belong to me, and that's when I knew I'd have to produce my own programmes. So I did. And nowadays I have the CBE, and that has made me really proud.

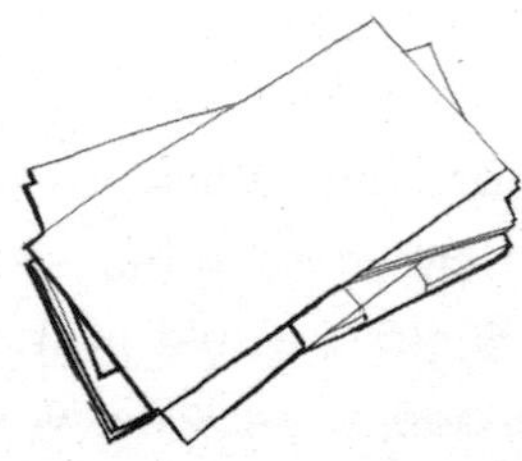

Mary J. Blige

Musician

10 July 2017

Music has surrounded me my entire life. When I was a little girl, my father was a musician and my mother was a singer. When I was four or five years old, I would hear my mother singing old soul and gospel songs, and she would sound just like the records. My dad was a bass player and he'd also play the piano. They had every record you could think of. So I was surrounded by it.

The first thing I'd say to 16-year-old me is, 'Stop playing yourself down, because you're going to be someone that people love and admire. I know you don't believe that right now, but trust me. Don't dumb yourself down to please everyone else, as you're never going to be able to please everyone. Just believe. Believe in yourself.'

I was just a typical teenager, not listening to my mother and not doing the right things. When I was 16, I wasn't thinking about anything, really, apart from singing. My dream was to sing, but it was just a dream at that point. I was really just trying to survive.

Music was going to be the escape route for me and my family. Of course you want it to happen immediately, especially when you live in an environment like we lived in.[2] You want it to happen so you can get your mom and your family out of the projects. You want to make money, so that everyone can get out of that bad environment. You want it to happen quickly and not to be squandering it.

Being in our environment, music was the thing that made us happy – singing in the house or at the block parties. It really was all about music. It was very hard to get hold of the songs you loved and heard the DJs play at the block parties. It was, 'How do we find that song? That song was hot! How do we find out what it was?' Now you can get everything at any time. There was no Spotify where you could go off and listen to one song off the album. You had to go and get the album, and listen to it – unless it was a single. We really appreciated it at that time.

The music that saves us, I don't think we look for it – it finds us. I was five years old when I first heard Stevie Wonder's *Songs in the Key of Life*. When I heard that album for the first time, it just found me. You feel so good listening to whatever lyrics Stevie is singing.

I felt like that was my music. It didn't feel like it was my mother's music or my father's music; it felt like it was my music. Mostly what catches me are the lyrics and the vocals. That is why *Songs in the Key of Life* was so important to me. There was a page with the lyrics, and me and my sister would go off and learn the lyrics to 'Knocks Me Off My

2 Blige grew up in The Bronx in the 1970s.

Feet', 'Pastime Paradise' and 'Summer Soft'. And then, when I heard Anita Baker's 'Caught Up in the Rapture', it was one of the most beautiful love songs I'd ever heard. The same with Chaka Khan's 'Everlasting Love'. When I was growing up, that was the music that found me.

I was always singing at home. I would have a hairbrush as my mic and I would be singing Teena Marie songs into the mirror we had in the bathroom. The brush was my mic when I was a little girl and I would be singing in the mirror – like a lot of little girls do right now are singing to Beyoncé. I was singing to Anita and Chaka and Melissa Morgan. I guess I was a performer then – or a practising performer then. I loved to do it.

I was seven years old when I got on a talent show in elementary school. I sang Peaches & Herb's 'Reunited'. My music teacher, Miss Sweeney, was the one who pushed me to be in the talent show as I never wanted to be in the front; I was always trying to be in the back. It was people pushing me that did it. Friends would always ask me to sing, sing, sing. That is something I had to grow in confidence to do.

Singing turns you into a better person. When you can open your mouth and something comes out of it that makes you feel confident and good, it turns you into another person – a better person. It gives you confidence. When I was younger, I could sing way better than I can sing right now and I could mimic anybody. Anybody. Any male or any female singer. It gave me confidence. It gave me strength. It gave me freedom.

My rebelliousness really messed up my education. When I was in eleventh grade, I dropped out of high school. I definitely regret it. I really wish that I had finished getting my education. Then again, I look at it and ask myself if I would be this person if I'd finished school. Would I be this Mary J. Blige today?

I am not ashamed or embarrassed about dropping out of school – it was just a mistake that I made. I would tell anyone who is trying to make it in music, especially the younger people or those trying to get into the business, to get their education first. You cannot be on top of your business if you can't read the contracts properly, speak to your manager or deal with people properly. I own my mistake and am not embarrassed. It was just a mistake. That's it.

I would tell my younger self that not everyone is going where you are going. You can't share everything with everybody and everyone is not always happy for you. I learned that one early.

I've learned to be careful with music – it either builds or it destroys. I've done 13 albums in my career and what it has taught me is this: music is one of the biggest forms of communication. You can build something with it or you can destroy something with it. Our words are super powerful. I have to be careful with what I am putting out there because there are people out there listening to music at home and it's helping them to stay alive or to get out of a bad relationship. Even if I am going through something negative and feel like venting, I have to make sure that it's not going to hurt anyone else. I have to pray and make sure that my message is strong.

Ozwald Boateng

Fashion Designer

19 March 2012

I was a very happy, confident teenager. I used to make people laugh – I could be very funny. And I was good at sport; running, football, cricket. But I wasn't a jock. I was cool and didn't live for sport – that wasn't the whole of me, I was very much a character at school. I was never 'Ozwald who's good at sports', I was just Ozwald. For a while I seriously thought I might make a life out of football – I was a good winger and then became a striker. But then I hit 16, went to college and discovered women, and it all went to crap.

At 16 I was studying computing at college, firmly believing computers were the future. But I'd been interested in clothes for a long time – my mum actually bought me my first suit for my fifth birthday. It was a double-breasted purple mohair suit. And at the same age, my father told me I was going to go and do wonderful things in the world. So I had this expectation from a very early age. There are so many things

I'd do differently if I could do it all again – from people I've worked with to design choices I made. But the experience of getting it wrong taught me so much. Would I like to be more successful than I am today? Yes, but the wealth of experience I have is partly to do with not getting it right every time.

I was the only black man on my course, but I'd been almost the only black kid at school too. There weren't many role models for black boys in general – I remember seeing Muhammad Ali on TV, and there was a black guy on *Rising Damp* and in *Love Thy Neighbour*. Those are the only men of colour I remember. But growing up, that was just the norm. It didn't worry me because I didn't know anything else – I just knew I had a talent. The doors opened for me and I went for it.

There was no reference point in fashion for a young black man, but I had enough early success to know I was doing the right thing. I was just 17 when I had my first magazine article written about me. I opened my first studio when I was 24 and had my first shop in Savile Row when I was 28. That shop had a cultural impact, and I recognised that, but my colour was never at the forefront of my mind – it was at the back. At the front of my mind was, 'I'm going to make great suits, I'm going to revitalise a very old tradition, and I'm going to begin what I expect to be a global process.' Now my clothes often get picked for big moments – weddings or awards, big days. That's a big thing for me and I love to hear that. When I started I wanted to create something special for men. I wanted to make every man look beautiful.

My father was a big influence on me. My parents divorced when I was young, so I didn't rebel against my father – the time spent with my father was time when I wanted to hear what he had to say. He always looked smart and he always wore suits. So to me, the suit meant respectability and success. It created a confidence. He was a headmaster and had a way of expressing himself. He told me from a young age if you believe in something 100 per cent, rather than 99.7 per cent, you can make it happen. And if something comes easily to you, that's probably what you're supposed to do. Well, when I was 16 I discovered fashion. And my father was like, 'What are you doing?' He wanted me to go to university and become a doctor or a lawyer. So I said, 'Hang on a second, I'm just taking your advice.' He was not happy. It took me many years to persuade him I'd made the right decision. That was a very difficult pill for him to swallow, but in the end, he did. Now he always says to me if he kicks the bucket, he'll do it a happy man. And I tell him he has to delay kicking the bucket for a good while yet.

I'd tell my younger self he should listen to other people more. I probably could have avoided a lot of mistakes if I'd listened to more people. I might not have married when I was 23 – I'd tell my younger self to wait until he was about 30! But the other side of that is that I was very determined and had a strong sense of my own voice – I think if you haven't got that, you can easily be misled, especially when you're young. I always felt that something big was going to happen. I was fearless – much more than I am today. As you get older, you become aware of the complications, but when you're 16, nothing can go wrong. And I was so committed – I used to regularly walk two or three miles across London to buy my fabric then walk home again, just to save my bus money.

As I've got older, I've become more aware of the cultural impact of what I did, as a young black man in the industry, and I've come to recognise that I can be an inspiration for other people. Success can conflict you and there comes a point where you feel a need to give back. I was lucky to have a great support network when I was starting out, but not everyone has that. I can give back to other people by providing them with something like the rules of life my dad gave me.

If I could go back and relive a moment, it would be the fashion show I had in Savile Row in 2002. I had a marquee the full length of the street, completely lined with models. I remember the excitement of that. At that time, the only other people who'd been able to close off the street like that were The Beatles. We did the show, then I had all the models in this beautiful room, about 50 guys, and they were cheering with the excitement of the experience they'd just had. I remember the energy in that room – it was electrifying. And I just stood there, wondering what the next day would bring.

Philip Glass

Composer

29 January 2018

By the time I was 16, I was at the University of Chicago and I was starting to write music.[3] It was a very good university but it didn't have a good music department in those days – it was a very academic university. To further my interest in music, I would go to the music library and copy out the scores and learn everything I could. Chicago was a great city for music then – the jazz scene was very much alive. I heard all kinds of people there, like Billie Holiday, and it had a very good symphony orchestra, so I could go down and hear a new work by Bartók. It was a good place to be.

My love of music started very young. There was always music in the house. My dad had a little music shop in Baltimore. In those days you didn't have such a thing as a megastore. My dad's store was like a candy shop and very small. He'd bring the records home and we would listen to them, and then he'd take them back to the shop. The old

3 Glass entered university at 15 due to an accelerated college system.

78s. That was the only way to hear new music in those days – you didn't hear it on the radio. So we heard all kinds of things – he listened to everything from jazz to symphonic to contemporary. When I came home for vacation I'd work in the store and I became the buyer. I didn't think of music in terms of genre, just in terms of good and bad. To this day, I have a very cosmic taste in music.

I was three years younger than everyone else at university; I was 15 and they were at least 18, but the oldest kids kind of took care of me. My family were far away in Baltimore, and they knew that. I had tonnes of friends; I could find them in the library and the cafeteria – they were all over the place. I had a lot of fun there and by the time I was 19 I'd done all my academic studies[4], so I could go to Juilliard in New York and just study music.

When I went to Paris in my twenties[5] we studied Bach and Mozart. Because the language of music took a big step when they were working, it became a very powerful form. There isn't any popular music that goes beyond the harmonies of classical music – they're just not there. When I came back from Paris to New York – I was about 30 – I didn't teach music. I was already writing. If I had to do commercial music, it didn't take me much time. I gave myself a time limit of two hours, in fact, so I could make a living writing commercial music[6] while I was also writing an opera or music for a film or a piece of theatre. I had a command of the language of music due to my training.

---

4 Mathematics and philosophy.

5 Glass won a scholarship to study with the esteemed composer / composition teacher Nadia Boulanger.

6 Including TV ads and cues for *Sesame Street*.

My younger self wouldn't be surprised that I don't go out a lot, though he was more outgoing than I am now. But even when I was younger, I didn't go to a lot of parties – I realised if I stayed out too late, I couldn't work the next morning. I remember when I came to London in the nineties, there was a lot of house music. The problem with the house music scene is they didn't get going until one in the morning, and I preferred to be asleep by then. But I stayed up and went to listen, because it was the only way to hear the music. I had lots of fun doing that and I worked with all kinds of people and did arrangements for people like S-Express. But now my work time is so important to me, and I have lots of children and like to spend time with them. I need to get to bed early – around midnight – then I get up around 6am and I work all day. I'm not seen outside of my house much.

The teenage Philip would be very surprised that I could make a living making music and that I can go out and play 30 or 40 concerts a year, all over the world. I had a day job until I was 42.[7] I'd move furniture for three days, then for four days I'd stay home and write music. You could do that in those days. I was very surprised when the day came that I didn't have to do that anymore.

The young Philip would be impressed that I got to know and work with Ravi Shankar. I was his assistant for a while. He was someone I admired – he was composing and out playing, all the things I wanted to do. I was in touch with him for 40 years, up until two or three days before he passed away. If I had to go to Los Angeles, I'd go early and have lunch at his house. He always had young people around. He was a born

7 Glass had a moving company with his cousin – *Time* art critic Robert Hughes was once astonished to find him installing his dishwasher.

teacher; he couldn't stop teaching. After lunch he'd say, 'Let's go to the music room.' And we'd go down there, four of five of us, and we'd sit down and he'd actually start giving a class – he couldn't help himself! Those were priceless visits for me. He was quite an amazing guy.

I knew many great people. So many of them are gone now. I knew Doris Lessing for 30 years, and Allen Ginsberg was a good friend for a long time. I'm now older than they were when they died. Leonard Cohen – I knew him for many years. The last time I spoke to him I asked him when he was next coming to New York. I hadn't seen him in a while. He said, 'This old car isn't leaving the garage again.' At the time I didn't really understand him. I think he was really saying goodbye. I never saw him again. He died about a week later.

I would have liked to have had more time to get to know my father. He was killed by a car when he was 67, so not that old. He didn't get out of the way quickly enough and someone knocked him down. But generally, I don't look back on my life. I think about what I'm doing next week and don't look through the rear-view mirror. A lot of dollars I might have missed, a lot of people who have gone – there's nothing to say about that. I have a lot of things I still want to do. I get up very early and work all day. I'm running out of time. I'm 80. If I'm going to write 12 more symphonies, I'd better get going.

Rufus Wainwright

Musician

23 March 2016

When I was 16, I was completely incorrigible and fanatically driven. I was so horrifyingly insecure that I acted secure. And I was quite beautiful, actually. I was a looker. If I could talk to that boy now, I'd just congratulate him on surviving. The odds were pretty stacked against me, considering my delusional state about how the world worked. But maybe that delusion saved me a lot of trouble. I believed in something that didn't exist and had this feeling that I was going to be a unique creation that everyone would love. I would have the answer to everything. I would conquer the industry. No one would care that I was gay. The truth turned out to be the opposite, on pretty much every point. But I just kept plugging away.

I might reprimand my younger self a little bit for the fact that I was 100 per cent dedicated to my career and my art, and to conquering show business. Maybe that was necessary to get there, but I think along the way I could have stopped more to smell the roses. Just enjoy the now. But I was always setting goals. You know youth is wasted on the young.

I officially said 'I'm out' to my parents when I was 18, but I knew it from the age of 13, and they knew too. I was sneaking out of the house, wearing weird clothes and getting strange phone calls. It was a turbulent period. My parents could have handled it much better, but looking back, I'm a bit more forgiving of that now. It was the late '80s and AIDS was everywhere, massacring everyone. But neither of my parents apologised. My mother died a few years ago and I don't think my father will ever apologise. But your parents are your parents – they're not supposed to make you feel better. My grandmother, God rest her soul, she was from Georgia in the South and somewhat racist, and not the smartest tool in the shed. But she was very loving, and she said she knew I was gay but she loved me and it didn't matter. So my simple, racist, Southern little grandmother was actually the most helpful – there you go.

Not to sound too old-school gay, but I'd advise my younger self to get to the gym right away. I didn't really hit the gym until I was about 35. It's been great, but if I'd started at 20 it would have been a lot easier. But that wasn't part of my persona back then – I was a romantic dandy, smoking cigarettes, and I'm not sure I'd go back and change that. But it would have saved me a lot of money now.

I think I'd still really like the teenage Rufus. He had a spark. What I love most about that 16-year-old was that he was always game. He would try anything. Whether it was a play or singing a song, wearing a weird outfit or dyeing my hair purple, I would try anything. And that's the kind of kid I like now. Even if they're naughty and subversive, at least they're engaged in what life has to offer.

I'd tell my younger self to listen to my grandmother. At one point, she put me on her knee and said, 'Rufus, you are a special child and you will have a lot of opportunities. You are very privileged. Some people are going to hate you for that, so you have to be ready to deal with that. People will want to take you down.'

It would have been nice not to have this period of addiction happen,[8] but your journey is your journey. In retrospect, I think there was too much drinking in the house when we were small children. My mother was a wonderful woman, but the drinking was ever-present.

If I really wanted to impress the 16-year-old me, I'd tell him I'm writing my second opera now. I became an opera fanatic when I was 13, and that music was my religion, my saviour, my resting place, everything to me. And a shared love of it brought me so close to my mother. So to be writing my second opera now, with the first one quite successful and the new one eagerly anticipated – that little guy couldn't have had a better outcome.

My younger self would be completely freaked out by the idea of being married,[9] and having children.[10] He would not be into that. I didn't want to have a boyfriend – I wanted to be a total loner. But life does change. One thing I always wanted was the next, bigger, better adventure. When you're

8 Wainwright struggled with drug addiction in the early 2000s.

9 To German artistic director Jörn Weisbrodt.

10 He has a daughter, Viva Katherine, whose parenthood he shares with 'deputy dad' Jorn and her biological mother Lorca Cohen, daughter of Leonard.

a teenager, it's drugs and alcohol and rock'n'roll, hanging out with your crazy friends. After that, it's establishing a career. Then when that's done, it's like, 'What's bigger than this?' Maybe it's having a real relationship. Then it's kids. We're at an interesting juncture now – maybe the next big one is death. But to my 16-year-old self, my husband, my beautiful daughter – they would mean nothing to him. I'd have to reassure him with the opera thing.

Of all the relationships in my life, the one with my dad has changed the most. It was very difficult for a long time. But we seem to have found a plateau where we love and respect each other, though we still have to be somewhat mindful of our wounds. I think he was always proud of me, but that was coupled with a tremendous jealousy because his career was over by the time mine really took off. He had to step aside, which to this day he refuses to do, and he wasn't very good at masking his resentment. To be fair, my mother wasn't particularly kind to him when we were growing up. She didn't speak highly of him, and that's the worst thing any parent can do to the other. But I forgive her wholly, because he was the love of her life and her heart was broken.

I've spent three-quarters of my life in the public eye, and it's tough when you hit 40. It doesn't matter how well you've taken care of yourself; there's a constant scrutiny. I have terrible moments of insecurity, but I feel like I made the right choices in terms of my music – opera kind of supersedes all that and fulfils me completely on every level. So all I have to do is grow a beard, and I'll be fine.

I'm doing the Judy Garland Carnegie Hall show again at the end of this year. It's ten years since I did that show. My mother was still alive. I was finally in a real relationship. That was possibly the happiest time of my life, my first Judy Garland period. So, fingers crossed, here comes the second.

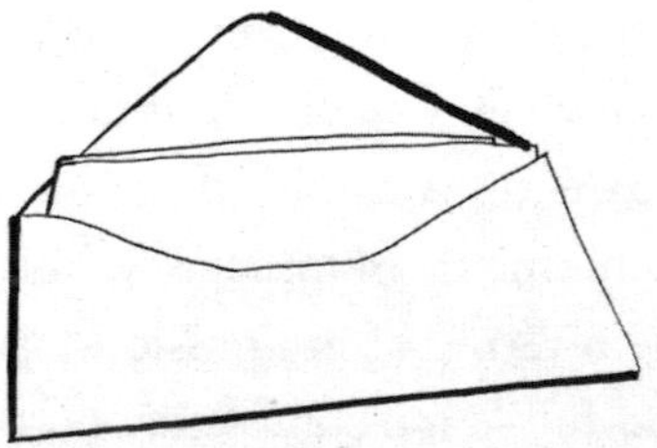

Shania Twain

Musician

21 August 2017

My early teens were difficult. My parents were separated and my mum and I were staying in a battered women's shelter. We stayed there for a year, and it was the most difficult period of my life. Growing up in a turbulent household brought out a lot of defensive characteristics in me. I was always waiting for the next argument or fight, and I also felt very protective of my mother – I was often directly involved in those fights, which could make me very aggressive if I felt backed into a corner at school.

I was very shy and very socially awkward. I was also very insecure – I didn't have a lot in common with the other kids, because I was just a music nerd. And I was embarrassed about my upbringing and how we were always scraping by and struggling to pay the bills, so I rarely brought a friend home with me. Early on, music became my therapy, somewhere I could go and be safe. I think that's how I survived it all, why I'm not a drug addict or a nutcase today.

From an early age I was always the little singer in the family. From the age of eight I would go and sing folk and country songs at clubs at the weekend. Sometimes even until two or three in the morning on a school night. I didn't enjoy being in those places at all, I developed a lot of stage fright. Sometimes there were strippers going on before me, and by the time I went on everyone in there was quite drunk. It wasn't an environment for a child. I did love the music – I was very passionate about it, but I just wanted to do it in my room, on my own, writing songs and singing to myself. I liked being alone and quiet. I didn't want to perform in public. But my mother was trying to help me get exposure, so that I could eventually become a professional singer.

There was definitely a transition in terms of the audience once I was fully developed – very developed – at 16, but I took it in my stride because I was so used to performing by then. I never mingled with the audience, so I was safe in that regard. But the changes in my body – I found those very difficult. I was such a tomboy, and I was definitely not the pretty daughter in the family. I was very athletic, but suddenly I didn't want to be bouncing around playing basketball at school with the boys. I was more self-conscious and uncomfortable about the eyes of the boys on me than when I was onstage. It wasn't until I went into the music industry that I really felt the sexist intimidation of exposure.

A major turning point in my life was when I was 22, when my parents both died.[11] It sounds odd to say, but it turned out to be something I made the most of. I had a lot of revelations that year. One was that I realised how much of the performing I'd been doing for my mother, and I didn't really need that for

11 Jerry Twain and Sharon Morrison were killed in a car crash in Ontario in 1987.

myself. But by then my friends had all gone off to college and I felt I'd missed the opportunity to do something productive, something tangible, like getting an education. Suddenly, not only did I not have parents, I had nothing but this music career, in which my chances of succeeding were incredibly low. So I really had to put myself to the test. And when I finally fully committed to my music career without the pressure of my parents, I felt that was a very positive change, and it led to the most productive 20 years of my life.

Once my career took off, the world become more accessible. I didn't get lost in just being the artist, I educated myself. I'm a good self-motivator and I'm very disciplined. I ran a lot, I wrote a lot and I read philosophy and psychology. I've always had extreme curiosity and I gravitate towards similar people. When I met my first husband[12], that was another turning point, which was crucial in the next 15 years of my life. We had such a good verbal relationship, we talked a lot. He was very stimulating, and I need to be stimulated. I learned so much in that relationship. And now I'm married again to someone who is such a thinker. I need that.

I don't think I felt confident that I was going to make it until I made my first album with Mutt Lang, *The Woman in Me*.[13] I wasn't sure at the beginning if it would work, because it was quite an unusual collaboration. Once it started, I felt that what we were creating was good, but when we had real success with it,[14] that gave me a much greater confidence about the future. After the release of 'Man, I Feel Like a Woman', it started

12 Rock producer Mutt Lang, who produced and co-wrote her breakthrough second album.

13 In 1995.

14 20 million global sales.

getting so big. I just thought, 'Wow, this is bigger than I ever imagined it could be.' Everything started spinning. And I was over-working, so it felt like a frenzy.

If I could go back, I'd cut myself some slack when my marriage started falling apart. I went into a black hole for a bit, I went into shock. It was a bit like when my parents died. But I was angry with myself for not getting over it right away. I should have said to myself that it was okay to feel bad for a while and not apologise for it. I just wanted to hurry up and get over it and I think that was a mistake, but I did get through it. I have a son, so that helped me persevere. And once I caught my breath, I was able to be creative again. That's how I escape. Some women go to the spa for 'me' time, for solitude – for me, indulgence is locking myself in a room and writing songs. I have no inhibitions when I write – I can curse, I can vent, I can be completely honest. So it's a helpful thing to be able to do in the darkest times.

In my forties, I really didn't worry too much about getting older or how my looks were changing. When I hit 50, gravity really started to take hold. I think you come to a point when you're mature enough to accept that it's one of the things in life you just can't control. I couldn't control my parents dying, I couldn't control my marriage falling apart, I couldn't control getting Lyme disease and losing my voice. And I can't control ageing. Once you get to your fifties, you have to accept some things are just out of your hands. Hey, it's time to throw those old bras away. You just can't wear them anymore.

Werner Herzog

Film Director

13 February 2017

At 16 it was obvious that I would make films but of course I failed to get anything off the ground. I realised I had to become my own producer or I'd never make a film, so I started working night shifts as a welder in a small steel factory. That's how I made the money to fund my first film. But of course during the day I was in school, so there was not too much sleep in those two and a half years.

I was in high school, a classical school. We had nine years studying Latin, six years of Ancient Greek and some English at the end. I hated it all. Everything. The idea of gaining knowledge did appeal, but I never trusted textbooks and I never trusted teachers. I'm completely self-taught, including cinema. I've never read a book on film-making.

When I was child, I didn't even know cinema existed. I grew up in the remotest mountain valley in the Bavarian Alps. I saw my first film when I was 11, but it was not really satisfying. A travelling projectionist came by our one-classroom schoolhouse and showed two films. They were both lousy. One was about Eskimos building an igloo, all paid extras who didn't know how to handle snow and ice. I could tell because I'd grown up in snow.

I excluded myself from music when I was young because I was harassed by a music teacher. I disconnected myself from music for four years. Then there was a void, and I felt a hunger to fill it. But you never can. It's the same with books. You read a wonderful book and you believe the pile of unread books will somehow be smaller. But on the contrary, the unread books pile becomes larger and larger after every great book you read.

I never saw a great film when I was young. I saw some mediocre pictures like *Tarzan* and *Zorro*, the cheap '50s version. But it was clear to me that I was some kind of a poet and I would use that quality to make films that would be different. I always had the feeling that I was the inventor of cinema. But I also wrote poetry and I have written prose – *Conquest of the Useless*, *Of Walking in Ice* – which I think will survive all my films because of the substance and calibre of the prose. There is no one who writes prose like me these days. I write better than all the others. But I always recognised that making films was my destiny.

I was not a neurotic boy. Not then and not now. I was just as stupid as anyone else at that age. But I do not want to remember the teenage me. I wouldn't want to meet him, for God's sake. I don't like to go circling around my own navel – I've never done that. I feel uncomfortable looking at myself. I do not like to look at my own face in the mirror. I do not like self-scrutiny.

I was not ambitious as a boy, but I did have stories and ideas coming at me with great vehemence, so I had to deal with that. I've never had any career. A career would mean planning the next steps and building something, and I've never done that. I was always very curious about the world because the world I grew up in was very limited, and I wanted to know what was beyond the mountains and the valley. I'm curious about the landscapes we don't usually see, like North Korea.[15] I've been to many places because of the projects I've done. I just made a film about volcanoes, *Salt and Fire*, and I went to see salt flats in Bolivia, which are just not from our planet. They're like science fiction – a completely different landscape. But I'm not a traveller or an adventurer. I've just done the slalom of life and I've done it well.

I do not like any notion of adventure – the concept expired at least a century ago. It's obsolete to speak about adventure, when you can go down to your travel agent and book an adventure trip to visit cannibals in New Guinea. It has become as obscene as that. When I'm making a film and there are certain obvious risks, I assess the risks for the sakes of the people who work with me. And I'm good at that. It's rumoured that I'm reckless and adventurous and it's not like that. I've always been very, very prudent. There are these myths that I jeopardise the lives of the people who work with me, that I push people over the brink. But statistics are on my side; in the 70 films I've made, not a single actor has been hurt. Not one.

Everything that I have done is wonderful. No, I am not being sarcastic. I truly love all my films. They couldn't have been better. Sometimes, the ones that have a limp or a stutter I love even more. You cannot ask a mother, 'Which of your seven children do you love most?'

---

15 Herzog explored the active volcanoes of North Korea for his 2016 documentary *Into the Inferno*.

I have had to explain things about film-making because I have faced a huge onslaught, a gigantic avalanche, of young people who want to ask me things. I try to give a systematic answer. I run my Rogue Film School, which is the antithesis of what you see happening worldwide in film schools. It's a guerrilla style, a way of life rather than a list of practical advice. You won't learn any practical things in my school, with two exceptions: lock-picking and forging documents. It has been life-changing for almost all of my students. I tell them to form secret rogue cells everywhere. They gang up and they make very good stuff and win awards at festivals. One of them outdid me recently by making it to the Academy Award shortlist. You see, I never make it to the shortlist. My students surpass me, which I find absolutely perfect.

Of course, I have got older and I have moved on, but the essence of my films has not changed. If I could go back, I would not do *Aguirre 2*, *3*, *4*, *5* and 6, but all my films come from the same family. If you woke up in the middle of the night and turned on the TV, you would know within 120 seconds if it was one of my films. The first thing you would recognise is that they are better than the others. No, I say that frivolously; it's a provocation.

When my older son was five, I had a really good telescope. One night there was a full moon. We looked at it together and you could distinguish the mountain ridges and crater rims. To see him discover the mountains on the moon – that was a fine moment. That is where movies come from. Always the sense of awe. That is the birthplace of cinema. Showing your little son the mountains on the moon – that is something I do in all my films.

CHAPTER 3:

Self-belief

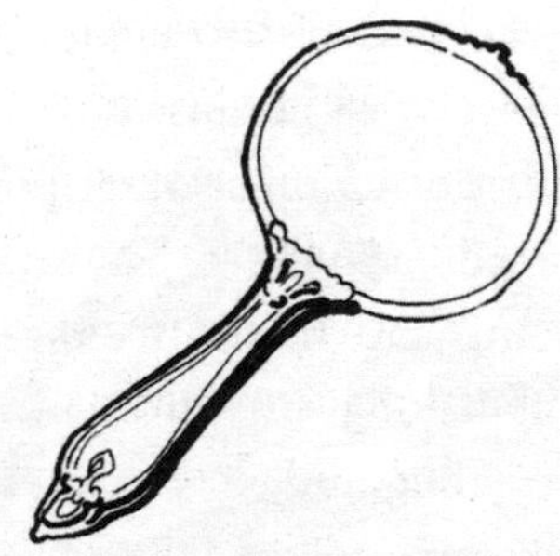

Val McDermid

Author

15 August 2016

At 16 I was preparing for my Oxford entrance exam. I was very driven and pushed myself in everything. I played hockey for the first eleven in the East of Scotland. I played guitar and sang in folk clubs. I won debating prizes. Everything I did, I wanted to do really well.

I was very much of the working-class generation that thought education was the key to doing well in life. My parents were bright people who passed their exams to go to high school but they had to leave at 14 because their families couldn't afford it. They never got to reach their potential, so they very much encouraged me not to be trapped by circumstances. But my parents had mixed feelings about my going to Oxford. It was a long way from Kirkcaldy – the only time we'd gone to England was a weekend in Blackpool. And it was a long way intellectually as well. So I think they were really a bit nervous for me, as well as very proud. But I think they saw that I was always going to go my own way.

I became aware when I was at Oxford that I was drawing a line between my past and my future. I couldn't articulate this when I was 16, but I think I wanted to spread my wings because of my sexuality. There were no lesbians in Fife in the '60s. I knew I felt different, and quite lonely, listening to Leonard Cohen and Joni Mitchell on my own, feeling that sense of both alienation and unhappiness. I thought my difference must be because I wanted to be a writer. If lesbians aren't visible in your culture – on TV or in books and films – it's very hard to come to that understanding by yourself. I'd spend hours walking with the dog along miles of coastline – days full of nothing but me, my dog and a book.

I did go out with boys. That's just what you did. I went to parties, did the illicit drinking, a wee bit of smoking dope. On the face of it, I was the life and soul, but I knew I was going through the motions. The music I was listening to was a far better reflection of how I really felt. And I was singing in folk clubs, where you'd meet people hanging out in the back room – people like Billy Connolly and Gerry Rafferty. It wasn't glamorous at all, but I was playing with people who were serious about what they were doing. If I hadn't been a writer, I'd have liked to be a musician.

I was lucky going to St Hilda's College at Oxford. Compared to many of the men's colleges, it felt much more egalitarian. I went to a fortieth reunion recently and one of my old friends said, 'We all thought you were so exotic.' Because I was from Scotland! I did think of myself as a fish out of water – I had to learn how to speak English because no one understood my Fife accent – but never exotic. At the same time, I never felt inferior. The main thing I learned from my parents was that no one is better than you. My father was a great Robert Burns man, and I grew up with that philosophy, 'A Man's a Man for A' That'. Call no man your master.

Towards my final year at university, I started learning about feminism. Reading Kate Millett's feminist classic *Sexual Politics* was like having a lightbulb going on above my head – it gave me a totally different view. I started hanging round with feminist groups, and that's where I learned about lesbians. And I realised that's where I belonged. Not much later, I had my heart well and truly broken in my first real relationship. It was one of those star-crossed, doomed things, which ended badly. I had to be emotionally tough about it. You had to be careful who you talked to about such things then. There was a lot of hostility, really quite nasty homophobia all around. So I just had to get a grip and get on. But that heartbreak stayed with me a long time, reverberating through my life.

If I'm honest, I'm still a bit of wary of the world and I still hold back a bit. Many women struggle to let go of that imposter syndrome; waiting for the moment when they turn round and say, 'It's not really you we wanted!' When I went for my Oxford exam, the woman asked me how long I'd lived in Shetland. My heart contracted in my chest and I thought, 'They've got the wrong person. It should be a lassie from Shetland sitting here, not me.' I almost shouted, 'I've never been to Shetland!' She said, 'But it says here you went to Fair Isle Primary School.' I said, 'That's just a name!' That was a terrible, terrible moment, and it's never quite left me.

I think my 16-year-old self would be taken aback by the life I've had. I was always ambitious, but where I've ended up is beyond the dreams I had. I feel a bit like the Ugly Duckling – 'Me, a swan? Ah, go on!' I'd like to show off to the teenage me, on her way to St Hilda's, and tell her, 'One day they'll make you an honorary fellow of this college.' If I told her they'd make a successful TV series of one of her books[16] she'd just think I was making it up. Stuff like that doesn't happen to people like us. I still think that. Sitting in a tent being interviewed about my writing by Scotland's First Minister! Ridiculous!

If I could go back, I'd like to have more time with my dad. He died when I was 32, the week before my first book came out, so he never actually held it in his hand, though he knew it was coming. He'd have been a fantastic grandad. There was a time after I was at Oxford when there was a feeling of distance between me and my parents, probably because of this huge experience I'd had that they hadn't. But I think that shifted back as I got older and realised the emotional closeness was more important that the intellectual one.

If I could go back to any time in my life, it would be when my son was born. He's not biologically my son; I was in a relationship with his mother. Before he came along I had a real worry about how I might relate to this baby I had no biological tie to. When he was born, he was put into my arms first because his mum had a difficult birth. And I looked into his face and he looked up at me and that was it, I was gone. It was unconditional love, forever. And the absolute feeling of that moment has never wavered, even though he's never read any of my books!

16 ITV's *Wire in the Blood.*

Andrea Bocelli

Opera Singer and Composer

10 December 2018

I was a very vivacious teenager, even a bit naughty, always willing to crack a joke and have a laugh. As they say where I come from, I was 'always up to something'. When I lost my sight[17] I cried, but only for a short while. I then set aside any form of self-pity and decided I needed to be positive and optimistic about life, finding ways to explore it. This did not affect my musical training in any way. People may perceive it as my main issue, but it never was and never is.

I would not say I had any teenage 'angst', but I was restless and I was always curious about everything, as well as stubborn. Maybe at times, as part of family life, there may have been the odd spark, some arguing with my parents or my brother, but overall we were a united and peaceful family. Love always prevailed and mutual fondness would soften any kind of friction that might have emerged.

17 As the result of a sporting accident, aged 12.

I think I was an ambitious teenager, and a dreamer. I have always wanted to earn my living with my music. It was an ongoing ambition from the time I was in secondary school and also later during my university years. I succeeded, albeit many years later, after I turned 35, after lots of hurdles and hearing 'NO' many times had severely tested my pipe dreams.

I owe my parents an awful lot. My father Sandro and my mother Edi moulded my character, offering me an education that was invaluable during my whole life. Among the many teachings I received, I would mention the determination not to give up. This is what my parents showed during my mother's pregnancy, when the doctors advised her to have an abortion because the baby would be born with severe illnesses. She ignored their advice and carried on with my father's support. Without their courage and faith, I would not be here today to tell the story.

My father and I were very similar in character. We were both strong-natured and we have argued over time. Even though there was never any family opposition to my passion for music, my father did not think I could succeed and support myself relying only on my voice. He used to say, 'If you enjoy it, sing, but you must first get an education!' He also used to try and restrain my youthful eagerness (and sometimes my recklessness) with his fatherly love and typical parental apprehension. I only understood that later, once I became a father myself.

The first time I was onstage I was about eight years old, during the end-of-school-year concert. I remember a small wooden stage in the school hall where I spent the first five years of my studies. I was anxious and emotional and I sang

'O Sole Mio'. That was the first applause outside the family circle. I was still in short trousers, at the age of 12, when my uncle insisted I took part in a summer competition run by the Caffè Margherita in Viareggio.[18] I won and that was my first success, and the first time I felt the affection of an audience. Many years later, onstage at the Sanremo Music Festival, I felt the enthusiasm of the audience and I understood that, maybe, my career was at last taking off.

If I met the teenage Andrea today, overall I think I would like him. Maybe the difference between us would be the impetuousness that I've learned to tone down over the years. And a pinch of recklessness that at the time made me take some risks, especially in sport, and that I have learned to contain as I developed a sense of responsibility. I would envy the teenage Andrea his youth, but the young Andrea might envy other joys that come with middle age.

As a young boy I was agnostic. The young Andrea would probably not understand that today I believe in faith and great values, and in the need to be pious every day. Over the years I have come to believe that faith cannot be acquired effortlessly; just as any other discipline, it requires commitment, perseverance and sacrifice. To be committed to faith means we need to comply with simple deeds that may even appear tedious. If we want to improve our faith, we have to submit to prayer. The young Andrea would not have understood this at the time.

Out of all the performances I've done, I would probably show the young Andrea the concert in Central Park, or one of the operas I have interpreted all over the world – this was always my dream, which I nourished with plenty of

18 A Tuscan seaside resort.

enthusiasm and little hope. Or possibly my duet with Luciano Pavarotti, or with José Carreras or Plácido Domingo.

Something difficult to fully grasp as a teenager, but that becomes very clear as we grow up, is that notoriety itself is not a value, and fame can be an obstacle in acquiring true humanity. It is legitimate and wonderful to be able to dream, but as an adult one must never lose touch with reality; unless we keep both feet firmly on the ground, we risk losing our way.

Earlier I said the young Andrea used to say he was agnostic, but that was a ploy to avoid the real issue. In adulthood, some pressing existential questions cropped up. Reading a small and wonderful book by Tolstoy, *A Confession*, later followed by all his other masterpieces, helped me a lot along the path to faith. To believe that life is determined by chance is not only unsuitable but illogical and not very sensible. The basic rationale that allows us to take the right path when reaching the first fundamental crossroads is: to believe or not to believe. To my mind, this is a choice and there is no alternative.

If I could have one last conversation with anyone it would be my father – to thank him. It would be enough to have him near me and to sense his smile. Any other words would be excessive.

I try and focus on the here and now, on each day. I never look back and I do not want to know what my programme is for tomorrow. As far as criticism is concerned, I fully respect other people's opinions – it is impossible to please everybody! Artists are subject to positive and negative criticism during their career – that's life. I have already told you what I think about fame – I do not consider it to be a value. As for priorities, children always come first. This was clear to me from the moment I became a father. If I could go back and relive one moment in life, it would be the moment I held my firstborn in my arms for the first time.

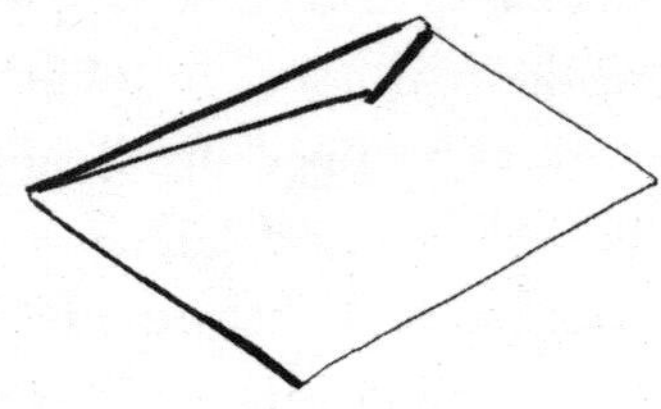

Diane Abbott

Politician

24 June 2013

At 16 I was preoccupied with my GCSEs, though I was regarded as quite a naughty girl. I certainly wasn't the teacher's favourite. I think now I'd be able to say to my younger self that that had a lot to do with being the only black girl in the class. That shaped the way the teacher looked at me, and it took me years to understand that.

I'd definitely tell my younger self not to worry so much about not being a size six, not looking like Twiggy and not having waist-length blonde hair. I wish I'd realised that beauty comes in all sorts of varieties. I fell for a lot of the beauty myths of the time. And when I look at old photographs of myself, I see I wasn't fat at all and I was much prettier than I remember.

My parents had gone through a very acrimonious divorce. My mother had to leave us and she'd gone a long way, to Yorkshire, because she wanted to get far away from my father.

I stayed very loyal to my mother and understood why she felt she'd had to leave, though my brother, who was younger, felt she had abandoned him. I had to do all the cooking and cleaning while I studied for my exams – my father hadn't heard of modern feminism. I did struggle with that role. I didn't question that I should be doing it, but it was all very stressful and very difficult.

My clear goal was to go to Oxford or Cambridge. For no particular reason – neither my mother or father had been to university; they both left school at 14. No one was especially encouraging me, but I was determined. In the novels I was reading, people went to Oxford or Cambridge. And I remember school had taken us on a trip to Cambridge once and I was blown away. The undergraduates in their striped scarves – to me they looked like gods and goddesses. I thought if I went to Cambridge, I too would become a special, remarkable person. In reality, when I got there, I felt so alone among these privileged, white people that I thought at first I'd made a horrible mistake.

I've been a very determined person from quite a young age. I'm not sure where it comes from. When I first talked about parliament, it was like when I talked about Cambridge – people didn't think it was realistic.[19] It was only when I became the Labour candidate in Hackney that things began to change.

I don't resent getting older. I hated being called a girl when I was in my forties and fifties – I found it patronising. I worry about my physical health, but I don't worry too much about looking older. I do think, though, there's a point as you get older that men stop seeing you. Middle-aged women become

19 In 1987, she became the first black female MP in Westminster.

invisible. As a public figure people pay attention to me, but when men don't know who I am, I'm invisible to them.

One of my happiest memories is when I had my son christened. I had it in the chapel at the House of Commons with all my family. I remember sitting in the chapel and Trevor Phillips leant over to me and said, 'Normally when there's this many black people in this place, they call the police!' It was a great day. Jonathan Aitken, whom I had worked for before I was an MP, was the godfather. It wasn't so much that we got on well, but I thought he'd be a good person for my son to have as a godfather – I thought he might help him in later life. As it turned out, he went to prison. So of all the people I could have chosen, he was really the wrong one.

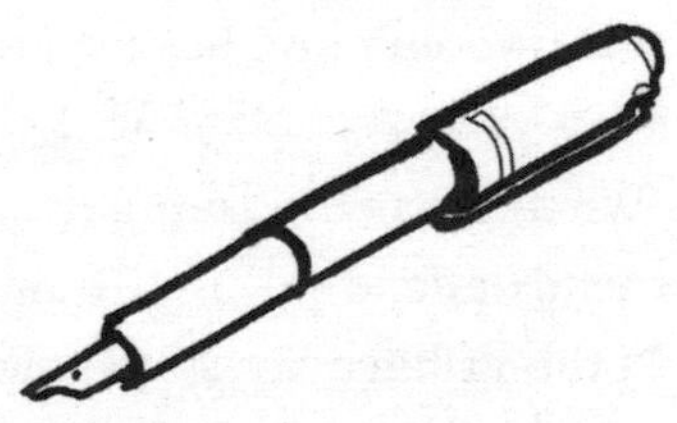

Imelda Staunton

Actor

22 December 2008

At 16, I was pretty sure that I wanted to be an actress. I'd done all the school plays and I'd done drama outside of school with an inspirational drama teacher. I wasn't angst-ridden because I knew my purpose. I was always pretty gregarious, the fun one in my group. I had access to boys from the age of about 11 – we did school plays with the boys' school across the road, so it wasn't hard to get our hands on them. But because I had my passion for acting, I wasn't obsessed with boys and there weren't any huge dramas.

If I met my younger self now, I think we'd have lots in common. We'd have the same sense of humour, the same group of friends and we'd live in the same part of London. I'd be glad I didn't have her spots, though.

I didn't mind being an only child when I was a kid, but as I've got older I've become aware of the adjustments I had to make, which brothers and sisters would have helped with earlier on. I didn't have the emotional vocabulary that sibling rivalry teaches you, so I had to learn I couldn't have my own way all the time and that when friends say they hate you and love you in the same breath, I shouldn't take it too seriously.

I was a lapsed Catholic by the time I was about 14. My parents were both first-generation Irish and had taken me to church as a girl and sent me to a convent school, but they were starting to lapse by then too, so they didn't mind too much.

I'd tell my young self to get tough quick, because you spend your whole acting life being rejected. There was a job I really wanted two years ago, and I wrote to the director, which I've never done in my life before, and I didn't get the job. I thought 'Right, okay – they weren't interested at all'. Part of you thinks, 'But I've got to this stage in my life – surely someone would show an interest?' but no, they didn't. I remember wanting desperately to work at the Royal Court and not getting that. I knew I just had to take whatever the next job was. I've learned to take the knocks better, but I was always quite good at taking criticism.

I'd tell my younger self to have the confidence to fail. You have to go through your own struggle and survive it. I think the most important thing is having the confidence to fail. It's all very easy to be successful, but if you can fail and carry on and learn from it, you'll learn a lot more from that experience. If things are bad, they won't be bad forever, and if things are good, they won't be good forever.

I'd love telling my younger self that one day she will meet a very tall, dark, handsome Yorkshireman and one day in rehearsals he will look at you and know that he wants to marry you. I'd assure her, ambitious as she is, that in the end she will value her marriage over her work. When we got married, we decided there was no point being married if we were going to be apart, so in 25 years, the longest we've ever been apart is very recently, for five weeks. Some couples spend their lives apart – it simply doesn't work.

I'm very proud that I didn't miss anything when our daughter Bessie was growing up – her father and I were around all the time. If one of us wasn't there my mother was, so there was no real guilt. I'm very happy about that and I'm extremely proud of her now. It wasn't perfect by any means, but we were there.

I've had my dreams fulfilled in the last few years. *Vera Drake* was the ultimate experience for me. It was lovely that so many people liked the film and it was a huge success, but that year was the best year of my working life.

Lord Jeffrey Archer

Author

19 August 2013

At 16 I lived in the West Country, in Weston-super-Mare, and went to a boarding school in a small town nearby. I was generally very contented. I was, of course, doing my O-Levels, but I was more interested in running the 100m for England. It's a boys' preoccupation more than a girls' one – boys are more interested in sport than study at that age. I didn't work hard enough at school, and I put about 50 per cent of the blame for that on myself. It was only later I discovered what hard work was.

I had a good life, though me and my mother were very poor – my father had died when I was 11. I still remember the school chaplain coming to the class to tell me, and of course I was shattered. But my mother was a stalwart. She took over and got on with life. She wasn't a giver-upper, that one. I adored her, and I was very happy. We might have been very poor, but as a child you only know what you know. I had no idea then how she was struggling. I grew very close to her after my father died, and my success and different kind of life later made no difference to our relationship. I always admired her work ethic and ambition and I always thought if she'd been born a generation later, she'd have gone to university and had a very different life, probably as a journalist. Much, much later in life, I was able to say thank you for everything, by buying her a house and making sure she lived comfortably.

I was a very energetic teenager – my mother called me a 'jumping bean'. I'd been bullied as a young child and then took up gymnastics and running – I took them very seriously, perhaps because I didn't want to be bullied anymore. I wasn't bright enough for self-doubt. I think the mother of the teenage Jeffrey would be very surprised, as my wife Mary was, that I became a writer. I was very outgoing and I wanted to be a politician – I loved the energetic side of life, making things happen. Writers are the opposite extreme. They sit alone in a room, hour upon hour, producing their work.

I was at Oxford when I got the idea of becoming a politician. I enjoyed public speaking and trying to make things happen, so it was an obvious step. As for the party, I don't think you can have the sort of free enterprise attitude that I have and be a socialist. I've been described as a left-wing Tory, which I think I am. Perhaps I'm more of a natural independent. I've fought for different causes that my party don't agree with all my life, and some of the politicians I've most admired straddled the centre ground. I liked Harold Wilson more than Ted Heath when I was in the Commons.

My younger self was very naive about the problems other people go through, and it was years before I realised that most people have massive problems. Prison taught me how privileged I'd been and how many good friends I had. I also realised how lucky I was to have the God-given gift of being a storyteller, and I wrote three books in prison. When I was young I charged about thinking I would live forever and that I could change the world. I probably made some mistakes policy-wise, but some things I got right. I fought for women's rights all my life – I prayed that the Duke and Duchess of Cambridge would have a girl so we would finally have a daughter automatically first in line for the throne. That would have been a landmark moment for me, because I fought so hard for that for so many years.

It may shock people, but I wouldn't want to go back and change anything about my life. When you make a mistake, by all means burst into tears, but don't spend the rest of your life looking back. Stand up, brush yourself off and get on with it. There's no human being alive who wouldn't like to go back and change their life but you can't, so get real and live in the real world!

My toughest time was when I was thrown into debt.[20] My wife was a don at Oxford, we were a comfortably-off middle-class family and we'd just had our second child. Then I lost everything, including my job. The two worst things in life are illness and debt. I went quiet, got my head down and worked to clear it – it took me seven years. If I could go back, I'd tell my younger self to ask for advice from older people. I now surround myself with intelligent, well-informed people. If I have a problem, I phone an expert and they tell me what to do. But I've always been a believer in fighting. Even when things were at their worst, I was confident that I'd be out of it in three

20 In 1974, after investing in a fraudulent scheme.

years. The big turnaround was writing *Kane and Abel* in 1979 – that changed my life completely.

When I finished *Kane and Abel*, publishers started bidding for it and the Americans bought it for $3,200,000. This was when I was still in debt, and it literally changed my life overnight. A very intelligent woman at HarperCollins told me, 'A year today, this book will be number one in every country.' I told my wife and we sat and thought, 'What did that really mean?' Then it came out in the UK and sold a million copies in the first week. We looked at each other and I said, 'Look, we've been up to the top and down at the bottom. Let's just keep our heads down and keep going.'

I'm quite fit for a 73-year-old. I still go to the gym three times a week and I can run a mile in nine minutes. I'd advise any young person not to smoke, and I'd say that especially to women – you'll regret it in 20 years when your face is lined. Personally, I have to live to 78 to fulfil my contract because I still have three novels to deliver. Though Dickens died in the middle of a book!

John Lithgow

Actor

9 February 2015

I was a young aesthete. As a teenager, I wanted to be a painter and was feverishly creative. I did woodcuts and created my own Christmas card enterprise. I was a curious mixture of very shy and quite outgoing.

By the time I was 16, I'd lived in eight different places. I'd been the new kid in town, over and over again. My family was peripatetic, so I'd worked out all sorts of strategies to make friends. When I was 16 we arrived in Princeton, New Jersey, after my father got a job at the McCarter Theatre. By the end of the year I was elected president of the student council and had somehow managed to make myself an enormously popular kid. I was cast in the leading role in the big school play, so theatre jump-started my social life.

I was a good survivor, but it was not a happy period of my life. I was in a constant stage of anxiety, saying goodbye to friends and arriving as the new kid in school. But in retrospect,

I see that that made me a social animal and probably made me an actor.

Most of my heroes were painters. I worshipped Norman Rockwell and when I outgrew him, I moved on to Picasso and the Abstract Expressionists. I became an ardent museum-goer, which I still am.

I was a curious hybrid American-Englishman. My father was a producer of Shakespeare festivals, so my acting heroes were the knights – John Gielgud, Laurence Olivier, Alec Guinness and Michael Redgrave. I listened to recordings of Olivier playing Othello and Robert Stephens as Benedick, with Maggie Smith as Beatrice.[21] I was quite the Anglophile and have gone on to play lots of English roles.

I didn't want to be an actor. I acted in my father's productions as a child and played one of Nora's children in *A Doll's House* when I was two and a half. I don't remember a single thing about it, but I'm told I was very good.

My shyness kicked in around my love life. I was hopelessly inept and had a total lack of confidence. My advice to my younger self is just to lighten up – and to find the most sexually active man on campus and get good advice from him.

I would tell my younger self to rely on his talents. I was a resourceful kid and immersed myself in my own projects, and that is still completely typical of me. I am in *A Delicate Balance* with Glenn Close on Broadway, but am spending my days on a new short story to incorporate into my one-man show. I do one-night stand gigs, and they're all mine. I am not waiting to be hired. Actually, that is advice my younger self gave me – stay creative and find projects that don't depend on other people.

21 In *Much Ado About Nothing*.

I come from a very lefty family. My parents were good FDR Democrats, my older sister is a terrific fire-breathing Democrat, and those are my politics too, but I'm rarely an activist. You won't find me making grand statements. My nature is dominated by conflict avoidance. I never get into political arguments, because I'm cursed with always seeing everyone's point of view.

I modelled my ambitions on my father, who was my great hero. I grew up in a regional, classical repertory theatre family and figured that was my future. I never dreamed I would act on Broadway, be in a movie or star in a television series, so life has been a series of marvellous surprises. My younger self would have been very astonished and very proud of the career I've had.

At the age of 20 I raced ahead to adulthood and got married. It was a long marriage, 11 years, and I have a wonderful son, so I have to discipline myself not to consider it a mistake in my life. It is something that defined me. If I could take younger myself in hand, I would tell him to be patient – but it is very hard to tell a 20-year-old he is not an adult yet, especially after my crazy childhood, which had a way of persuading me I was an adult. I had to take the situation in hand a number of times.

I don't consider myself a brave person, but as an actor I will take on anything. I've played a lot of people I disagree with and I'm always being hired to play racist politicians. When I play a villain, I regard that villain as the hero of the story. I'm a character actor, which means I am ready, willing and able to play parts completely different to myself and play them with empathy. That's why I played Roberta Muldoon in *The World According to Garp*. Probably my most famous role, Dick Solomon in *3rd Rock from the Sun*, was literally an alien. How could that be any more different?

I worked with Robin Williams in *Garp*. He was a dazzling person and remarkable to work with. Talk about aliens – Robin was on another planet. We did not remain friends. We were friendly but I rarely saw him – he went out into the big wide world. In terms of people who have influenced my life, it's the people who have stayed in my life. A wonderful actor you will never have heard of, Donald Moffat, an English émigré from my father's company, was a humble man but with such skills. Since then, I've subscribed to my personal motto, 'Always cultivate humility – you never know when you're going to need it.'

I've learned a great deal from both of my wives. My current wife of 33 years has been the strongest influence on my life. If I could go back to live one moment again, it would be meeting her. That was a peak moment. We fell in love with each other absolutely instantly. That hadn't happened to me before. That was pretty unique.

CHAPTER 4:

Inspiration

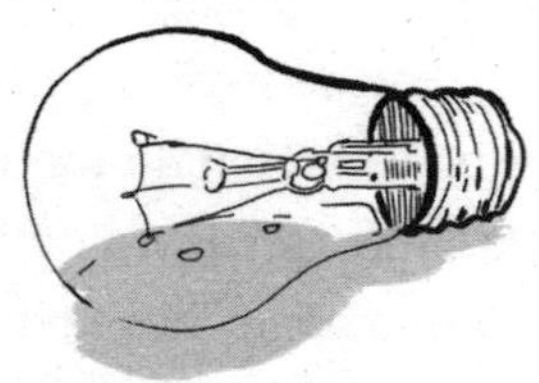

Mavis Staples

Musician

7 July 2014

As a child I would sing to myself all the time. I first learned 'You Are My Sunshine' and 'A Bushel and a Peck', and then it was anything I heard on the radio. I first sang in front of an audience when I was eight. We sang our song 'Will the Circle Be Unbroken' at my aunt Katy's church in Chicago – we were just so happy to sing somewhere other than our living room floor. The people liked us so much they clapped us back three times. It was the only song we knew and we had to play it three times. Pops[22] said, 'Shucks, these people really like us – we're going home to learn some new songs.' And we did. The rest is history.

If I met the teenage Mavis now I'd see a very humble, friendly girl. By 16 I'd already been singing with The Staple Singers for many years. I was singing on records and in front of thousands of people, travelling the country – my sisters

22 Mavis's father, Roebuck 'Pops' Staples.

and I always had different gowns and robes to wear. Life was beautiful at 16 – everyone wanted to know me and my friends wanted to talk to me, but I never got on any star trip. Pops taught us not to get a big head and not to think we were better than anyone else.

I grew up with many of my peers. Aretha Franklin and Dionne Warwick were childhood friends and I lived in the same neighbourhood as Sam Cooke and Lou Rawls. Sam had five brothers and one sister, and Lou's uncle, Reverend Rawls, the founder and pastor of the Tabernacle Missionary Baptist Church. We'd sing there or stand under the streetlights and sing doo-wops.

I'd tell my younger self she has so much to be grateful for. I'd tell her, 'God has blessed you by giving you this gift. You don't even know what keys to sing in, you don't know music, but for you to be able to go out and sing the way you do, to have people admire you across the world, you are blessed. You have many, many wonderful days ahead. Love and treat everybody right. Keep your head up when things don't go the way you want them to go. Have faith and think positive. And whatever the problem is, you can survive it because you're a strong girl, you're well loved, you have faith and you can conquer anything that comes your way.'

Bob Dylan and I became very close. He was just a little folk singer when we first met, an average kid, but he knew The Staple Singers. He asked me to marry him but I told him I wasn't old enough. Neither of my sisters were married, so I couldn't jump the gun. I did like Bobby – he was really cute with his curly hair. I admired him so much for his writing. I thought he was a genius.

If I could relive one day, it would be when I first met Dr Martin Luther King. It was the early '60s – we just happened to be in Montgomery, Alabama, and Pops took us to the Dexter Avenue Baptist Church. Dr King said, 'We are glad to have Pops Staples and his daughters here this morning.' Boy that felt so good. Pops told us that he liked this man's message and that 'If he can preach it, we can sing it'. From then we began writing freedom songs. We started marching with Dr King and we'd sing 'Why? (Am I Treated So Bad)' before he spoke at meetings.

I've met presidents – Obama, Clinton, Carter, and I even met President Kennedy – but none of them topped Dr King. If I could go back and do that all over again, God have mercy, I certainly would. To meet this great man, shake his hand, to be in his presence. For him to love our music, I can't ever forget that. I can't ever live that down. That was my greatest moment. I last saw him a month before he was assassinated. When we lost Dr King I thought I just wanted to go on with him. I was heartbroken when we lost him. He was such a great man.

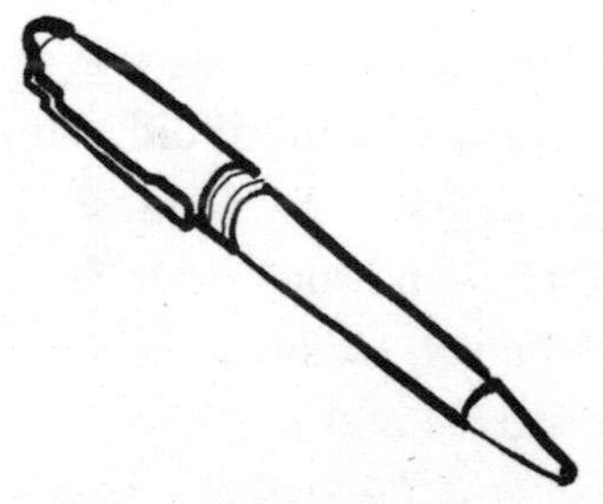

Archbishop Desmond Tutu

Cleric

5 December 2011

As a teenager I looked like my mother – stumpy with a large nose. She was not very educated but she was a wonderful, compassionate, caring person. I've always hoped I resembled her in this. I was the only boy in my family, with two sisters, one older and the other younger. I was delicate healthwise. In fact, at 16 I went down with TB and was in hospital for 20 months. So I was maybe pampered at home after that.

We had fun in my family. I did a few household chores, like fetching water and making tea for the grown-ups. I liked reading. My father was headmaster of our school and encouraged us to read. He let me read comics – *Superman*, *Batman & Robin* – this was unusual, since conventionally most teachers didn't like us to read comics. This fed my reading appetite and I grew to like reading. But I wasn't a bookworm, as I also liked playing. We had tiffs with white kids, because we lived in segregated areas and there was a hostility between the races – we tended to be the ones who got the thin end of the stick.

I think I would rather like my younger self if I met him now – he was rather fun. I was probably quite bright in class, and I had some special friends. One became editor of a big South African magazine, *Drum*. We enjoyed playing soccer with tennis balls. I had many friends and one or two girlfriends!

God has a funny sense of humour. I wanted from an early age to become a physician, and at 16 I was even more determined because I contracted TB and wanted to find a cure for this scourge. I would have been in seventh heaven to qualify as a doctor, but black people did not then have a wide choice. For instance, you couldn't become an engineer or a pilot or even a train driver – these were jobs reserved for whites. That is why I said God must have a sense of humour. Quite frequently, when I'm sitting with heads of state in their imposing offices or residences, I have to pinch myself and say, 'Hey, this is the segregated township urchin – look at him now!' Never in my wildest dreams had I ever imagined that we would be where we are.

Despite my passion for becoming a doctor, I could not take up my place in medical school because my family could not afford the fees. So I went to train as a teacher. I enjoyed teaching until the apartheid government introduced Bantu education, a deliberately inferior system meant to prepare black children for perpetual serfdom. Leah, my wife, and I resigned our posts. She went to train as a nurse, but I did not have too many options and could say I became a priest by default. But perhaps growing up in a Christian family meant that one absorbed certain things unconsciously.

I was influenced by some remarkable people as well as

my mother, the most important influence of all. The first Anglican priest I met was an amazing man, Father Zacheriah Sekgaphane. I might be idealising him, but I really don't recall ever seeing him angry. When he went to take services on the farms, he was usually treated like a big chief. He had his own hut and was served a sumptuous meal after the service. I recall that he never sat down to his meal on those occasions without first checking that we lesser mortals had been provided for. Looking back, I think I wanted to emulate him for his caring for the unimportant.

Another major influence on me was Trevor Huddleston.[23] During my 20-month stay in hospital with TB he really was amazing, either visiting me every week or sending someone else. What that did for my self-esteem was incalculable – that a white priest could take time off regularly to visit a black nonentity was mind-boggling. I have, I think, tried to emulate him in his concern for justice and standing up for the downtrodden – he made me feel important and affirmed.

My teenage self would be amazed to hear about my first visit to Britain in 1962. What surprised Leah and me most was being treated as human beings, courteously. We were bowled over when a London bobby addressed us politely, as 'madam' and 'sir'. It was such a novelty that we would accost a police officer – a white one at that – to ask for directions even when we knew where we were going, just to savour the novelty of being addressed as madam and sir!

When you are right, as we were in opposing apartheid, it is easy to become self-righteous. I depend on the love and prayers of so many, and when the size of my head is in danger

23 The English Anglican bishop known for his anti-apartheid activism and 'Prayer for Africa'.

of swelling, Leah and my children are quick to bring me back to terra firma. Leah has a noticeboard which used to be in our bedroom that reads, 'You are entitled to your wrong opinion!' But, more seriously, I think I was more strident than I need have been, forgetting that we catch more flies with honey than with vinegar. Perhaps I could have won over more whites had I been more conciliatory.

The Anglican Church is like any other denomination. It is God's church and ultimately nothing will prevail against its true teaching. We will recover our true vocation as servants of the kingdom, remembering that we exist ultimately to advance God's kingdom of righteousness, love, compassion and caring to be there on the side of the poor, the hungry and the despised, exactly where our Lord and Master was and is.

My younger self had dreams, but what has happened in our lives and in the lives of all who were oppressed and now are free has exceeded all of them. And in a real sense, all of us – black and white, disadvantaged and advantaged, oppressed and oppressors, willingly or unwillingly – all of us are now free. South Africa, the repulsive caterpillar, has become a gorgeous butterfly that could host one of the most successful soccer World Cups. Our beautiful land, which was an international pariah, has metamorphosed.

Dame Julie Walters

Actor

12 September 2016

At 16, I was at Holly Lodge Grammar School for Girls in Smethwick, which sounds very posh and wasn't by any stretch of the imagination. A lot of people chose not to send their kids there because they thought it was so rough. But I loved it. I really hated my primary school, a Catholic preparatory school. The nuns slapped you about the head. I was frightened of them – how could I learn anything?

When people don't feel like they have a place, school life is difficult. But I was good at sport and I made people laugh. I was never in school plays, but I would fool around and entertain people. I didn't work terribly hard. I played basketball, hockey and was a runner – 200m Worcestershire Champion in 1966! I watched so much of the Rio Olympics it exhausted me. I ran all the races with them, not breathing – and that was very hard in the 10,000m. When Mo Farah fell over, it really hurt.

I was interested in boys, but too lacking in confidence to push myself forward. Some girls at school were like women in their thirties, but I was more like someone of about 11. I would advise my younger self not to worry about how much boys fancy you. I was always terribly flattered if someone fancied me. That seemed more important than what I thought about them. I'd tell my younger self 'No! Really look at them. Don't worry, there are plenty of them. Don't take any shit.'

We were a working-class family without a book in the house, but we all did further education of some description and my brother went to Cambridge. That was because of my mother's drive. We were expected to do something with our lives. We weren't going to work in a factory or a shop, though my dad was a builder and my mum packed chocolates in Cadbury's – she wasn't having that for us. My mother wanted me to be a nurse. 'You can go anywhere in the world!' she'd say.

We lived in an end-of-terrace house in Bearwood, Smethwick, which is now one of the most deprived areas of the country. It was a big, freezing old house, with a park at the end of the road. I was never allowed to go there because there were strange men, according to my mother. I didn't know what that meant until somebody did try to abduct me when I was a child. We were playing in the garden of a big old empty house. And this man found us and basically assaulted us. 'Lift up your dresses,' he said. Nothing terrible, but he was trying to take us. I didn't fully realise until I wrote about it in my autobiography. I recently wrote to one of the other girls, and she's had nightmares about it.

It was incredible to be 16 in 1966. I recently saw Ron Howard's documentary on The Beatles, and you could see all the girls screaming. I never did that, but 'I Want to Hold Your Hand' was playing when I was first kissed. It was just gorgeous – a great time. Then at college I embraced hippiedom. I loved it. I had the long hair, huge bell bottoms, that Indian effect – the smell of patchouli is really evocative for me. I smoked dope. Everybody did. I liked it. Free love.

I knew nothing about politics at 16, but Enoch Powell's 'Rivers of Blood' speech was about Smethwick. I didn't take it all in until I met my first college boyfriend. There was an anti-apartheid demonstration and he said we should go. I said, 'Should we?' and he said, 'What, do you condone apartheid?' I had to find a dictionary to look up 'condone'! Then I tried to look up 'apartheid', but didn't know how it was spelled. So I was educated mainly by him.

Reading Germaine Greer's *The Female Eunuch* confirmed all the things I'd felt. Here was someone more intelligent and older writing about how women were treated as second-class. And I'd grown up feeling that. I remember my mother saying, 'You must work – you don't have to get married.' She was like that from life experience rather than from reading about it. Strong women talking about that really affected me.

I didn't look very far ahead, but when I started nursing, it felt like a career for life and it wasn't what I wanted. I lay in the bath at home and said very quietly, 'I want to be an actor.' People told me I should be on the stage, but I'd never said it out loud. I still didn't know what to do about it, but I'd said it. Then my boyfriend told me about a course at Manchester Poly. I left nursing. Mum went mad, of course. But I felt I could make it as soon as I went to drama school.

I really feel for my younger self. I want to put my arm around her and say, 'You're all right, you are mate!' I can feel her innocence. I feel for women coming into the business. It is a tough old game, full of rejection and people commenting on you physically.

The Everyman Theatre was a wonderful place. We felt like we were changing the world. Willy Russell, Alan Bleasdale, Pete Postlethwaite, Bill Nighy, Matthew Kelly, Antony Sher – a fantastic group of actors. And Alan Dossor, who recently died, was the most extraordinary director. This was a theatre that was about community – it was for the community. We went out around the area doing pub shows. We embraced the community, and they loved it.

A lot of my roles have dealt with class. I was very conscious of the class divide; I remember visiting my brother in Cambridge at 16 and thinking it was another world. I remember feeling quite angry at middle-class people and their privilege. 'Middle-class actresses? You should be fucking good – you've had all the privileges.' Which is a load of rubbish, of course. Acting isn't about that. Although nowadays, getting to drama school bloody is. People can't afford it.

Meeting Victoria Wood was like a gift. From the moment we met, we just laughed at the same things. We would look at people and laugh – not in a nasty way, but we'd see the human frailty and how funny it is. I knew I'd met someone very special. I was very lucky to meet her. I thought, 'If I could write, this is what I would have written.' It was like she could see inside my head. I still can't get my head around the fact that Vic's gone – I can't get my heart around it, either. She was such a powerful presence. And for me, personally, we went back such a long way.

Educating Rita was massive for me. It was like a parallel to my own life. I never thought the film was very good at the time, because I'd done it onstage, which was very different, but it opened up my career. Then Alan Bleasdale's *Boys from the Blackstuff* was completely groundbreaking television. To be part of that, which also felt revolutionary, was incredible. And I met Alan Bennett very early on, a wonderful person to work with. I was so lucky.

People are really nice to me. You can say I'm loved, but it's not really loved. I don't know how you define it, but it is nice to feel that people are affectionate – that's lovely.

I've been with my Grant for 31 years. It was instant. He moved in the night we met and never moved out. I was pissed in a posh bar, saying, 'I bet nobody here's a member of the Labour Party.' And he turned round and said, 'I am actually.' I looked at him and thought, 'Oh, he's a bit of all right.' I probably said it as well, being drunk. I remember saying something ridiculous like, 'Look at the size of this man's neck!' He walked me home, and that was it. He mended my washing machine. What more could a girl ask for?

My younger self would think it was wonderful that I live on a farm. Living in the country was always a fantasy. My own patch of green – I still love it. I love the peace and I love walking and being out in all weathers. In the dead of winter it's fabulous, watching it change. These days, a role has got to be good to make me want to leave my home.

Sir Michael Palin

Comedian and Author

31 August 2015

When I was 16, I was spending most of my time away at public school in Shrewsbury. I'd been there a couple of years, so I'd got past the bit when you're treated as the lowest of the low. I was doing a bit of sport, rowing quite a lot, getting terrible bum blisters on the Severn. I was settling down. People liked me because I was able to make them laugh. Some of the teachers perhaps saw a glint in my eye, a cheekiness, that they liked. I had an accommodating nature and tended, and still tend, to see the good in people. I was deliberately approachable because I was so curious about people.

At 16 everyone's looking round for girlfriends, and I was quite lucky. While on holiday in Suffolk with my parents I caught sight of a group of girls being led out to swim in the cold North Sea by some striding male figure at quarter to eight in the morning. There were three trying to make the best of it, and a fourth who didn't look pleased at all and was storming along with the most marvellous, rebellious look. And I thought, 'She's great – I like her.' My friend Richard contrived a situation where I threw a ball at him in the sea but deliberately missed and hit the girls instead, and it worked! I got together with her that summer, and we had a little summer holiday romance. That was the first time I met Helen and our golden wedding anniversary will be next year.

The teenage Michael would be astounded that the boy who sat around watching comedy on TV grew up to write some of those jokes himself. I was born and brought up in Sheffield – not the centre of the cultural world. My and my friends used to look at the names of scriptwriters as the credits rolled – the idea that one day I'd actually meet Spike Milligan and become a sort of friend of his, that would be quite unbelievable.

I don't think I've changed much. If I met my teenage self now, our conversation would be around things that make us both laugh. If I was looking for modern comedy he'd go for, I think I'd show him Alan Partridge and *The Fast Show* – he'd like that way of delivering jokes. And he'd like Vic Reeves and Bob Mortimer – the silliness, the invention and imagination. I'd look for the real spirit in young Michael, bubbling under the conventional respecter of rules. I'd like to find the rebel in him. If I had to show him bits of Python, I don't think he'd like my bits best. He might be a bit embarrassed by them. Like me, he'd find Cleese hilarious. He'd probably say to me, 'Yes, you can be funny, but clearly the big presence in that show is Cleese.'

I first met John Cleese when he was in *The Frost Report* in 1965. I clearly remember walking behind him on the way to a restaurant we were all eating in, in Shepherd's Bush. John was walking with Terry Jones, and he suddenly put his hand out and just pushed Terry over a wall into someone's garden. It was a wonderful moment. I thought, 'This is someone I really need to know.' I was probably terrified of him at first – he was so very tall and so very, very good at what he did. I thought John was in another league, and I didn't think we'd ever work together. But when he instigated Python, he rang me and asked me to get the others in too.

All the Pythons came from the provinces. None of us were on a career course to do what we did. Our fathers were policemen, insurance sellers, steelworkers. We envied the ease which with the metropolitan crowd controlled everything but were determined to take a new approach. We were critical of what was mainstream and London-based, and taste was London-based. We weren't the first – Peter Cook and Dudley Moore's *Beyond the Fringe* was perhaps even more important than *The Goon Show* in that sense.

Realising Python was coming to an end was quite hard. After the third series, John decided to quit and there were two feelings in my mind. One was, 'Oh God, how will we earn money?' The other was that perhaps he was right – maybe we were running out of originality. The forest fire that had blazed so brightly was dampening down. John was the first to realise the material wasn't as good anymore. It was a difficult time.

As you get more popular, you realise there are people who like what you do, and you feel a responsibility to them. When we were first making the Python shows, I wasn't aware that I was creating an audience for Michael Palin stuff. I didn't feel a bond of trust with the viewers. But later, after

I'd done *Ripping Yarns* and travel things, I made a show, *Palin's Column*, that didn't really work, and I was conscious of feeling I'd let my audience down. I don't think you can ever get that early freedom back. Those early years writing comedy after university, I just wrote as much as I could, and tried everything. It was hit-and-miss but there's was a feeling of, 'Let's just do it.'

The '60s were a good time to write satire – the establishment was very clearly defined, so it was easy to have a go at it. Now we're told anything goes, there's a place for everything, so where does satirical humour find its place? Who are the people you're trying to send up? I think the joy has gone out of comedy. Maybe we've lost our way – maybe we can't see that the people we should be sending up are the people who run the big high-tech companies who tell us we can say whatever we want in the utopian, new, Internet-based culture. Because what they're really doing is making sure that no matter what we're doing, they're making money out of it, which is why I value the BBC. These are scary times and everything is for sale. I've watched the triumph of marketing in every sphere, from red buses to cricket pitches.

If I could go back to any one point in my life, it would be to a day during my school years. I got quite good at rowing in the end and eventually our team won the school regatta. I remember being very nervous the night before, and then we were out on the water on a sunny day, looking across at the other boats on the water alongside us, and everything just went right. It was a wonderful feeling, just fantastic. I had one of my first beers in the tent afterwards. And nothing has tasted as good since.

Richard E. Grant

Actor

21 January 2019

When I was 16, I had a sudden growth spurt and had to take time off school, as I suffered from acute pain in my legs. I was pipe-cleaner thin and grew my hair as long as possible as I had acne, which I was told would disappear by the time I was 18.

I had a lifelong passion to be an actor and made shoe-box theatres, with scenery and cut-out figures attached to lollipop sticks. I progressed to glove puppets and then marionettes. My parents gave me Pelham Puppets[24] for every birthday and Christmas, which proved lucrative as I did shows at kids' birthday parties in the school holidays and in a full-sized puppet theatre in our garage.

I always wanted to be an actor, but I had no clue as to how to go about it. I was good at art and model making, so my father encouraged me to consider architecture – but I failed every maths exam, which kiboshed that idea. He then

24 Wooden marionette puppets made by English puppet maker Bob Pelham.

suggested I become a barrister, as I was so argumentative and he said it required acting skills.

I did school plays with Zindzi and Zeni Mandela.[25] None of us believed that their father would ever get out of Robben Island alive, let alone become president two decades later. Waterford Kamhlaba United World College of Southern Africa,[26] had 27 nationalities and an ethos of tolerance, multi-faith acceptance and multi-racial openness and inclusivity. The injustices of apartheid in neighbouring South Africa had a profound impact. Prejudice and ignorance based on someone's skin colour is ludicrous and abhorrent.

After my parents' acrimonious divorce, my father became a violent alcoholic. His personality switch at night culminated in him attempting to shoot me at close range, after I'd emptied a crate of his Scotch whisky down the sink. He drunkenly lurched when he pulled the trigger and mercifully missed. There was no treatment nor AA meetings available, and the social stigma was such that everything was kept secret. Christmas was invariably a nightmare, with everyone on tenterhooks, so I've made up for it as an adult by celebrating Christmas to the max.

Neil Armstrong landing on the moon in 1969, when I was 12, made an indelible impression. It was about proving that what had seemed impossible could somehow be achieved. It has been a lifelong passion to go into outer space – it looks increasingly unlikely to happen, but having the dream is everything.

Being teased for wanting to be an actor and being accused of 'playing with dolls' inadvertently helped inure me to the

25 Zindziswa and Zenani, daughters of Nelson.

26 In Swaziland, where Richard grew up

derision and rejection that's part and parcel of an actor's life. Once I got used to being told, 'You'll never make it', it strengthened my resolve to prove those naysayers wrong. Where that determination and self-belief came from is a mystery, but wanting to prove yourself is a very powerful force. I would tell my younger self, 'Never give up' and 'Don't try and imitate anyone else.' I'm just grateful that my teenage dream came true, in spite of being pants at maths.

London is the epicentre of the theatre world, so it was always my plan to come and live here and try to make it as an actor. My parents periodically brought me to London when I was growing up, and we saw as many films, plays and musicals as could be crammed in, which left an indelible impression. When I emigrated to England in 1982, the directors I met observed that I spoke like someone from the '50s, which reflected the time-warp effect of growing up in Swaziland. I can only assume that this has influenced my getting cast in period dramas.

I had two role models – Donald Sutherland and Barbra Streisand. He was very tall, gangly, long-faced and funny, and didn't fit the Robert Redford movie-star mould. My final drama school assessment was that I was too tombstone-featured to make it as an actor and should concentrate on becoming a director. Having seen Sutherland in Robert Altman's *M*A*S*H*, it felt like a dream come true when I got to meet him and subsequently work on three of his films – *The Player*, *Prêt-à-Porter* and *Gosford Park*. Streisand was likewise derided for her unconventional looks, but her astonishing talents and determination were inspiring. I finally got to meet her in Los Angeles in 1991 and was delighted that she asked even more questions than I do!

I genuinely thought that my entire career would be in the theatre, and never thought I'd ever be in films. That all changed in 1985 when I was cast in an improvised film for the BBC alongside Gary Oldman and Adrian Edmondson called *Honest, Decent and True*. The day after it screened in 1986, I got a new agent, Michael Whitehall, who introduced me to casting directors – one of whom, Mary Selway, auditioned me for *Withnail & I*, which completely changed my professional life.

Almost without exception, every job I've had is a direct result of being in *Withnail & I*. I am so indebted to the writer and director Bruce Robinson for taking a chance on a complete unknown, and for the decades-long friendship that's ensued. I'm allergic to alcohol, so it's ironic that I'm identified for playing a drug-addled alcoholic.

I am utterly and completely gobsmacked to have been cast in the final episode of *Star Wars*, 41 years after I first saw it as a drama student! And it would really surprise my younger self that I've either got to meet or work with most of the actors and movie stars I grew up admiring and reading about in *Plays and Players* and *Films Illustrated*, the monthly magazines that I subscribed to. I remain as starstruck as I ever was.

I never thought I would ever risk falling in love or having a child. The experience of my parents' divorce was so cruel and pain-filled, but as John Lennon wisely quipped, 'Life is what happens to you when you're busy making other plans.' My late father gave me some advice that has proved to be invaluable. He advised that 'If you have five true friends, consider yourself a rich man,' the wisdom of which I've come to acutely appreciate. He also said, 'Good manners cost nothing and maketh the man', which was another fine piece of advice.

The film from my back catalogue I think is most underrated is *Wah-Wah*, which I wrote and directed. It had an exceptional cast and took five years from script to screen, but regrettably it opened on the same weekend as *The Da Vinci Code* and got 'drowned' by the tidal wave of that movie's success.

If I could have one last conversation with someone, I would want to speak with my mentor, Bunny Barnes, who died 11 years ago. She was my piano and English teacher, with whom I became lifelong friends. She believed in and encouraged me to pursue my dreams of becoming an actor, and the collection of letters we wrote to one another over decades continues to be a great source of wisdom, gossip and hilarity. Her love for classical music inspired, informed and educated me.

I've kept a diary ever since I was ten years old, in an attempt to make sense of the world. It helps whenever I get panicked or feel out of my depth – there is always the reassurance that no matter what you're currently troubled by, you can somehow wiggle your way through. It's also proof that I've met the people I've long admired and I've been to extraordinary places along the way.

Tim Peake

Astronaut

16 October 2017

At 16 I lived in a small rural village in West Sussex and all my thoughts were taken up with being in the cadets. I loved it. It had an army section and an air force section. I loved being in the army section and all the adventurous outdoor activities at weekends: camping, hillwalking, climbing. But I had a huge passion for flying, so I tried to sneak off with the air force at every opportunity and jump into a plane and go flying in a glider or a small tandem-seat trainer aircraft. That took up most of my time outside school.

At various stages I suffered from the usual teenage angst. I worried about school work – I wasn't a particularly gifted student and I wasn't at the top of the class, so school was often a struggle for me. Then I came to a bit of a crossroads when I was 18. I was set to go to university when I was offered a place at Sandhurst. I thought a lot about it then decided to go straight to Sandhurst and start flying. I couldn't contain my excitement. I think now that if I hadn't started my flying career so early, I probably wouldn't have had the operational experience as a test pilot, which turned out to be the key to me becoming an astronaut.

I was painfully shy with girls and probably still am. The idea of going to ask a girl out was terrifying – far more frightening than going into space. I did have the odd girlfriend, but it was never an easy experience, and it took me months to work up the courage to ask anyone out. Then I had a bit of real heartbreak – an early girlfriend got leukaemia and passed away at the age of 21. She was much more than a girlfriend really – she lived two doors down from me and we'd been friends our whole life. Losing such a close friend at such a young age, having to face that and the emotions it brought out – it was very tough.

What's quite surprising is that there's no military background in my family. My father was a journalist and my mother was a midwife. Both grandfathers were conscripted into the army in the Second World War, but they weren't career military men. So I have no idea where my early interest in the army, and in flying, came from. My father used to take me to air shows – that's the only thing I can think of. I watched fantastic displays at those shows and marvelled at the engineering. I loved building and testing model aeroplanes; I bought one kit, and thought I could design and build my own better, so I spent many hours experimenting after that.

I can still remember my very first flight. I was about 13 and it was a Chipmunk aircraft. I remember that feeling of bumping along the grass, then accelerating, then the smoothness as it took off. And you were in control, feeling it respond to your commands – that was just exhilarating.

I always knew what I wanted to do with my life. I felt very lucky that way, seeing friends really struggle, wondering what they should study, what they wanted to do. For me, the air force stood out like a beacon as a route to follow.

Life became more complicated for me after I joined the Space Agency, because that's when my wife and I had our first child. For me, becoming a father was a more life-changing experience than going into space – it completely changes your outlook and your perspective. If I'd been younger and without children, going to live on the International Space Station would have been no problem. And I did leave my dream job as a pilot to go to a situation where there was absolutely no guarantee that I'd ever be picked for a mission. That was a risk, but it worked out.

The hardest thing about living in the Space Station for six months is the feeling of complete helplessness. If something were to happen to your family back on Earth, you couldn't be there. It's not like you're cut off from them – you could call every day if you wanted, and you get a weekly video conference. And six months is what you'd spend away if you were in the army and posted overseas. But what I found hard was the idea that I wasn't in a position where, if my family really needed me, I could be there for them.

To me, the space station was never a lonely place. It's an incredibly busy, vibrant place, which always keeps you motivated and energised, so the time goes by very quickly. You do feel very detached, but that's not the same as lonely. You're very aware that you've really succeeded in getting away from it all. You've left the planet, but that also brings a sense of peace and tranquillity. Music can be very powerful and it can evoke strong emotions, so I would be cautious about listening to anything too emotional. I used to listen to very lively upbeat rock when I was working out.

Becoming well known would have been a shocking idea to the young Tim. We're used to being quite guarded in the military, so to have a complete reversal of that, where you're an ambassador interacting with all kinds of people and doing lots of public speaking, was strange. I was very nervous about that at first, but I've come to really enjoy it. I love telling the stories about the mission – it was a great experience and I like telling people about it.

A 16-year-old Tim would be amazed, shocked and delighted if you told him he would end up going into space. I loved astronomy and looking up at the stars. And I was always questioning things, all the big questions about the universe, the sources of life and light. But I wouldn't want him to know in advance – it's a scary prospect and I think it would change his outlook on life. I've enjoyed the journey in my life, and I've never looked too far ahead.

The moment I'd like to live over again was when I was 21. I'd gone through the gruelling selection process for becoming a pilot – the medicals, the interviews and flying training. It's a very tough process, especially for a young man. Then you have to wait to see if the air force are going to take you. I was called into an office and sat in front of the chief flying instructor. I'd seen people before me come out, some very happy and some very disappointed. The instructor was a man of few words, in true military fashion. He just said, 'Well done, Peake – you're in.'

Wilbur Smith

Author

28 May 2018

My teens were a pretty miserable time, and reading became a sneaky pleasure for me. In those days, all the heating and cooking in the house was done with wood, and one of my chores was to go off with the tractor and trailer and a gang of guys who'd cut the wood and load it on, and I'd bring it back. I always used to sneak a book down the front of my shirt, so I could perch up on the tractor with a big hat on and read my book even in the middle of the day. My father never caught me at it, because I could always hear his car coming.

As a child I preferred being on my own, reading whenever I could. As soon as I was able, I started to read books myself, starting with *Biggles* and *Just William*. Soon I was lost in the worlds of C. S. Forester, with his exquisite tales of Horatio Hornblower and adventure on the high seas. My mother struck up a friendship with a public librarian in Bulawayo, Zimbabwe, in Northern Rhodesia, almost 800 miles south of where we lived, and every month a package of new adventures would arrive on the freight train. From that moment onwards I always had a well-thumbed novel in my pocket. I could dive into books and find gripping tales of death and danger, and the heroism and savagery of this continent we called home. I loved the romance of Africa.

When I was 16 I was stuck in a horrible boarding school. However, when I got to university, that was special. By the time I was 18, the gates of heaven had opened for me at Rhodes University in Grahamstown, in the Eastern Cape province of South Africa. Suddenly there were girls who didn't wear gym slips and walk primly to church in crocodile formation. Up until that moment, I had never dreamed of how soft and warm these gorgeous creatures were, or how sweet they smelled.

I remember a used convertible I bought that was very popular with the ladies. I lived in Matthews House, part of Founders Hall, but I soon found my way to the leading women's residence, Oriel, named after Oxford's Oriel College. I fell for a girl who was in her second year. Her boyfriend was a lawyer in Port Elizabeth but she took a shine to me, a bumbling first year, naive and eager to please but longing for adventure and new experiences. Within a week I discovered, to my joy, that the mouth wasn't the only way to give pleasure during sex.

The only saving grace of my boarding school was an influential English teacher who took time to talk to me about the books I read and focused my mind on what was I trying to achieve in writing a story. He liked to have a structure in the classical style: beginning, middle and end. The idea of picking the story up and letting it go, and then picking it up again in the middle, and then at the end to engender excitement and tension, of not giving too much away at the beginning, of letting characters develop themselves and keeping some mystery about how it's all going to turn out, were all formulas that he proposed to me. Of course it's the way you take them and employ your own instincts that makes all the difference. If there's a genius in writing, that's where it lies.

I was very fortunate to have two wonderful parents. My father was a man of action and my mother was an artist, a very gentle person who loved books and painting; I have many of her paintings to this day. My father taught me about the outdoor life and my mother gave me the other side of the mirror, with music and books – before I could read myself, she'd read to me every night. My father thought that reading too much was unhealthy. He only read non-fiction, mostly manuals about how to fix things on the ranch.

In 1962 I was 29 and, sitting in the bedroom of the bachelors' lodgings where I lived, I stared at the twentieth rejection letter I'd received for the novel I considered was my masterwork, *The Gods First Make Mad*. As I screwed it in my fist and prepared to tell my agent to stop submitting it any more widely, I faced a troubling thought: my father might have been right and books were a waste of time. A few years later, I returned to my love of writing and never looked back.

I remember the first time I saw someone reading my first novel, *When the Lion Feeds*. I was in the departure lounge at Heathrow in 1964, after a disheartening trip to London when I realised that the red carpet of success was not going to be laid out for me after publishing one novel. An attractive woman was reading my book, and I was so overwhelmed that I walked over to her and said, 'Excuse me, you're reading my book.' She looked at me and, putting the book down, said, 'I'm sorry, someone had just left it here.'

I would hope my 16-year-old self would look at me now and see something in himself where all of this would have been possible. Writing fiction on my own terms, in my own way, and never doffing my cap to another is something my younger self would be pretty pleased about. I think he would look at me and say, 'You jammy sod – save some for me!'

I'd tell my younger self, 'Be careful what you wish for, and if you don't have the chops to deal with the trappings of success, go and work for someone else.' The criticism and the uncertainties of self-doubt will gobble you up. I've made a lot of mistakes, but unfortunately they are the only way to learn. Fail again; fail better. Move on; learn.

If I could go back in time, I would like to watch my mother and father drinking tea on the veranda of our house again, talking about what had happened on the ranch that day. The happiest times for me now? It's simple: waking up next to my wife Niso on the first day of writing my next novel. Pure bliss.

Viggo Mortensen

Actor

25 March 2013

I remember my first year of school, when my family moved to the United States from Argentina. They had this thing in the morning: a pledge of allegiance to the flag. I didn't know the words and mumbled them. The teacher said, 'You – you don't know the words!' That was embarrassing. After a few days I realised it was 'Liberty and justice for all.' That's it. I know it now.

Before school started each day, the kids used to gather outside on a grassy sidewalk. At that age, the kids tended to be in groups of girls and boys – it wouldn't do at all for you to be by yourself. I'd stand near groups of boys, so it seemed to the girls in particular I wasn't standing alone. I hadn't grown up with these kids, so I was an alien life form – that's what it felt like.

I had no intention of being an actor. I've always been kind of happy being by myself and I was a teenager in my own quiet way, living in my own world. I didn't really go out destroying property – I mean, I did a little of that, like throwing snowballs at police cars, but not much. I never had problems with animals of any kind and I didn't mind getting lost, but I would run from crowds of people. Acting would have been the last thing I'd have thought of doing.

My heroes were explorers, ancient Greek heroes or cowboys like Martín Fierro.[27] Above all, they were the players for the San Lorenzo football team. I always had a thing for explorers, the people who went to places other people hadn't been to and tried things other people hadn't tried. If I was 16 right now, I would be really interested in the guy who skydived, Felix Baumgartner.

I wanted to learn how to act, as a kind of a practical thing – I was interested in movies and since I was very little my mom had taken me to see them a lot. In the first years that I tried acting as a career, I kept having screen tests and it got down to me and one other person for a lead role in a movie, but I kept going. I didn't have to deal with playing a major part in a movie for years, so I learned the craft but didn't have to go to premieres, which was probably good for me.

If a girl liked me, it was kind of terrifying – as I wasn't one for parties or social interaction, I was awkward in how I would interact. I used to wear pyjama tops for shirts because they were comfortable – I think people thought I was really strange. One time I actually wore a big floppy hat, but that was in my hippie days. I was 14 or 15 with very long hair and a big floppy hat with a pheasant feather sticking out of it. With adolescence I became a little more impulsive. Whenever

27 A Gaucho character from Argentinian writer José Hernández's epic poem of the same name.

I would have a girlfriend, I would always think I'd be with that person forever. The top three things I would tell my younger self to look forward to are: falling in love, having a son and travelling.

Is there anything I should definitely have avoided as a teenager? Drug use, not that I was terrible. Actually, scratch that one because I don't entirely disapprove of it. Of course I have regrets about things I did or didn't do, even as an adult, but I think everybody has that. I've gradually learned to be more in the present, learn things and move forward. Otherwise you go crazy.

CHAPTER 5:

Family

Grayson Perry

Artist

17 October 2016

I was already a transvestite by the time I was 16. I took my stepmother's clothes, changed in the toilets behind Chelmsford Museum and walked up and down the high street in make-up, a mini-dress and a wig. I was just acting on an instinctual desire, a need to play a role. It was very sexually exciting, a big turn-on. Adrenaline is a great aphrodisiac. I got the wig from an advert in the back of the *Daily Mail*. It was about £1.50 – a shapeless, brunette, very wiggy sort of thing. I'm sure the *Daily Mail* would be happy to know they facilitated my sexual fetish.

At 16 I was a complete mess. That was probably the epicentre of my adolescent woes, my *annus horribilis*. My mother had a volcanic temper and when she found out I'd been in contact with my real father for the first time in eight years, she erupted. Within half an hour she'd packed up all my possessions and was driving me to my father's house. She dumped me at the top of the road. He wasn't even there – he was away working. His wife took me in and I ended up sharing a room with their lodger until she found out I'd been wearing her clothes and threw me out.

Getting in contact with my dad came out of chance. A friend of mine at school was going out with a girl who said her stepfather was my dad, so my ears pricked up and I put feelers out through her and went to visit him. It was interesting but disappointing. My male role models weren't great. My dad was an emotional coward. And my stepfather was a violent ignoramus.

I wasn't a very sophisticated teenager. At 16 I was still watching war films and wanted to be a jet pilot. My plan was to join the army. I had a very well-developed interior fantasy life. I did a lot of drawing. But I didn't relate that to any wider career context. I was in the cadets and saw the army as an easy transition. Lots of transvestites overreact, try to cure themselves by doing something manly; there was a bit of that going on. Then halfway through my 16th year I got my first girlfriend, I stopped going to cadets and my art teacher said I should apply for art college. Almost overnight I changed my ideas. I thought, 'Actually, that sounds good – doing something I like. Wow!'

I wish I'd had the emotional intelligence when I was younger that I have now. Perhaps I could have said things to my mother or father that would have made their lives easier. My mother would have had a much better life if she'd left my stepfather when I was 16. But I was very fucked-up then. And my relationships with my parents just got worse. I see my father about once a year. My mother died this year, and only half her children went to the funeral, and that was out of morbid duty. She was... a difficult woman. And mentally ill. And it wasn't our job to fix that.

I don't think I'd tell my 16-year-old self everything is going to turn out okay. In a way it would be lovely to put my arms around him and tell him not to worry, but then he might relax and he wouldn't be driven by the demons I was driven by. Confidence is the most valuable commodity on Earth because it allows people to reach their full potential. But I wouldn't be the artist I am without all those years of self-doubt and anger. Fear and anxiety powered me through those times. Anger is a force that motivates you. I still use it now, but in a much more measured way.

If I met the 16-year-old Grayson now I might tell him to be nicer to people. Some of my friends tell me they used to find me funny but scary and after a few drinks I could be vicious to people. I had the temper from hell. And I was articulate enough to pull people to pieces. I went on to have very taut relationships with art dealers, with arguments and fall-outs. One of my mottos now is 'It's nice to be nice'. Because people will be nice back. I think because I was so hard on myself I was hard on other people as well. I was struggling all the time, and I was very negative and cynical. That's still a big part of what I do, but now I think being nice is fun and makes the world a better place.

The 16-year-old set to join the army would not get it if I told him his future was in ceramics – it's so random. I didn't go to college to do ceramics but took an evening class in it because it sounded fun. I wasn't overly blessed with self-awareness as an artist – I just got on with things. I think that was helpful when I was young, and I'd tell my younger self to go with his instincts. That would be a lovely thing to say, because you're not sure of anything when you're young and your mind is just plastic. To be guided by your intuition, that's an asset.

I felt relieved to have a daughter because I wouldn't inflict my own problems about masculinity on her. I was so aware of the dysfunction I'd grown up with that it had been a worry regarding becoming a parent. I was a textbook dad in her early years. My wife would read out passages from parenting manuals, and I'd say, 'Right, this is how we have to do it.' I took everything on board. One thing I'm good at is playing, so I taught Flo to play. I think being good at playing is an under-celebrated part of life. I felt quite sad when she became less huggy as she got older.

The thing I find most poignant is the idea of doing things for the last time. And you often don't know you're doing something for the last time, perhaps because it's the last time you're physically able to do it. Or it could be the last time your child sits on your lap. Most of the things I enjoy doing I can still do, but I do miss anonymity. Fame means that as a transvestite, I can no longer be an anonymous man in a frock walking down the street. I'm now 'Grayson Perry, public property', and I am very nicely accosted by my mainly middle-class fans. I didn't realise how much I'd lose when I became famous. I miss the thrill of being that weird bloke in a dress who's slightly dangerous and ridiculous.

Chelsea Clinton

Author

20 August 2018

When I was 16, I was definitely a nerd. I was preoccupied with my reading and my studies. I also went to ballet every day after school, and I was quite serious about it. I remember clearly my mother coming into my room in the evening and telling me I shouldn't be doing my homework – I should be out with my friends and needed a bit more balance in my life. She was completely correct, of course. But I was so curious and loved school.

I'd like to go back and reassure my 16-year-old self, moving from Little Rock, Arkansas to the White House, so worried that I'd never make any new friends. My two best friends, both called Elizabeth, came to stay with us for a week or so during those first months. And for the first time my parents let me have a phone in my bedroom so I could call my friends whenever I wanted. When I wasn't doing schoolwork or at ballet, I was on the phone talking to my friends back in Little Rock. We talked a *lot*. My parents did everything they could to allow me to nurture those friendships through my teenage years in Washington. They were very important to me, and they're still my closest friends today. I was a bridesmaid at both their weddings, and we've always been deeply connected to each other.

I was never resentful about any restrictions on my life when I was a teenager. I don't find resentment a helpful or comforting emotion, and I always understood that the secret service had a job to do and respected them. When I had to have protection, I understood why. In fact, I was quite grateful to the secret service people and the way they treated my friends – particularly the boys, who were utterly fascinated by them. They were always so patient, answering endless questions about their training and weapons, and what they would do in all these different situations my friends dreamt up for them.

I watched *The West Wing* when it came out and I just remember thinking, 'I wish politics really operated like that.' Especially today – the idea of general agreements over shared goals and intense debate about how to reach them. Today in my country we don't have a sense of shared ends – it's quite the opposite.

I think if you met the 16-year-old Chelsea today you'd find her friendly – I was always very friendly. I understood it was my responsibility to help people overcome their preconceptions about me and wanted to show that I wasn't snobbish or hoity-toity. I was a blend of outgoing and quite geeky. I wasn't shy or reticent, but I was not outwardly confident either. I've always had a strong sense of myself inside, but I've never been brash or loud.

I was very aware of the comments about my appearance in the media when I was young. I've thought about this a lot, especially as bullying is on the rise and we have a President who's normalising hate. I was picked on at elementary school by some not very nice people – generally boys – who made fun of my appearance or locked me in my locker to see if state police would show up. But I'm so grateful looking back, and I feel this so deeply, that when it happened to me in Washington, it was these older men saying these mean things to a 12-year-old girl. I mean, it was crazy – why were these old men picking on me? That said nothing about me and a whole lot about them. Something clearly hadn't gone right for them in their lives and they were now trying to bully a child. That helped me understand early in my life that when we are verbally abused by other people, it's not about who we are, it's all about the bullies.

I miss my grandmother Dorothy so much. I loved her so much, and I talk a lot about her to both my children. She was such a huge part of my life and who I am now. She had a life I couldn't imagine. She was born to teenage parents who struggled and abandoned her for the first time when she was three. Then, when she was eight, they basically gave up on her and her much younger sister completely, and put them on a train from Chicago to LA, to go and live with their grandparents, who were harsh at best. When my grandmother was 14 she was told she had to start supporting herself, so she found a job and got herself through high school, graduating with honours. She was so determined and went on to create a home of hope and love for my mother and her brother. She was very wise, but she was also so much fun to be around. I wish she could have got to know her great-grandchildren, but

I find it very moving that she was born before women had the right to vote and lived long enough to see her daughter enter the race to be president.

My 16-year-old self would be very surprised that I'm such a public person now – I used to be a very private person and expected to lead a very private life. It was partly because of my grandmother that I became a more public person. She once told me that I was Chelsea Clinton and there was nothing I could do about that, so I could either do something positive with all the inevitable attention or I could just live in a smaller way and learn to bear whatever *Page Six* [28] was going to say about my rather boring life. My mother told me to take serious criticism seriously; it's important to be open and receptive to the thoughts of your family and friends, the people who care about you. It's equally important not to be curtailed by the criticism of bullies who don't know you.

If I could go back to any time in my life… am I going to give the answer that every woman gives? It's when my children were born. I'd always hoped to be a mom, partly because I'm so close to my own mother. That moment of pure love and gratitude and joy – I've never felt anything like that again, and nurturing that bond has been the best part of my life.

---

28 The infamous gossip section of Robert Murdoch's tabloid *New York Post*.

Baroness Shami Chakrabarti

Politician and Lawyer

20 October 2014

When I was in the sixth form, I was already quite interested in the things I'm interested in now. I cared about the world and wanted to make a difference. I was a bit on the earnest side, maybe a bit grim and worthy – I probably took everything, including myself, a bit too seriously, which is a bit like the way some people perceive me now. But it's not true now – I'm much more fun these days. This interview finds me at the right moment in my life. I have a lighter attitude, I know who I am and that my time is short, so I make the most of it. I walk in the sun more than I used to.

I was short and Asian, so the younger me wasn't very different from me in my forties. I wore Doc Martens and my dad's jacket with the sleeves rolled up. My friends and I weren't obsessed with spending lots of money on clothes; we wore donkey jackets and made our own stuff. I liked to read and listen to music, and I've always loved the cinema.

I think those things are related to caring about the world. If you grow up in a suburb, a lot of your window on the world comes from cinema. I still think great literature or art can move people, even on ethical issues, more powerfully and in a more lasting way than politics or legislation or speeches or journalism. I also liked depressing indie music when I was a teenager. It had to be serious – a bit of The Smiths, a bit of Joy Division. What else would you expect from the grim and worthy Chakrabarti?

My parents were migrants from Calcutta and came to London and found friends from all over the world in London's 'bedsit land'. They were very aware of the wrongs of the world, but they were also very optimistic – they were proper internationalists. They didn't have much money, but what they had was spent on fun and hospitality rather than on stuff. I think that's partly why I believe in human rights, no matter where people are from. They also believed in British justice, though neither of them were lawyers.

When I was about 12, I remember watching the news about the Yorkshire Ripper and saying something to my dad about what I hoped they'd do to that monster when they caught him. He said, 'You can't possibly believe in the death penalty. No justice system in the world can be perfect. If only one person in 100 is wrongly convicted of a terrible crime, imagine that person is you. You've been through every appeal and failed. Even your family doesn't believe you anymore. You're on the way to the electric chair, but you didn't do this thing. You might call out to God, but no one is listening.' Something clicked inside me, and that was when I began my journey. I realised I cared about the world and hoped that one day I'd be able to make a difference. I didn't articulate it as being about human rights at the time, but I was already concerned about the abuse of power and what it would feel like to be the one person who was falsely accused or picked out by the crowd.

Growing up in England in the '70s, I was well aware of racism and the National Front. I was aware of economic injustice, but I didn't think much about gender injustice. It's not a competition of injustices, but now I think of all the injustices on the planet, gender injustice is the deepest, the most entrenched and perhaps the one that my generation of women have not done enough about. I think if a Pankhurst met a Chakrabarti, she wouldn't be desperately impressed with her achievements.

If I met my younger self now, I think I'd find her quite precocious, quite argumentative and very serious. My motto these days is 'Everyone's equal and no one's superior.' I'm going to get Google to translate it into Latin so everyone takes it seriously. And I'd tell that to my younger self – 'Come on, you can be confident without being arrogant. Be angry but don't be chippy.' And I might tell my younger self to be more of a risk-taker. Maybe I'd become a screenwriter instead of a lawyer – that was a dream of mine in those days. I wasn't always 'The most dangerous woman in Britain', as *The Sun* called me. I mean, I had actual mates. I still see some of them today.

I hope the teenage me would be pleasantly surprised that at 45 I can still learn new things and make new friends and change my mind on things. I don't think I'm too set in my ways. If I told myself when I was an undergraduate studying law that I'd be head of Liberty, that would be her dream job. If I didn't work for Liberty now, I'd be sitting in the pub every night complaining about threats to our rights, so what a privilege I have. But that 19-year-old law student would not believe that decades in the future she'd have to make an argument against torture and in favour of keeping the Human Rights Act in a great old democracy like Britain. That would truly shock her.

If I could go back in time, I'd have a long, last conversation with my mum. I'd just ask her questions and try to hear more of the stories about her youth in India – what her aspirations and hopes and regrets were. And what she wanted for me. But there you go, that's the difference between what you can do in your imagination and what you can do in real life.

Davina McCall

TV Presenter

10 June 2013

By 16 I was still in my 'teenage angst phase'. At school I wasn't working as hard as I could have done – I was going out a lot clubbing and partying, and not telling my parents where I was. My parents had separated and I was splitting my life between France with my grandparents in the holidays, and England with my dad and stepmum in term-time. My dad and stepmum were great – they gave me diaries and discipline. They weren't heavy-handed, but they gave me boundaries. In France there was no discipline, which I loved, because I was 16 and wanted to go mad. I was just left to let loose. My grandparents would go to bed early, at 10, and I'd get up and go out and come home at about 5. I didn't have an eating disorder, but I was very thin because I took a lot of speed. So after my time in France, I felt like I needed a month's holiday when I got back. Basically, I had to detox in England.

I was in the grip of my first true love with a boy called Ti when I was 16 – he was my first true love. But what's quite funny when I look back, is how you put yourself through such emotional torture. I was such a people-pleaser because of my upbringing and having to constantly adapt my behaviour to my mother's state of mind, that I think I ended up trying to do that with everyone. Actually, with Ti, I think I lost myself a bit. I just tried to be what I thought he wanted me to be. And it makes me sad to think about that little girl, who thought she was so grown-up and mature. I think we should be who we are and be proud of it.

I loved my mum, and I know she loved me. When I was younger we had a better relationship. She was an active alcoholic, so I spent a lot of time reading her mood to make sure I didn't get her angry or upset. Sometimes she was really good fun and sometimes she was really not. I only saw her in the holidays and I had a great stepmum, so bizarrely, I didn't miss her as much as I did when I got older and had my own children and wanted to talk to someone, or when I had a girly problem. But our relationship by then was a bit strange – she sold a few stories to the papers, and I didn't trust her anymore. My stepmum is amazing, but I did spend quite a lot of time trying to get my mother to mother. But she couldn't do it, and I feel now that I was asking an impossible task of her.

When I thought about doing this interview, it made me feel incredibly sad because I was full of angst when I was 16. I didn't have a job or a mortgage, but I did feel constantly stressed. I had this fear of abandonment, this 'if you love me, I'll love you back' feeling. And thinking about that, I wanted to go back, give myself a big hug and tell myself it was all going to be okay. And when I thought that, I realised that's exactly what a mother would do. I would do for my younger self what my own mum couldn't do for me; I would mother her.

I'd tell my younger self to go to university. I struggled with the last two years of school and didn't think I could do years of further education. I'd relish the chance to learn now, but at that time I wasn't into learning at all – I think uni is at the wrong stage of life. I would love to go now. I look at my friends and they made such good friends at university. But then again, lots of my friends were jealous of me at the time, out working at 19, living on my own.

I'd tell my younger self not to worry so much about transient things. I try very hard not to read anything that's written about me, good or bad. But when I was doing my BBC chat show, I kept getting sympathetic looks in supermarkets or on the school run – the pity face – and I thought, 'Oh God, what have they written now?' On top of that, I had all the raging hormones of pregnancy to deal with, at the same time as thinking my career was coming to an end and wondering what was I going to do now. On the other hand, the pregnancy did make me think that, in the scheme of things, nothing is more important than this baby.

These days I don't think I'd get as upset. I know now that you go through periods in life when people can't stand you – the press said I just shouted all the time – but then it passes and it's okay again. Also, I know better what I'm good at now. I don't think I'm great at talking to famous people – to be honest, I get nervous. I'm much better with real people. The thing I cherish most of all now in my life is talk time, when someone listens to me and then I listen to them. Most of all, I cherish time with my children.

My Granny Pippy brought me up in my formative years with extremely strong manners and morals. Even though I went massively off the rails,[29] I think my foundations were strong and that was thanks to her. I really hated myself when it got really bad, because she'd made me believe I was a good person, and I could see that the person I was becoming was not good. It was that utter self-loathing that got me clean. I knew I was still in there somewhere. My moral compass was always there, and I came back to it eventually.

When I first wanted to be on TV, I was definitely seeking validation – people on a mass scale saying I was good. But when it happened I realised fame doesn't give you validation. It has to be an inside job. I'm very lucky that I didn't go on TV until after I got clean; there was no falling out of nightclubs by then. I was just reading Richard Bacon's book and his friend basically sold him out for £20,000. His best friend! He was 21[30] – so young. When I think of the things I was doing at 21 – thank God I didn't get into TV until I was 25, when I was drinking soda water. I got married, had kids and became, as far as the media was concerned, incredibly boring.

I wouldn't change anything about the amazing ride that was *Big Brother*. I learned enormous amounts from it and I really love and cherish the experience. And in retrospect, I'm so glad I finished on a high. I think if it had gone on longer at Channel 4 it would have flickered out and been really depressing. It was the perfect ending.

---

29 McCall was a heavy cocaine/heroin user in her early twenties.

30 When he was exposed for taking cocaine by the *News of the World* in 1998 and had his Blue Peter contract terminated.

Bear Grylls

Adventurer and TV Presenter

22 June 2015

At 16 I was at Eton and trying to find my identity. I found school hard, especially being away from home. At around that age I was starting to find my niche, which was climbing and martial arts. I remember getting a bunch of friends to do karate with me and they were all stronger and fitter than me – gradually they all quit, but I stayed with it. I loved the training and the discipline. It was the same with climbing – we set up these mini mountaineering trips to Scotland and I just loved it, fighting your way up a mountain in the wind and rain.

It was around 16 that I found my Christian faith. I wasn't brought up in the church, but I had a natural faith when I was a little kid. I always believed in something. Then when I went to school I thought, 'If there is a God, surely he doesn't speak Latin and stand in a pulpit?' But when I was 16 my godfather, who was like a second father to me, died.

I was really upset and said a very simple prayer up a tree – 'If you're still there, will you please just be beside me?' And that was the start of something that grew and grew and it's become the backbone of my life. I'm more convinced than ever, no matter how crazy it sounds, that there is a God and he is love. It's a very personal relationship. I still don't go to church very much, but I start every day on my knees praying by my bed, and that's my grounding for the day.

Believing in God definitely makes me less scared of life in general. People say I'm not scared of anything. Well I am – I'm scared of lots of things. After my skydiving accident in the military,[31] I still have to parachute quite a lot and I find that hard. But having a faith reduces my fear hugely, because I'm not alone – I'm fighting these battles with the creator on my side and that's amazing. My faith definitely plays a part in my love of the outdoors – I see miracles everywhere I look, in mountains and in the jungle. And I think I have less of a fear of death as well, because I see it as going home.

I'd tell my teenage self to appreciate having his dad around. He died when I was in my early twenties, and I'd have loved to have him around for longer. He was a wonderful dad, really cosy and fun. He was the man who taught me to climb at a young age and he really encouraged me to go for things. He told me to look after my friends and follow my heart. If he'd lived longer, I'd have shown the gratitude you don't always show when you're young. I have three boys now and I appreciate more than ever everything he did when I was a boy and the values he gave me.

I would also tell my younger self not to fear failure. I went to Eton, and like lots of schools it was a bit of a survival

31 A fall that doctors worried would paralyse him for life

exercise – especially if you weren't naturally sporty or super clever, and I was neither. It took me some time to gain any confidence. So many kids around me – and I was the same – were terrified of doing anything different, in the class or on the sports field. We never took risks. But that's the opposite of life, where you have to forge your own path, embrace risk and prepare to get things wrong.

By the time I joined the military, I had the confidence to do things my own way. After school I joined the army as a private rather than as an officer. All my school friends who joined went in as officers, but I wanted to go in at the other end. It looked more fun – I've never been very good at drinks parties or that side of things. I wanted to be muddy up a mountain.

If I met the teenage Bear now, I think I'd see a shy young man trying to figure himself out. I used to try to wear trendy clothes and spike my hair. If I went back to talk to that boy I'd say, 'That's all just window dressing, and you're not very good at it anyway. Don't worry about that side of things – just love what you do and keep smiling. And don't worry if you don't want to go to university. School is such a small part of life.' My dad used to say, 'Don't peak at school or you'll mess up the rest of your life.'

I think the thing about my life that would really surprise my younger self would be my work encouraging young marines, handing out the green berets to them when they pass out. I remember trying out for the Royal Marines when I was 16, and turning up at the train station, very nervous with my little bag, surrounded by all these big burly guys. I did eventually pass, though when I finally left school I didn't take it up, and I joined the army instead. But if you'd told me then that I'd go back one day as a colonel and stand on the parade square where I did press-ups in the mud when I was 16 and encourage the young marines – I could never have called that. But I was there doing it last week and really felt that my life had come full circle. I definitely felt my dad smiling down on me.

The younger me wouldn't have understood the TV personality thing. Fame was not a goal. I didn't even watch TV. If someone told me I'd be involved in that, I'd have said, 'Really? It doesn't sound very fun. And it doesn't sound in line with the values you have.' The public recognition is the downside, but we do actually have lots of fun exploring the most incredible wildernesses. And if someone had told me when I was a boy scout that one day I'd be Chief Scout, I'd definitely have said, 'You've got to be joking.' I was a terrible scout who didn't get many badges at all.

If I wanted to impress the teenage Bear, I'd tell him about climbing Everest. I really aspired to do that when I was young – it was a dream of mine. I'd warn him to brace himself for the pain of going through SAS selection. That was a long, two-year road and I failed selection the first time. If I'd known in advance how hard that was going to be, I would've questioned embarking on it. But once you're in, you're in.

I know Ranulph Fiennes well, and he always talks about the importance of preparation. I come from a slightly different place; for me, the adventure begins when things start to go wrong. I'm not one of these meticulous people who loves the preparation and the planning. A lot of the great adventurers are, but I like having to work things out as I go, improvising and being caught out.

If I could go back and relive any time again, it would be tempting to go for the summit of Everest, or the moment I passed SAS selection the same day as my best buddy, or some of the times climbing with my dad when I was a kid. But in the end, I think I'd go for a time on our family hideaway on the little island we own in North Wales. It's a twenty-acre place, with no electricity and no communication. Just me, my wife and our three sons – Huckleberry, Jesse (named after King David's dad in the Bible), and Marmaduke (named after a First World War fighter pilot). Those are precious, precious times. Picnics, lots of laughs, messing around on the rocks and swimming. Just us guys having fun. And no crocodiles or snakes.

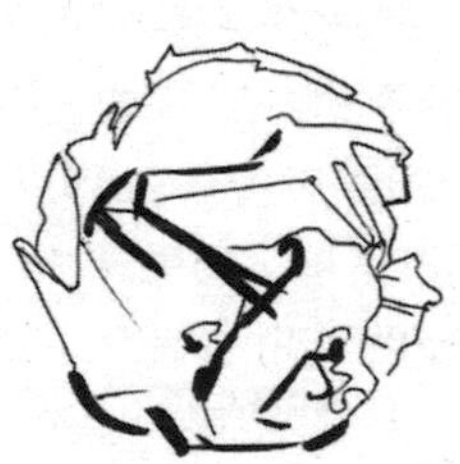

David Cameron

Former British Prime Minister

25 July 2011

I'd like to tell my 16-year-old self that it's better to try and fail than to not try at all. It makes you a stronger person. For a lot of young people, the idea that you shouldn't try at something because you might not succeed is pretty seductive, and I was no exception. At school, there were some subjects and some sports where I didn't always put the effort in but instead just went through the motions, drifting along rather than giving it everything.

I took my family for granted. If I could go back, I'd tell myself 'You don't know how lucky you are.' A lot has been written about my background, but the great privilege of my upbringing wasn't the wealth – it was the warmth. We all got on, we were all there for each other. There was so much love and support. I'm not sure we all appreciated that enough at the time. I know I get criticised for talking about how important families are to society, but I'm just saying it as I see it and as I experienced it. When you've got a strong family behind you, it makes it easier to cope with the things life throws at you.

I lived in the shadow of my older brother. He was three years older, went to the same school and was a huge success on the sports field and almost always the lead actor in school plays. It was great to have that kind of role model and I was incredibly proud of him, but like many younger brothers, I always found myself a few steps behind. If I could give my younger self some advice, I'd say, 'Don't worry about it; your life is not predetermined, you'll find your own feet in your own way.' It was not until I left school that I felt I was breaking out of my brother's shadow and doing my own thing.

My dad had an amazing ability to always look on the bright side of life. He was disabled, had short legs, not enough toes and no heels, yet he did everything with us – tennis, swimming, holidays – and was always the most tremendous fun. Because I grew up with him, I'm not sure I even realised how amazing he was – and if I was 16 again, I'd tell him. His optimism was infectious. He always told me, 'No matter how bad things are, you can overcome them if you have the right frame of mind.' It was the perfect advice for a future politician. In a typical morning, you can wake up to being criticised on the radio, read bad headlines over breakfast and then get skewered in the House of Commons. But throughout it all, you've got to focus on the big picture, do the right thing and remain optimistic.

My travels to the Soviet Union were incredibly formative to my political worldview. When I was young I didn't care that much about politics, let alone have ambitions to be prime minister – I wasn't one of those people who'd mapped out their career on the back of an envelope. But my travels around the Eastern bloc after I left school had a massive impact on me; I'll never forget the greyness of life under Communism; the lack of choice, freedom and expression. I began to develop a political consciousness, a sense of what was right and wrong, particularly relating to the importance of freedom and the state being there to serve the people and not be their master.

David Tennant

Actor

19 February 2018

At 16, it was all about O-Levels and coping with adolescence. I had a very happy childhood; I was very fortunate to be brought up by good parents who gave me a great deal of astute wisdom for life. But I didn't really enjoy adolescence, because I was always aware that I was waiting for adulthood to start. I found the lack of control over your own affairs as a child annoying, and that just became more pronounced during the teenage years. I knew I definitely wanted to go to drama school. In fact, I think I got my first acting job at 16. Or even at 15, in an anti-smoking ad. Then I did an episode of *Dramarama*[32] for Scottish TV. We went to the Isle of Skye for four days, and I stayed in a hotel on my own for the first time. I was old enough not to need a chaperone; I was my own boss – it felt like a glimpse into adulthood.

My mum and dad were a big influence on the way I saw the world. I wouldn't have admitted it at 16 though – that's

32 An ITV children's drama series.

when you start thinking your parents are just utter losers. But I think deep down, even then, I knew. They gave me a world view that was based on a Christian outlook – they were Christian in the right sense, genuinely Christian people in terms of the way they believed in equality for all, treating everyone with respect and kindness, with a 'do unto others as you would have them do unto you' attitude. On the whole they were quite free of the right-wing attitudes that sometimes come with Christianity. They were liberal and forward thinking. I cherish the way they comported themselves in life.

Doctor Who was a big influence on the young David. I liked superheroes too, but *Doctor Who* was my great passion when I was a kid, maybe because I could identify with the character. I could never identify with the Incredible Hulk, though I loved the comics, but The Doctor felt like someone I could aspire to being like, and maybe he'd want to hang out with me too. I think it's very important that there's a kids' hero who is not a jock, and that was something I came back to a lot when I was playing The Doctor. Finding out I was going to play the role all those years later was just surreal. Something which had been so important to me as a child was going to be a big part of my adult life – it would, in fact, in a way end up defining it.

If you met the 16-year-old David now, you'd wonder why he thought all that Brylcreem was a good idea – you'd be mystified as to why he thought that was an acceptable way of presenting himself. I did have an interest in clothes – I remember discovering charity shops, and the opportunities they gave me were quite exciting. I sported a bootlace tie at one point, probably to emulate Bono or Jim Kerr. That was one of my favourite things, worn with a bolero jacket

I'd got from a charity shop. And my favourite shirt was a hand-me-down in a paisley pattern – red shot with black. So surprisingly, I was quite out-there, bolder than I realised. I remember going out to a nightclub in Paisley – Toledo Junction I think it was called – and being accused of being a weirdo, which I think vaguely translated into being a goth in those days. Which I wasn't, but I suppose in a sea of shellsuits... In fact, I got smacked in the face. Just for being a little bit dapper!

I think I was quite outgoing within my group of friends, but not particularly when I was outside my gang, my comfort zone. Despite the boldness of my bootlace tie. I remember the roar of hormonal confusion. My head was full of mince most of the time. I was churning, not at ease with myself, but I think I was good at masking my anxieties. I think I still do manage to do that – it's only my very closest confidantes who get a glimpse of what's underneath.

When I was 16 and wanting to be an actor, it still felt like a bit of a ludicrous idea. I didn't know any actors, and people all around me were saying, quite rightly, 'This is a daft idea. You won't make a living.' It was sound and proper advice, but there was a little part of the teenage me that thought they might be wrong. It would be nice to go back to him now and tell him, 'You're in your mid-forties now, and you're still getting away with it.' Though I still don't know how much longer that'll last!

I remember the pleasure of the first paid job once you leave drama school. The shock of realising, 'Right, that's it now, there's no more 'bits'. You're on your own, and if you can't make it work now, you'll have to do something else. Life won't be what you've always imagined it would.

For me, that first job was the Scottish People's Theatre tour, doing a bit of Brecht in a van. Getting a wage packet, with actual money in it, in a little brown envelope, gave me such a sense of achievement. I was a grown-up person making my way in the world.

I left drama school in 1991, so I'd been a jobbing theatre actor for quite a few years before I did *Casanova* and *Blackpool* around 2003. TV definitely makes a difference to your profile – suddenly you're flickering away in everyone's living room and opportunities start to open up. When I got *Doctor Who*, I quickly became very aware that life had changed. It is unique in terms of the level of attention you're suddenly getting – it's incomparable to pretty much anything else. Very rarely is someone getting a job on the news. I became public property in a way I'd never imagined. I remember thinking about all the times I'd been in a room when someone off the telly came in, the ripple that went round the room – 'Ooh, look who it is', with everyone looking and pointing, while the famous person apparently noticed nothing. Actually, when you are that person, you're thinking, 'Keep your head down, keep going till you get to where you need to go.' It doesn't feel empowering at all; it just feels scary and nerve-wracking.

If I could have a last conversation with anyone who's gone now, it would be my parents. Pretty obvious really – they're so fundamental to who you are. And you miss the mundane, the phone call to catch up. You can never really appreciate that while it's happening, because you're just living it day-to-day. I think the loss of a parent, especially the first time... it's so bewildering. The loss of one of the fixed points on your life. You always know it'll happen one day, but you can't prepare for the scale of that loss. And you never quite get over the fact that they're not there. Neither of my parents died suddenly – they both had pernicious illnesses that took them relatively slowly, so there was no shock. I don't know if that's better or worse. It's no fun watching someone you love suffer, but the advantage is that you can make sure you're around and you can prepare, as much as that's possible. But you never really get over it.

Prue Leith

Chef and TV Presenter

1 October 2018

At 16 I was at school in South Africa, just shifting my passion from horses to boys and parties. We lived in Johannesburg, in what would seem now to be a very luxurious style, but in those post-colonial days it felt normal – all well-off white families in South Africa lived in nice big houses. I was the daughter between two brothers. My mother was an actress, my father was a businessman. We were a ridiculously happy family, all very close. We didn't have a lot of outside friends, but we did a lot together as a family. I think we had an idyllic childhood, and I would attribute all my success to being constantly encouraged as a child. No one treated me differently because I was a girl – I was just expected to do well.

My mother[33] was very glamorous and I resented that. I wanted a fat mum who came to the school fetes and made

33 The actress Peggy Inglis.

cakes, like all the other mothers. One day my headmistress told me she'd asked my mother to come to talk to the senior school about Shakespeare. I thought, 'Oh God, I'll die.' I stood right at the back, thinking it was going to be the most embarrassing day of my whole life. She was about 45 at the time, and she came on and played the 14-year-old Juliet in the balcony scene. Then she played the old nurse with the arthritic back. Then she played Hamlet. She was completely mesmerising. We were all just agog. I walked out of that hall feeling so proud, thinking, 'My mother's an actress. Of course she can't come to the school fete – she's far too important.' It completely changed the way I saw her.

Young white South Africans didn't go into the townships, so all we saw were lovely servants like my wonderful nanny Emma, who I absolutely adored. I can still remember how great it was being held by her. She wore a white pinny with a lace collar and I can still remember the feeling of her collar against my cheek. My mother was very liberal though – she was a founding member of an anti-apartheid protest group called The Black Sash. I remember her coming home after standing on the town hall steps, her black coat covered in splodges after people threw eggs at her. She was trying to get black actors to be allowed to work alongside white actors in her theatre group. You couldn't have black musicians on the stage. You couldn't even cast a black man as Othello. Black people couldn't come to the same performances as white people – it was ridiculous.

If I could go back to the teenage Prue now, I'd tell her to be more sensitive about what it was like to be oppressed. We were the oppressors, so we never thought much about the oppressed. I'm ashamed to think how, when I was 16, I skipped down the street giggling away with my girlfriends, while venerable old black men would get off the pavement and walk in the gutter so these idiots, who didn't even notice him, could pass by. I thought I was liberal, but I had no idea what a non-segregated society was like until I came to Europe. I found it quite amazing, almost shocking, the amount of black people there were in Paris. I could just sit down with them in public and have coffee with them – I found it so awkward, because I'd never done that. I was amazingly selfish and amazingly unaware.

My father would be astonished that the teenage Prue, who kept changing her mind about what she wanted to do, would end up with the career path I've had. I'd wanted to be an actress, an artist, all sorts of things, but I never had any interest in cooking food. We had a wonderful Zulu cook, Charlie, for that. In my family, food was rather like money and sex – you didn't talk about it. It wasn't until I got to Paris that I found everyone was interested in food and took it seriously. When I was working as an au pair, I saw the care Madame took preparing fantastic dinners for her children, and I thought, 'Aha – food is something proper people really care about.'

I left *The Great British Menu* on the BBC after 11 years, intending to retire from TV. I'd sold my business and I was writing novels, so I thought I'd just write. Then along came *Bake Off*, and I couldn't resist it. I knew Mary Berry because she's a friend and I thought it was great for her. She'd worked so hard all her life, ploughing along, so it was fantastic at that stage of her life to have such wonderful success. Then I thought, 'Well, now I've got the chance to have that.' But I hadn't watched it and I had no idea what a phenomenon it was. I wasn't expecting the amount of attention, but I like it – I'm an egotist and I'm quite happy to be interviewed and photographed and have people in the supermarket say, 'Are you that lady off the telly?'

It was hard when my husband[34] died in 2002. We'd made the same mistake as my parents. We'd been so happy in the family unit, tucked away in our house in the Cotswolds, that we had hardly any friends. Rayne had always been somewhat reclusive; he barely left his study to even go into the garden, and no one except family came to visit. I didn't mind because I would go up to London a few days a week to work at my company,[35] then we'd all meet up at weekends. I didn't want to sell up after Rayne died, but it meant coming home late at night to a big empty house. I remember one night driving home in the rain from the train station, bawling my eyes out, thinking, 'What am I going back to?' But my brother was very good. When Rayne was alive and I was away, one of us would phone the other at seven o'clock. After he died, I'd often find myself reaching for the phone at seven. And sometimes I'd pick it up and phone my brother instead, and he'd say, 'Ah, seven o'clock – time for some brotherly love.' And gradually I made some local friends and then I got married again.

If I could go back to the happiest time in my life, it would be the summer of 1976. My son was not quite two. My adopted Cambodian daughter arrived when she was 16 months old. We'd been staying in a tiny flat in London, with no more outside space than a little balcony. And then we moved into this beautiful old house in the Cotswolds, and started revamping it. There's

34 The author Rayne Kruger.

35 Michelin-starred restaurant Leith's until 1995, then the Prue Leith College.

nothing more exciting than making your own nest. It was the year of the huge drought so it was very dry, but that meant the children were running around in the sun. They were very happy, and we were happy. It was just the most beautiful year.

CHAPTER 6:

Friendship

Joanna Lumley

Actor

27 June 2016

I was born in India, raised in Hong Kong and Malaysia, and went to my first boarding school at eight, which now seems paralysingly young. It seemed par for the course, as my parents had been brought up abroad and sent home to school. I especially loved my second boarding school, an Anglo-Catholic convent in the hills behind Hastings. The nuns wore blue stockings and were brainy and lovely. There were 70 boarders and I was happy as a clam.

We were very innocent teenagers. By 16, we may have kissed a boy on the cheek. One day a girl was rumoured to have 'done it' and we were awestruck. I was a bit spotty and had problem hair. The music was fabulous – it was the beginning of The Beatles, The Everly Brothers and there was still a bit of Elvis going on – all listened to on Radio Luxembourg on borrowed transistor radios underneath the bedclothes. It was pretty darned thrilling! On Saturday nights we would dance to 45s on a Dansette in the school gym.

If we could, we would have all looked like Brigitte Bardot or Claudia Cardinale, with their tiny waists, stiff petticoats, cute expressions and pink lipstick. There was a lipstick called 'Pink Capri' and even the word Capri seemed too exotic to speak. We were besotted with the idea of riding on a Vespa, wearing silk scarves like Sophia Loren. Being mistaken for a French woman was the height of my ambition.

I would tell my younger self to concentrate; I was a show-off, a comedian and a clown. We were so vague and dim about the future – when people were revising, I drew pictures in my rough book. The idea of actually studying filled me with horror and I never wanted to go to university – I couldn't wait to get out into the world. I was already mad-keen on acting but usually had to play the men's parts because I was tall. So when Patsy started wearing moustaches in *Absolutely Fabulous*, it was already second nature. I loved making people laugh.

I'm pleased the lazy, lively little girl was a teenager long ago; if little Jo was 16 now, it would be a different story. There would be the tyranny of social media. Girls are worried about their weight, what people think of them and what they should be wearing, and that is horrifying. Those things didn't matter a jot to us. Dipping our petticoats in sugar water so they went stiff was the nearest we got to trying to look nice.

In those days virtually anybody could be a model. London was swinging, and suddenly one was in the middle of it all. We did our own make-up and hair and went everywhere by Tube. We were in control of our lives. There were not many rules – when I got a Mini, I'd drive where I needed to be and just leave it in the middle of the road! Our flat in Earls Court seemed like paradise, even though we shared rooms.

We were poor as rats, but happy if we could scrape the £9 rent between four of us. There was an extraordinary, slightly hippy-ish feeling that money was not the object. I think today money is the object, and that has turned the world into a different place – quite sour, hard-nosed and harder-hearted.

I was 21 when I had my son. Having someone in your life that's so much more important than yourself changes things hugely. I'd just started acting and suddenly had to pay the bills, put food on the table and buy baby clothes. That sobers you up. Before, one was quite dizzy. There were times when I was absolutely skint, particularly before *The New Avengers*, which came when I was 30. Trying to get work is the hardest thing in the bloody world, and when you're an unemployed actor, people see the desperation in your eyes. But playing Purdey, I worked solidly for two years with the best directors and actors. It was sensational.

Jennifer Saunders and I are as close as can be. In *Ab Fab*, Edina and Patsy are inseparable, and in real life, although we are grown-up women with husbands and children and are both now grandmothers, you can't put a cigarette paper between us. Playing Patsy, spanning 25 years, has been the best fun in the world. We all love each other so much and we were so thrilled we were all still here to do the film. We have to cherish the people who bring us joy. We have to remember to say, 'By the way, I love you,' and tell strangers who've been kind, 'God, you're a nice person.' When a huge talent is taken away like Victoria Wood was, it reminds us. It is so sad to think that we will have no more of her incredible work. She had the most extraordinary skill.

I've always loved getting older, so being 70 is fabulous. I've always just felt like me, so the numbers are incidental.

You never lose the little you who is within you. We are like trees – we grow more and more circles and more layers as we grow older, but inside us is always the person you were when you were tiny. To be 70 and still working, I've been very lucky. Mind you, I have also worked jolly hard.

This year is our thirtieth wedding anniversary. My husband Stephen[36] and I look at each other and wonder how it happened. I'm hoping we will be together on our anniversary for a change, because often I'll be filming, or he'll be off doing an opera. But this year is huge – 30 years is wonderful.

I would tell my younger self that one is powerless until one decides to be powerful – any of us can put on a Batman cape. I'm not a lawyer, nurse, teacher or any of the things that are really useful, but when you are an unskilled person like me but have a kind of fame, you can use it to attract the oxygen of publicity towards something that will make other people's lives better. That is a great privilege I try to use responsibly. It is never for political reasons; it is for the good of the planet and everything it contains.

My happiest day was probably my twelfth birthday. It was a lovely spring day in the beautiful hills near Hastings, my parents gave me the pair of flat, cream-coloured sneakers I'd always longed to have and I was in a beautiful dormitory with lots of funny people. I remember thinking, 'I'll remember being 12 because this is the best birthday ever.' And I feel like I'm 12 every day – it's quite wonderful.

36 English opera conductor Stephen Barlow.

Sue Perkins

TV Presenter and Comedian

5 October 2009

At 16 I had two lives. I was very square, bookish and spoddy, but also spent most nights drinking two litres of cider in a disused car park with ne'er-do-wells. Both of them were the real me – I'm a shy, failed scholar but there's a side of me that's a loud, gobby nutter, which is the side that likes to do TV. I have to balance both sides or I start to feel a bit sad. Thankfully on *Supersizers Eat*, I get to be tanked all the time.

I envy the young Sue her simplicity. She loved books and had an enquiring mind but didn't apply that analytical process constantly to her own life, fretting and worrying. I had no perspective and in a way that was great. I was a very happy child and had a great, secure relationship with my parents and was very confident about who I was. Everyone has a crash eventually, wondering who they really are – for me, that came much later.

Mel[37] and I didn't have a pot to piss in when we started doing stand-up and writing for radio in our early twenties,

37 Giedroyc, Sue's comedy partner.

but they were some of the happiest days of my life. I began to think it might be possible to make a life out of just messing around. My career's been one of mistakes and wrong turns, but I don't mind that – it shows no media savvy, but neither do I. I'm incredibly shy and can't network.

People thought Mel and I were mad to give up *Light Lunch* on Channel 4 after two years – it was still going well and was a good secure job. But we were tired, and we wanted a life outside of TV. Ten years on, she's got a husband and two kids to show for it, and I've got a wealth of life experience that TV can't buy you.

I think people are easier around me now that I know who I am. Being gay is not my identity, but it calms people to know that I'm out and relaxed with myself. I probably knew at 16 I was gay, but only in a very latent way – I didn't have a girlfriend until I was 22. Instead I had a long-term boyfriend, who later turned out to be gay, too. He was a gorgeous man and I was very happy with him, sexually and romantically. So I wouldn't even say to my teenage self, 'Buck up, you idiot – you're gay!' because I was happy with my boyfriend and I've always had great relationships with men.

My 16-year-old self would not believe that I don't smoke and have never taken a class-A drug. I assumed I would be coked out of my nut for most of my twenties and thirties, but I found that when I'm working and 'in the moment' I'm incredibly happy and feel very free. In the last year I've stopped worrying so much about my place in the world. I spent two decades trying to make people like me and it was tiring, and you just come off manic and annoying. Now I accept that there will always be people who think I'm a wanker.

Dionne Warwick

Musician

7 May 2012

I had big plans when I was 16. I was going to be a prima ballerina, a concert pianist, a teacher or a photographer, and I still think any of those things could have given me as much pleasure as singing. But when I tore the ligaments in my foot and couldn't stand on my toes anymore, I knew I couldn't be a ballerina. So I changed my focus from my toes to my throat. I was born singing and come from a singing family, so maybe it was pre-destined. But it wasn't until I had a hit record, when I was 19, that I decided singing was definitely the way I was going to go.

I think I'd instantly like the teenage Dionne, and can say that without any reservations whatsoever. I had no real problem with liking who I was then, and it's always been that way. I attribute that to the amount of friendships I was able to make with people who are still my friends today. I had a very strong family around me, and family is the anchor of anybody's being. One of the biggest things the young Dionne will have to learn is the art of making decisions, and much of that will come from the environment she's been brought up in. Fortunately for me, I was brought up in an environment of love, support and promise.

There isn't much I could tell my younger self about the industry that would help her. Back then, there wasn't really a pattern – you either had it or you didn't. In the '60s, when I started, it wasn't the massive competition it is today. We were all comrades, and we all cared about each other and supported each other. And when I have an opportunity to go and see Gladys Knight or Smokey Robinson or Patti LaBelle – who all happen to be my friends – I take the time to do that.

The young Dionne would be overwhelmed if I told her what was going to happen in her future. She'd say, 'You're kidding me.' Aside from all the awards, there's all the people I've met – I've performed before kings and queens and with some of the major, major icons of our industry. At the time, I was so busy touring I didn't really have time to think about how overwhelming those things were, so I was able to handle them. That said, I quit every day. You get to a point when you're just so tired. But you know there's a room full of people waiting for you to do what you do, so you have to pull yourself together and get on out there.

I carry some strong formative memories with me. I still remember the first time I heard my voice coming out of the radio. I thought, 'Woah, wait a minute, is that really me?' And I still remember my first Grammy and first platinum record. I experienced some instances of segregation, which was really rampant in the '60s, but because I was always with my peers and those I revered as music icons at the time, it was just part of what I had to go through. I remember hearing about the death of Martin Luther King Jr. I was on a plane heading to a concert and when I got there, I was told that he'd been shot. I felt awful, absolutely terrible.

Sometimes this life can be hard because there is no privacy at all. I accept the appreciation for what I do, but I'm at the disposal of the general public. I do, however, draw the line when I'm with my children or grandchildren – if we're out having dinner, I expect to be able to eat in peace.

When I was 16 I always wanted to be 40. There was something very magical about that number for me – I couldn't wait to be 40, and now that I'm 70 I feel the same way. I'm not looking forward to 105. But that's the way God planned it, and that's the way you have to look at it.

Graham Linehan

Writer and Comedian

15 May 2017

At 16 I was lonely and insecure, bullied and unhappy. I was obsessed with science fiction, comics, music and comedy. I had an existential crisis every day. I was big and tall so I should have been confident. But I worried about losing my temper, so I tried to keep out of trouble by making myself look smaller, which gave me a permanent slouch. My school was all-male and violent – like living in a really bad area for 12 years. It's interesting to me that one of the first things we do as parents is prepare our children for life in a prison yard. The relief I felt leaving school was unbelievable.

I was around 16 when I completely lost my faith. Basically, I read *The Cider House Rules* by John Irving. Before that I was extremely religious and anti-abortion, and then I read that book and the central argument was so brilliantly articulated. I realised my understanding of the medical procedure was childish, at a 'killing babies' level. I thought,

'Wait, it's much more complicated than that' and then I grew up a bit. When you have something so fundamental as your views on abortion changed, everything else changes as well – it was like a row of dominoes. Maybe that's why the Catholic Church is so terrified by the idea of abortion being legalised in Ireland.

I don't think I'd be the person I am if I hadn't had those early years of believing all that religious stuff completely. And of course, as soon as you stop believing it, these very, very serious ceremonies and rituals suddenly seem hilarious. The idea of giving up every single Sunday, getting dressed in our best clothes and going to be bored solid for an hour and half – God, that seems so ludicrous to me now. Recognising the ludicrousness of that helps you see the ludicrousness of any kind of ceremony that pops up elsewhere. So you see it all over the place, these traditions which make people feel important.

My father was hurt and disappointed by my rejection of the church; he's maintained his faith and still goes to church often. We were at loggerheads for a while, but then we came through that and got to a place where we both accepted the person the other one was and reached an understanding. My dad's always been an incredibly warm, decent human being and if religion's part of his life, that's fine. I do love Pope Francis. He's awesome. We obviously disagree quite strongly on certain things, but I think he's done a wonderful job. He's so great, saying that nice atheists will get into heaven quicker than immoral Christians. There's definitely a bunch of cardinals in the Vatican trying to get him.

The Pythons were incredibly influential on me. When I heard the theme tune I would get this depth charge and was almost sick with excitement. They were extremely mysterious. Some of the sketches, you couldn't work out what point they were getting at, and I loved that. I've always loved people who make me work for it, who expect me to catch up with them, rather than dumb down for me. Then it was *Fawlty Towers*, an almost perfect work of art. With everything I do, I'm just trying to write 'The Hotel Inspector' or 'Basil the Rat', to press that joy buzzer so hard you think your head's going to fall off.

I think the thing that would make the teenage me happiest would be hearing there are lots of girls in his future, but I don't think he'd believe that. At 16, he's still two years away from kissing a girl. That feeling, of being ugly and just not an interesting person – I'd love to go back and tell him, 'Just hang in there. It'll be fine.' Music journalism will help and comedy writing will too. You'll meet interesting people and some of them will let you have sex with them.

I'm very proud of *Father Ted*, but I've learned that there's a point when you have to give things away to their audience. You can't own them forever. Arthur[38] and I once went to the *Father Ted* weekend in County Clare. Everyone dresses as priests and bishops and nuns, and it's fantastic. But after a while of looking around, I began to feel a sense of discomfort. I saw people dressed as priests laughing their heads off with someone dressed as a cardinal, but then they'd notice me and Arthur and they'd begin to look very self-conscious. We weren't dressed as priests, we just had normal clothes on. And we realised, 'We're screwing this up. Our presence is getting in the way of them pretending they're in *Father Ted*.' And we felt we should never come to these things because we

38 Mathews, Linehan's sometime co-writer.

break the spell. And that's been my thinking on everything. Once you've finished it, you have to step away from it and hand it over to the audience.

It would be good to tell the younger me he's going to write something that will mean a lot to Irish people – I'm very proud that Irish people kind of know *Ted* by heart. And I think it possibly went some way to changing Irish society, in a healthy way. I think we lanced a boil. You couldn't ask for anything greater for a writer – it's the ultimate. The only slight problem is, I'd have to admit to him, you'll only do this at the very start of your career.

The pleasure you get from kicking against the establishment gets very addictive, especially when you've been held back for years. When you're suddenly let loose, it's like a giant elastic band has been stretched and stretched and then it's fired. I feel like that's what happened to me when I was 16 and that propulsion has carried me all the way to here, aged 49, still wanting to kick as many pricks as I can find.

In terms of relationships, I'd tell my younger self, 'If you ever think of doing something that's not morally okay and just a bit mean, bear in mind that you'll think about it for the rest of your life. It may feel like a get-out-of-jail card, but it will bother you for the rest of your life. And if it doesn't, you might be a sociopath.' I was always very anxious about relationships, very aware that they'd probably end, so I'd end them, quickly. And I guess I had that thing of wanting to make up for lost time, because I hadn't had enough affection when I was a teenager. So I was looking around for years, and that made me unhappy and not a very good boyfriend. It's still a major cause of unhappiness. Every now and then my wife will hear me go, 'Urgh', and she'll ask what's wrong and I'll say, 'I'm just remembering something that happened 25 years ago.'

If I could go back to any time in my life, it would be those years of writing with Arthur. I don't think you get any happier than when you're laughing. Consistently, and so much that you sometimes can't breathe – that was what writing with Arthur was like. You'd go into work, you'd start laughing about an idea, he'd start laughing, he'd tell you his idea and you'd laugh more. I can clearly remember the endorphins just pumping through me the night we came up with the monkey priest who climbs up onto the bookshelves and throws things at people. We just could not stop laughing. It was just joy – total joy. We had a magical thing, but we can't get it back now. We're too different as people to tap back into it the way we used to. Writing alone is nowhere near as good.

Michael Winner

Film Director

9 April 2012

At 16 I was at my peak, and it's been downhill ever since. I had a showbiz column in 26 local newspapers and I was the film critic of the *NME*. The London Palladium had big stars every two weeks – Dean Martin, Nat King Cole, Bob Hope – and they weren't as protected from the public as they are today, so I just went round and met them all. I was, as I still am, extremely shy, but when I wanted or needed something I became this other person who was very determined. I'd known from the age of five I wanted nothing in life other than to direct films.

If I could go back, I'd pay more attention to my parents. My father was adorable and my mother, though a nutcase and addicted to gambling, was lovely. But at 20 I became a movie director. It was all-consuming – all I wanted to do was make movies, hang around with actors and have affairs with actresses. My parents, to put it horribly, just weren't as interesting. I regret that deeply because they really loved me.

When I was 17 I got a girlfriend. She got undressed in my bed in my home and she was stark naked and ready for a, you know… She said to me, 'Aren't you going to take your clothes off?' I hadn't even taken my shirt off – I was terrified. By good chance I met a nymphomaniac when I was 18 and she took no nonsense. She was determined to have a go, and that brought me into the sexual world.

If I met my younger self now, my first thought would be, 'He's very handsome.' Though I thought I was ugly. I'd also think him very shy. But if he told me what he'd already achieved in his young life, I'd think, 'This lad is something exceptional.' But I didn't see it like that at the time.

My younger self wouldn't be surprised that he'd become a successful film director because I always knew that was what I'd do with my life. I had no evidence for this but was quite certain, then I made it come true. If I went back and told him he would not only direct some of the greatest names in cinema but would be great friends with them, he'd think, 'My goodness, this is even better than I expected.' He'd be impressed at how many great friends I've made – Brando, Bob Mitchum, Orson Welles.

Oliver Reed was the most wonderful man I ever met. He was the most sensitive, shy person – he needed drink because he was so terrified of life and people. He didn't drink on set, but he did in the evening. We were on location in Germany and had to change his hotel room every night, because he'd spent the night pissing on the German flag and Heil Hitlering around the hotel. He'd come in in the morning, very quiet and gentlemanly, and I'd tell him I had to change his hotel and he'd say, 'But why?' He didn't remember any of it. He was adorable. I never cried at my mother's funeral, or my father's, but I wept at his. I was the only person from show business who went. All his so-called friends, like Ken Russell, who directed him in all these movies – they couldn't be bothered to go. Terrible.

I got on wonderfully with all these actors who everyone warned me were impossible to work with. Brando, Mitchum, Sophia Loren – they never behaved badly with me. Roman Polanski told me that Faye Dunaway was totally impossible when they were making *Chinatown*, but I can only say that to me, she was the most professional, wonderful person. But then, she did say in her autobiography that the film she made with me was the only one she ever enjoyed. I called her Fayzie. Burt Lancaster tried to kill me three times but he was my best friend, a wonderful actor – he just had a terrible temper.

I made some mistakes. I turned down *The Prime of Miss Jean Brodie*, *The French Connection*, *James Bond*! Why did I turn down James Bond? – it was madness. I never made a film that would have given me the credibility of a few Bonds. Nicolas Roeg told me I shouldn't look as if I enjoyed directing so much. I thought he was crazy, but the English apparently don't like somebody who enjoys it all. They like you to suffer and talk a load of rubbish about the intellectual side of the movie.

When I die, it's going to be '*Death Wish* director dies.' I don't mind though – *Death Wish* was an epoch-making film, the first film in the history of cinema where the hero kills other civilians. It had never been done before, but since then it has been the most copied film ever. Tarantino put it in his top ten films ever made.

Michael Winner

I finally got married last year. It was quite fun. We had Michael Caine and his wife for witnesses. And when the registrar said, 'Is there any reason why these two should not be wed?' I said, 'Well I'm not too sure about this.' And Michael said, 'For once in your life, just shut up, Michael.'

Roger Daltrey

Musician

5 November 2018

School ended on my fifteenth birthday. I was sent to the youth employment officer, who got me a job as an electrician's mate on a building site, but I never saw a wire – I just bled pipes. I thought, 'Fuck that, this is plumbing.' By 16, I was working in a sheet metalwork factory in South Acton. Calling it a factory is a bit much; it was more like an asbestos shed with 20 blokes turning out early computer cabinets, which were as big as tanks. They were some of my happiest days. Some guys were just out of Malaya and Korea, two wars we often forget about. The singing, laughter and camaraderie was so much fun, even though it was hard graft.

Those teenage years were full of angst, energy, testosterone and paranoia. I was bullied at school, so my 'flight or fight' switch was always on – if I ever felt threatened, I learned to get the first blow in. Perhaps I was quite an aggressive bugger, but I don't think I was a bully.

My imagined future was nothing other than becoming a rock singer – it was already my drive and my vision. I was 11 when I saw Elvis, but it was Lonnie Donegan that really hit me. One reason I got slung out of school is that I didn't want to know about anything other than music. And every night I was out playing with the band – we were just starting to get paid jobs in social clubs.

My generation missed national service by one year, thank goodness. I don't know where my life would have gone, but I would have been okay. I didn't mind a bit of discipline – I'd been in the Boys' Brigade, and in those days we were all being trained up for the next war. I learned the bugle and formation marches, but they also taught us how democracy worked. I became the company singer; because I'm little, the sergeant used to sit me on his shoulders and get me to sing.

We were a generation of builders who grew up with nothing – everything had been destroyed by war. When you have nothing, if you want something, you fucking build it. I made my first electric guitar, a copy of a Fender, and we were building a band. John[39] joined – we were different characters, but got on and he was a genius bass player. Pete[40] joined, and, fuck me, he was a different class altogether. He had the ability, through his writing and intellect, to write songs of a different calibre to anyone else. I happily gave up the guitar – it was completely incompatible with being a sheet metal worker and my hands were cut to shreds after unloading ten tonnes of steel. So that was the gang. And when Moon[41]

39 Entwistle.

40 Townshend.

41 Keith.

joined, it was the key to the starter. 'Vroom' – off it went, like a jet engine. Even then, our energy was different to any other band.

Even with all the anger, angst and paranoia there was always a deep respect, and that is why The Who stayed together. You can have all that stuff on tour, but when you get home, there's a deep caring for each other – it's family. Don't fucking get in the middle of it – you wouldn't last two seconds!

I've done what I always dreamed of, but I haven't changed inside from being that kid. Fame is a weird thing. We all wanted to be rich and famous, which we became, but you are still the same blokes. I don't want to be that star on a pedestal – I was always uncomfortable with that. I lock myself away in the country now and I'm a bit of a recluse, but that's out of choice. I like to be with the grandkids and the family.

I was 20 when I became a father. When I left my family, it was with the intent that I could do better for everyone – Jackie,[42] my son Simon, me, the band, my mum and dad, my sisters – if I followed my dream. Better than if I tried to do something I couldn't handle, which was being married with a kid in a council flat in Wandsworth. I'd look down at the band's van with the arrow and The Detours[43] on the side – it was luring me down. And as it happened, it worked out. I haven't been a perfect human being, but I hope I've learned from the mistakes I have made.

The main advice I give youngsters is to be aware of what you're getting into on social media. Because life is not

42 Daltrey's first wife.

43 The band's previous name.

looking down at screens, it is looking up. We are heading for catastrophe with the addiction that's going on in the younger generation. Your life will disappear if you are not careful.

My younger self would have loved 'Baba O'Riley' – it speaks to generation after generation. The bridge – 'Don't cry, Don't raise your eye, It's only teenage wasteland' – if that doesn't say more about the new generation, I don't know what does. But I'm inspired by the young people I meet through the Teenage Cancer Trust. They're fantastic.

There have been two 'lightbulb moments' in my life: the first was the music of Lonnie Donegan and the second was my GP, Adrian Whiteson, starting the Teenage Cancer Trust. Adolescents were being diagnosed with cancer and waking up in children's hospitals next to two-year-olds. I thought back to that period in my life, when I was so isolated, walking by the river every day and playing truant from school. I thought, 'Fucking hell, imagine if you had cancer and you were next to screaming kids on a hospital ward? Or even worse, geriatric adults.' It's something I'm determined to change with whatever life I have got left, but it's a hard, hard slog.

Young musicians today are much better trained than we ever were. Occasionally you see the sparks, like when Ed Sheeran first played for the Teenage Cancer Trust. He's a remarkable young man. To do all that on his own? People think it's easy – is it fuck! And he's a diamond of a guy. We've had them all play for us. Arctic Monkeys are going to be around for a long time, and I wish the Gallagher brothers would get back together. My advice to them would be that all the verbal that keeps you in the press is today's version of wrestling – it's not real, so get over it.

If I could relive any day, I'd like to go back and give Heather a proper wedding. We got married at a registry office on the spur of the moment. Then we went down the pub and had a laugh with Zoot Money, Steve Ellis and a couple of mates. I don't know if she'd want a proper wedding – it's more that I feel bad about it. We met 50 years ago this September. What's the secret? Ask her – I don't know!

I'd love to go back and have one last conversation with Moon. What would I say to him? 'You silly fucker!' No, I don't know if I would say anything – I'd just like to hug him. We loved him. We didn't know about rehab in those days; we did our best with what little we did know, but it was hard. A good day out with Moon could be one of the best and funniest days in your life. A bad day out with Moon could be your worst nightmare. But a good day out with Moon could be one of the best and funniest days of your life.

will.i.am

Musician

19 March 2018

I've been praying to my 16-year-old self, as well to as my 60-year-old self, every year since I was 17. Say you want to be a musician or a doctor or a preacher – whatever it is, you pray to that version of you in the future to keep you on the right path. As you get older, if you also pray to yourself in the past and stay true to him, you avoid making a lot of mistakes. That continuous connection to my younger self and my future self has helped me make every decision I've ever made. Am I going to go to a strip club tomorrow? Probably not, because my 60-year-old self is praying to me now and telling me not to do that shit. For the same reason, I didn't indulge in crazy activities, like having unprotected sex, when I was a teenager. And that little dude has kept praying to me since I was 16, pinging me the co-ordinates to get me to my destination, just like a sat nav. God does amazing miracles, but he cannot do things for you unless you are trying yourself.

I was at a school at 16 but got a record deal when I was 17. Me and my best friend apl[44], who I started the Black Eyed Peas with, we were relentless dreamers. People would tell us we sucked, but we just thought, 'Dang, you don't know what we know.' We had a different mentality. You can't be so arrogant as to ignore every critic – sometimes there's truth there. And you shouldn't just soak up praise – everyone telling you you're amazing can be kryptonite, it can cripple you. You have to know what to take and what to ignore. You have to be level-headed and not emotional. And there's nothing wrong with pressure – it's what makes diamonds.

My family and I lived in a stressful environment, and I became the master of my projects by not indulging in the things that cause stress and seeing every problem as a riddle to solve. I did that by disciplining myself and surrounding myself with people who would not add to the problem. My mom had a heavy hand about who I could hang out with. And my grandmother gave me an amazing prayer – 'We come before you as humble as we know how' – that helped me develop my praying style. It gave me my compass, so I always knew my true north. So even when you're hanging around a certain environment with certain folks, it doesn't mean you'll be thrown off course. That prayer is like my immunity, so if I'm around an affected area, I've had my Hep B and Hep C shots so I'm not getting Hep.

I don't think I'm political – I'm socially conscious. We grew up in a poor neighbourhood, and in the summer, when there's no school to feed their kids breakfast and lunch, poor folks can't feed their kids three meals a day and can only afford one meal. So my mother helped run a summer lunch programme

44 (Filipino-American rapper and producer Allan Pineda Lindo, a.k.a. apl.de.ap)

and signed us up to help. It was important that it was the community feeding the community, and not rich folks from outside the neighbourhood – that gave me my entrepreneurial spirit. My mom also had a job looking after the kids in the ghetto whose parents had three jobs and couldn't look after their kids after school. My uncle taught them basketball. That's why I went back to the ghetto I'm from to start my computer school and my robotics programme.

It hurts my heart when young people tell me they want to be a star. I know strippers who are stars, and there are prostitutes who are stars now. I don't know what the fuck the word 'star' means. When I was growing up I didn't want to be a star – I just wanted to take care of my mom. I wasn't even looking for a record deal – I got signed because I was good at improv and I got spotted in a freestyle battle contest. I didn't actively chase a record deal until Eazy-E,[45] who signed me when I was 17, passed away in 1995. We started the Black Eyed Peas and I thought, 'I know what a record deal is now – and we need one.'

I wrote 'Street Livin'' in 2015, and it was the first song I wrote without a beat. I wrote it on the aeroplane as a poem. I was going to China to raise money for my artificial intelligence company. I was thinking about the changing opportunities for my black ancestors over the last 100 years, how we've gone from coons, because that's what they called us, to cons, who are in and out of correctional facilities. For every song I write that's fun, like 'Boom' or 'My Humps', I have to write a conscious poem or an in-depth thought composition. We didn't do it thinking, 'We're going to win Grammys with this one' or 'We're going to sell out stadiums with this one.' We

45 NWA rapper who launched his own label Ruthless Records, in 1986.

can do stuff like *The E.N.D.* and know we can knock it out of the park. 'Street Livin'' isn't for the masses, and it's not about the numbers or the plaudits – it's about the issues.

When I first showed *Masters of the Sun*, my graphic novel, to Jamie Foxx, he didn't take me seriously until I proved to him that I was solid. And why should he? He's supposed to make me work harder, to go beyond my limits to get his attention. Just doing a book – I'm sorry, that's not good enough. Anyone can do a fucking book. But when I told him, 'Check this out – I brought my book to life with augmented reality,' he was like, 'What? Okay, let's do this.'

Of all the things I've done, I think the 16-year-old me would like the whole 'Street Livin'' project the most: the graphic novel, the augmented reality, the music and the video. He'd ask what company was doing the graphic novel and I'd say, 'That's us, bro – our own company.' 'What do you mean, our own company?' And I'd say, 'Yeah bro, we got lots going on, like our AI stuff.' 'What AI stuff?' 'Never mind about that – I'll tell you all about it when you're older. All you need to know right now is not to listen to the naysayers – focus. When things get hard, when your knees are about to buckle, keep moving, keep going. And do not give up.'

The first time I got jealous of an artist was when I saw Lin-Manuel Miranda's *Hamilton*. I was like, 'Wait a second, they haven't stopped rapping! They haven't taken a breath!' Everything is so perfect, from top to bottom and from beginning to end. Every line was complementary to the next line and the whole story was in rhyme. I was like, what the fuck!

The Voice is an amazing vacation – I love coming to the country and being around people who remind me of my

16-year-old self, dreaming about music. My dreams now are ginormous, but I had ginormous dreams then too, of looking after my mom. When I showed her the first house I bought, she was like, 'How much is the rent?' I said, 'Ma, I bought it.' I didn't know what a mortgage was when I lived in the projects. We paid $100 a month to rent out our home. I told her my house cost $5,000 a month and she said, '$5,000 a month? Will, that's like four years on the projects! You can afford that?' I said, 'Don't worry, I'm not going to flip. I know how I work under pressure. I'm good at it.'

My best friend apl, was adopted. He was sponsored at five years old, when he was living in a village in the Philippines. His adoptive dad was Scottish, and he brought apl to America when he was 14 so he could go to school and get eye surgery, because apl is half-blind. The reason I am who I am today is because I met him at 14 years old. I graduated from high school but I wasn't at the ceremony because it was at the same time as apl's and I wanted to see him graduate instead. He said, 'What are you doing here – what about your graduation?' I said, 'Nah, you've only been in America for four years – I wanted to see *you* graduate.'

If I could go back to any day in my past it would be the day apl's dad said to him, 'Son, I brought you to America to go to college. What college do you want to go to?' And apl said, 'I want to do music with Will.' And his dad called me in and said, 'I brought Allan to America to go to college and now he says he wants to do music with you. I think you should think about your career choice. If you're sure that's what you want to do, you're no longer welcome under my roof and you both have to leave by next week. Allan is now your responsibility.' I understand why he was so concerned and angry, after everything he'd done. And I don't know why I was so sure, but I went to apl and said, 'Don't worry bro – we're going to make it.' We were crying and could have buckled then, like we could have buckled when Eazy-E died and doors were shut in our faces. But we kept going, until one day we both went back to the Philippines together as the Black Eyed Peas. And the people who used to call this little kid 'Nub Nub' because he was half-black celebrated him as a Filipino national treasure. I saw how he felt. And I felt like it was me coming home, too.

CHAPTER 7:

Tenacity

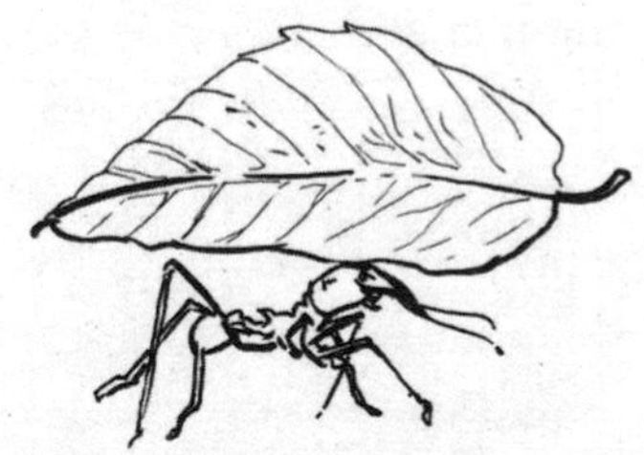

Olivia Newton-John

Actor

9 March 2015

When I was 16, I'd just left school and I was already singing in a little jazz quartet with three other girls, performing in clubs around Melbourne. We dressed like beatniks, the style of the day. My singing, my boyfriend and riding horses – those were the main things in my life.

I think I was a pretty optimistic person – I still am – but I was a little anxious. My parents separated when I was nine and we went from living in the college, with my mother being the headmaster's wife, to my mother and I living on our own. That was pretty traumatic. In those days, divorce wasn't so common – telling my friends was awkward. And there was some tension from some of my friends' mothers, which I now realise was because my mother was very beautiful. We never discussed it then, but now I can see that I caused her some alienation.

My father worked on the Enigma project at Bletchley Park but he never talked about it because he wasn't allowed to.

Just before he died he gave us children some tapes in which he talked a little about it, but he was still pretty guarded. I went to see *The Imitation Game*, the Benedict Cumberbatch film about the Enigma project, and it really made me wish I'd known more when my dad was still alive, so I could have asked him about it.

Until I was 15 I wanted to be a vet and work with animals. But I failed maths, so that was out of the question – thank goodness I could sing. I entered a TV talent contest when I was 15 and much to my amazement, I won. My mum wanted me to finish my education, but suddenly I was being offered all these TV opportunities and wanted to go ahead with my singing career. There was even a bit of controversy in the papers when I was offered a job on this kids' show – 'Should she take it or should she finish her schooling?' In the end, I took the job, and that was me set.

I went to London when I was 16 – it was the prize for winning the TV talent show. I found it totally overwhelming and wanted to go home and see my boyfriend. I didn't like London and said ridiculous things like, 'It's so cold!' I kept booking my flight home and my mother kept cancelling it – now that we were in Europe, she wanted me to go to RADA. But I wasn't too interested in acting and just wanted to sing. My poor mother, that was another thing she never got her way with. Now I look back and I wish I could tell her I'm sorry.

I had a lot of doubts about making *Grease* – I was the most reticent Sandy you can imagine. I'd just made this film called *Toomorrow* – it was going to be the next big thing, but it turned out to be pretty bad. So I was thinking about focusing on my singing career, which was going well, instead of doing another movie. I was also worried I was too old. I asked if I could do a screen test with John Travolta to make sure I looked age-appropriate – Sandy was 17 and I was 29. But John wanted me for the role and bent over backwards to accommodate me, and in the screen test it really worked between us. He's a lovely man and we had an amazing time making the movie – we'll be friends for ever.

I remember going to the premiere of *Grease* in LA – the crowds were insane. We were in an open-top car and they were all over us. I think *Saturday Night Fever* had just come out. Then we went to London and the car nearly got tipped over. But I've never been blown away by those things – I always remember someone telling me 'Tomorrow it'll be somebody else.' I have a great sense of reality and I had a good upbringing in Australia, where they like to keep your feet on the ground. I think that's important – life can be very disappointing if you believe your own handouts.

I got my breast cancer diagnosis the same day I lost my dad. I couldn't go home for the funeral because I had to have surgery and start my treatment. It was a very difficult time, but I had to take care of my health. I had a daughter by then – Chloe was just a little girl – so I had a reason to live and be strong. I went through a few really terrifying nights with a feeling of dread while I was waiting for my final diagnosis, but then I made a decision that I was going to be alright. And after that I had a deep-down belief that I would be.

I don't think I was able to deal with losing my father at the time – it was too difficult to deal with my illness and my grief at once, so I closed that drawer. Later, when I was ready, I opened it and started to cope with what was inside. After my treatment I went straight to Australia with a mind to retire, but music helped me cope. I ended up writing an album, initially with no intention of releasing it, but when it was done I decided to put it out, and it rebooted my career.

I've thought, 'That's it' many times. When I sang at the Sydney Olympics, that was one of the most amazing experiences in my life. And I thought, 'This is the pinnacle – there's nothing else after this.' But it didn't end there, and after 50 years in the business, I'm still going.

If I could go back and relive any time, it would definitely be the birth of my daughter. The first few years of her life were the most amazing time of my life. I had her quite late, when I was 36, so she was such a gift, and I'd like to relive that time to remember more of the details. I was there, but I was the family breadwinner, so I was always busy. I adored my daughter, but I should have spent more time playing with her.

Barry McGuigan

Boxer

26 March 2012

At 16 I was already caught up in boxing and was beginning to give up on school. I'd just won the national title, I was training at the High Performance Training Centre in Dublin and boxing was starting to take over my life. I enjoyed school, but in those days they weren't flexible – it was either school or boxing. I had training twice a day and was trying to help out my mum in the shop and to do my studies. I don't want to sound like a goody two-shoes, but though there were six of us siblings, I seemed to work harder than anyone else. Finally, I just said to my mother one morning, 'I'm not going to school today.' She went straight to wake up my dad who was still in a deep sleep and said, 'He won't go to school.' I had a chat with dad and said I couldn't do it all at the same time, and he let me opt out.

I don't regret leaving school at 16 – I carried on reading insatiably and through my boxing I ended up having the best education in the world. I met different people and cultures, and learned about history and places. I was one of the lucky ones, and didn't need something to fall back on when the boxing career finished. Because I'd read so much about boxing and its history, and had a pretty extraordinary knowledge of the sport, becoming a commentator was a natural progression.

I was a very ambitious, driven, searching teenager and was always looking to the future – that's the exciting part of being young. It would be good to go back and tell that teenager it would all work out. I can't say I knew I was going to make it – I didn't. I was bold, but I was also apprehensive. I didn't have a trade or anything, but I was determined, and the cards just fell the right way for me. Just after I left school, I won the Commonwealth gold medal and nothing could hold me back.

What happened with Young Ali was a tragedy, and a very tough time in my life.[46] I'd just got out of the blocks as a professional fighter, and it was upsetting and terrifying. I wasn't sure I could do it anymore, but I'd committed my whole life to boxing. My wife was pregnant and working six days a week. I had no money, no skills and no qualifications. My father was a great help then, as were all my brothers and sisters, and my wife. I'd like to go back and put my arm around young Barry going through that hard time, but I probably couldn't have helped him any better than my dad did at the time. I decided that if I re-focused and won the title, I would dedicate it to Ali.

Living in Ireland, the Troubles were with you all the time – you felt them in your tummy 24 hours a day. I was a Catholic

46 Barry's fight with Ali in 1982 put Ali in a coma, and he died five months later.

boy from the South, but I wanted people to be able to go to my fights and not feel any threat. I was in and out of conflict areas all the time, among the tricolours, union flags, murals and painted flagstones – the Shankill Working Men's Club and Gerry Storey's boxing club in the New Lodge. My father sang *Danny Boy* before my title fights because it was a song that belonged to everyone. Cynics said it was a commercial decision, but that was a load of bollocks.

There was a brief moment when I thought I might give up boxing. I got to the penultimate round in the 1980 Moscow Olympics, beat the guy to Edinburgh and back, and they didn't give me the fight. I was so pissed off I decided to have nothing more to do with boxing. I had a wild idea to open a hamburger joint, but that lasted three days. I couldn't stand it, so I went back into training and the thing I love. Boxing is a drug, and so is fame.

I often think about what would have happened if the boxing hadn't worked out. I love music and my father was a singer, so maybe entertainment would have been my thing. My two boys are both musicians, so it's sort of in me. I'm into words, too – when you're a commentator, you get bored of saying the same thing, so you look for several ways of saying the same thing. I like firing new words at people and have a gamut of books with unusual words in them. But you must remember to articulate to express rather than to impress. You don't want to be a pompous eejit.

If I could go back, I'd try to spend more time with my dad. I did spend a decent amount of time with him, but he was out at work a lot. After he died it was hard, but I grappled with it and decided to fight on. I never got to fight for the world title again; my career was derailed, and I knew something had gone by then – maybe it was my dad and maybe it was moving from Ireland to England. The truth is, I fell out of love with boxing, though it took a while to admit it to myself, because I knew life would never be the same again. There would always be a hole.

If I could go back and say anything to my younger self, it would be, 'Batten down the hatches and strap yourself in – it's going to be a fantastic ride.' I could never have imagined what was going to happen to me – that level of success and popularity, and 20 million people watching me win the world title on TV. And that girl across the road that I was madly in love with but she didn't know it – it's amazing to think I'd end up marrying her.

Jamie Oliver

Chef

17 December 2012

When I was 16, I couldn't wait to get to London and get my first job. I'd had a rough time at secondary school and didn't do well. I'm dyslexic – I don't know where I fit on the spectrum, but the school didn't bother too much, because mine wasn't the most severe case. I've always struggled with writing and I've never had the ability to concentrate long enough to read a narrative book – my letters get mixed up. I've never had a problem with imagination, but when I write my cookbooks I speak into a Dictaphone and have my editor take down what I say. I think it's fine to tell kids you don't need to be good at everything.

Most 16-year-olds aren't scared of much and I certainly wasn't, but I did worry about not getting a bunk-up – my love life was like a bloody desert. There was nothing going on, and they were running a bloody mile, basically. I wasn't very confident; my voice shook when I talked to girls.

I'd like to tell the 16-year-old me he'd end up with a model – he wouldn't have believed that. Though actually, I'd already met Jools by then. She'd joined the sixth form in my school, but every time I went to talk to her, I just sounded like Scooby Doo. So I just sort of avoided her because I kept sounding like a complete idiot. But a year and a half later, I don't know why but she had a change of heart and decided she quite liked me. And as soon as I found out, I was all over it like a rash – I didn't want to miss that opportunity. But when I asked her out on a date, I still sounded like Scooby Doo. She didn't understand me but laughed and said, 'Yes to whatever it is you just said.'

If I met 16-year-old Jamie now – well, he wouldn't be that different to the Jamie who was on TV when he was 21, on *The Naked Chef*. Undoubtedly that person had lots of annoying nuances that would jar with a 38-year-old bloke like me. I was incredibly enthusiastic and thought I could do anything. I was into my music, on my scooter and saying 'pukka' every five seconds. I was annoying, but I was genuinely being myself. Fifteen years, four kids, and a lot of responsibility later, I'm a much calmer person.

I'd like to sit down with the teenage me, have a pint, and tell him to stick to his guns and trust his gut instinct. He'd be in massive shock if I told him how things were going to go – working with governments across the world, all the different types of businesses he's involved in – that would scare the life out of him. When I was young I just wanted to cook, run a nice little pub in the country and have a nice wine cellar and good local beers – that's all I dreamed of. Then they made a TV documentary at the restaurant I was working in, The River Café, and when it came on TV, I was laced across the whole thing and it looked really cool. Then the phone calls started coming.

I'd warn the younger me that being in the public eye takes time to acclimatise to and that there are always going to be people who don't like you. I'd tell him, 'Don't turn into an arsehole.' I think I did avoid that. Even early on in my career, I had people around me who loved and respected me. I don't think I was ever a diva with them, though I may be the wrong person to ask – we always just got on and had a laugh. I'd remind the younger me that the showbizzy stuff is fine but it's all the other stuff that counts – the stuff we did helping kids who'd had a hard time into work with Fifteen[47] and the campaigns we've done – that's the meaningful stuff.

It's quite hard getting a balance. I used to work seven days a week and I loved it, but I probably wasn't a very good boyfriend then. So when we had Poppy, our first, we started from scratch and made weekends and holidays totally precious. After eight years, I actually think I've got my life more in balance than Jools – she could actually do less with the kids. Mums need a bit of a break as well – I need to get her up to the same work/life balance as me.

The idea of four kids would scare the life out of the younger me. I only ever saw myself having two, and I could barely see that. I never thought I'd have so many kids, ever. You always think you'll grow up in a family like your own. My wife is a hands-on parent and that's a tough job – I'm in complete admiration of what she does. But the thing I'll never get is why lots of wives are always trying to prove that their job is just as hard as the man's job. Men don't need constant

47 Jamie's non-profit restaurant, which offered training for aspiring chefs from disadvantaged backgrounds.

reinforcement about how brilliant they are – we just kind of crack on. But the girls do like to be constantly reminded how brilliant they are. It's not a problem – it's just that men are from Mars and women are from Venus.

I don't have many regrets, but I have done some of the dodgiest photo shoots in the world. Some of the shittiest ideas a photographer could force on you, like juggling vegetables and generally looking like a total knob. And they're all there online, to haunt me for the rest of my life.

I'd tell my younger self that when you're really uncomfortable, that's often when you do your best work. *Jamie's School Dinners* and *Jamie's American Food Revolution* were the hardest things I've ever done. Having to go into a place and bring up that world people hate, 'change' – you have whole communities of people hating your guts for about two months, before they see some benefits from what you're doing.

I never used to have a sense of mission, but over the years I looked around me and got wiser and more thoughtful. Back in the day I'd see a bunch of kids on a street corner and think 'yobbos', but then I had my own children and looked at them again and thought, 'They're someone's kids.' And if they had disrupted home lives and their health wasn't the best, maybe we could make sure they got one good hot meal a day. You can't do everything, but maybe you can do something.

I've had a fast, mad life. If I could go back, I'd take more time to enjoy that time when we had no ties, no responsibilities and no baggage – those weekends when we could just be selfish and have a conversation without being interrupted a million times. When I was 18, I took Jools to Crete and we had the most amazing week. I'd saved my money and was able to treat her, which was a really grown-up thing to do. That was brilliant.

Dame Stella Rimington

Former Director General of MI5

26 November 2018

I was a child of the war, having been born just four years before the Second World War broke out. We left Nottingham and went to stay with my granny in Wallasey, across the river from Liverpool, and we lived there when the docks in Liverpool were bombed. By 1951, when I turned 16, people were looking towards the future again. That was the year of the Festival of Britain, on London's south bank. It was to celebrate a new start. I remember a fairground and a Dome of Discovery that was full of new scientific inventions. I found it enormous fun. The government were saying, 'The gloom is over now, and we have something to look forward to.' Do I think we'll have a Festival of Brexit in a few years? I very much doubt it.

My father fought in the First World War and was subject to periods of depression. He was very fond of my brother and me, but he wasn't very communicative. I had a closer relationship with my mother. She propped us all up. She had worked as a midwife in the East End, just like the nurses in *Call the Midwife*, but she came from an era when women weren't expected to have a job after they married, so she gave her work up after the war. I wonder if she ever thought about what her life might have been like if she'd been born at a different time. It must have been very stressful, carrying the weight of two small children and a very anxious husband through the war. I regard her as an unsung hero.

I found work as a county archivist after university, but I did assume I would eventually get married and then my career would come second to my husband's. It did for a while. When he got a job in New Delhi, I immediately gave up work and went off to be a diplomat's wife. India was fantastic but I found the life rather boring – hosting tea parties and getting involved in amateur dramatics. When we came back to England, I expected we'd start a family, but it didn't happen. I suppose I was kind of a failed mother at that point, so when I managed to get a job as a typing clerk in MI5, my husband encouraged me.

I thought the MI5 work was interesting, but I was slightly bored because the women were very clearly treated like second-class citizens. I had a degree just like the men, but we were regarded as men's helpers. But as the '70s went on, and we had Women's Lib and the Sexual Discrimination Act, those vague feelings that it wasn't quite fair began to mount. Women like me became discreet revolutionaries. We were politely saying, 'Why are we not thought fit to do the real work?' And things began to change.

It wasn't easy for me. I split up with my husband when my older daughter was about 10. From then on, we were a single-parent family with two growing girls, and me in a full-time, 24/7 kind of job. We managed with a combination of au pairs, nannies and the lady down the road. It was a bit hand-to-mouth at times, I admit. My daughters talk about it sometimes, usually very generously – they say that it was good to have a mother who was doing something, but it wasn't as cosy a childhood as they might have had.

The end of the Cold War was a time of vast excitement and great hope. Suddenly the world began to change radically and everything I'd been working against began to crumble. Gorbachev had started an avalanche, which led to the total collapse of the Iron Curtain. It was a bit like 1951 again, that sense of the world opening up. But I'm not optimistic about the future right now – I feel the world is in a very worrying state, with the rise of nationalism, people retreating behind borders and the uncertainty of Brexit. Things feel very unstable; the golden hope of the late '80s has not been fulfilled.

I was told I'd been made Director General of MI5 just after the end of the Cold War, and getting that job just felt like part of a series of amazing things that were happening. I was very excited, thrilled and surprised. The government then decided that, for the first time ever, they were going to announce the appointment and tell people who I was. So after years of being very cautious about telling anyone what I did, I was on the front page of every newspaper. It was a very strange period, actually, a mixture of elation and alarm. My mother was stunned. I hadn't talked to my daughters about what I did, though I think they had their suspicions. Their friends were all saying, 'Oh, I read about your mum'. I had one friend who was very hurt. She was traditionally left-wing and thought the services were the enemies of the people, so when she found out what I'd been doing all those years she was very upset and didn't speak to me for ages.

We tried to combat the press's initial image of me as a James Bond housewife superspy, and I think we were making some progress. Then, of course, the new Bond film had Judi Dench as M, and she was said to be modelled on me. So rather than knocking the James Bond thing on the head, it became quite fun.

If I could go back and relive one day, it would be the day I went to meet the men who had for so long been our enemies, the KGB. The idea was that we would help them legislate the secret services so they could operate in a democracy. But really, it was like talking to the deaf and they saw us as extraordinary creatures from another world. I was the only woman at the table, of course. At the concluding speech one of them said, 'In your country you have a woman prime minister, a lady queen and now a woman leading your intelligence service.' There was a sense of 'you must be mad', but still, that was one of the most amazing things that ever happened to me. I didn't think it would ever be possible to go to Russia – I thought the Cold War would last for my lifetime, yet there I was in the British ambassador's Rolls-Royce with the Union Jack flying on the bonnet, driving through a snowy Moscow night to have dinner with the KGB. It was something straight out of a novel.

The 16-year-old Stella would be completely amazed by the way my life has gone. Some of the things I've seen, she didn't even know existed. Her world was much smaller, of course. She'd have worried that my life wasn't safe, because she came out of a world of fear and saw it turn into what looked like a new peace. And everything I've been involved in has not been about peace – it's been about protecting against threats, but that hasn't made me a more fearful person. Quite the opposite in fact.

Tracey Emin

Artist

11 August 2008

Life was quite complicated for me when I was 16. I was homeless and spent part of my time sleeping anywhere I could in London, until eventually I went back to Margate and lived in a DHSS bed and breakfast. This was a very, very sad and depressing time, but to counterbalance it I dressed on the wild side. All my clothes were either handmade or second-hand. I would dress in a cross between Christian Dior's 'New Look', '60s miniskirted beat girl, and very occasionally I'd go completely crazy and do the total Goth.

I think if some people saw me at the height of my white-faced Goth look, they'd probably cross the street. Punk wasn't long over and there was still an attitude of rebellion. But personally, I'd feel very sorry for me – I'd take me under my wing and try to help.

I'd tell my younger self to use condoms. Have fun. Don't expect boyfriends to sort everything out – they can't. And don't let your love life take over – concentrate on your education.

When someone tells you that you can't do something because you haven't got the right qualifications, understand that there's always an alternative way of doing things. For example, when I was 17, I was told I would never be able to go to university because I didn't have O-Levels, but I managed to get a portfolio together and I learned to draw, and even though I didn't have the qualifications, my determination showed I had conviction in what I wanted to do.

As a teenager, things are always magnified. It's like everything you are doing is on a tightrope, but the majority of things are always going to be okay. Only life-and-death situations can be catastrophic and difficult to deal with – and that's at any age. You have to go through these emotions and feelings to understand about life, and that's your own personal journey.

It might look like I made a mistake leaving school at 13, but I'm sure if I hadn't, I wouldn't be as successful an artist as I am now. I feel sorry for teenagers that have to fill their minds up with so much exam work that they're probably not interested in. It would be wonderful if you could just learn what you wanted to know. No exam is worth killing yourself over, ever. If you don't get into university this year, go the next, and go travelling.

I'd tell my younger self, 'Don't steal and try to be as honest as possible at all times. And never bite the hand that feeds you. And stop smoking now. It really is a waste of time.'

If you are in education – school or university – get a part-time job doing the closest thing to what you like doing. So if you like reading books, get a job in a bookshop. If you like food, get a job in a restaurant. If you like clothes, get a job in a clothes shop. That way you learn about something that you like as well as earning money.

I would tell the young Tracey, 'Make sure that no one spikes your drink with acid, drives you 15 miles outside London in a van, and has sex with you virtually without your knowledge, let alone your consent.' I think that's the kind of thing you should avoid at all times being a teenager. Crabs are another good thing to avoid – which, can I say, I've never had!

Mary Robinson

Former President of Ireland

6 August 2018

I grew up wedged between two sets of brothers – two older than me, two younger, five of us born in six years. So by the time I was 16 I was a tomboy, and I had a strong sense of equality and justice. My brothers always claimed I was the favourite; my parents made it clear that they wanted me to have the same opportunities as my brothers, but the wider Irish society in Mayo didn't give me that same sense.

I had very few options as a teenager and I was expected to either marry very young – which I had no interest in doing – or become a nun. I was quite religious in those days and my family were very much so. And we had nuns in the family who had lived very full lives in England and India. When I finished boarding school, I told the Reverend Mother I wanted to become a nun, but luckily, she told me to go away for a year and think about it. My parents were so pleased with me that they sent me to Paris for a year. Of course, that changed everything and I came back wanting to study law.

I adored my father – he was a wonderful doctor. I used to love going out with him on evening house calls. He'd tell me stories on the way there and then he'd go in, leaving me reading in the car. Eventually he'd come back out of these poor peasant houses with no electricity, and I'd watch him stand in the dim light of the front door, talking to the mother of the house. He'd be bent over, listening very patiently. And I waited and waited, wanting him to come back and tell me more stories. But he'd stand there for 20 minutes, because he knew that listening was very important as a doctor. I think it was because of him I called my memoirs *Everybody Matters*, because he firmly believed that. I grew up believing it too – no matter how poor, how old and how inarticulate – everybody matters.

My mother died very suddenly of a heart attack. It was a terrible loss to me. She only saw two of her grandchildren, including my eldest daughter Tessa, who was named after her. Then she died two days after Tessa's first cousin was born. My mother was the life and soul of the family, the heart of the family and she influenced me more than I knew. When I was campaigning to be President of Ireland, I realised I'd have to let people get to know me. I'd been very private before that; I was a naturally shy person. But the more I really talked to people on a personal level – opening up, becoming more friendly, warmer and a better listener – the more I became like my mother. That changed my approach to public life, and I've never gone back.

I went to Harvard Law School in 1968 after I graduated from Trinity. That year made a huge impression on me.

American law students were trying to avoid the draft and condemning what they called the immoral war in Vietnam. I was impressed by their idealism, seeing young people who were determined to do things and to really make a difference. That was very different from the Ireland I was used to, where young people waited their turn. Then you were 30, and you still waited your turn. Then, in your mid-forties, you might be allowed to take a role with some responsibility. That's why, when I came back to Ireland in 1969, and there was a senate election, I queried why the candidates were always elderly male professors. And my colleagues said, 'If you feel so strongly, why don't you go for it yourself?' I very much stood out as a young woman of 25, arguing that we had to open up Ireland and liberalise the country.

If I was to give my younger self advice, I'd tell her you can't change things too quickly. The first thing I did when I was elected to the senate was to pen a bill to legalise family planning. I was denounced in newspapers and churches – Nick[48] burned the hate mail I got. The archbishop in the city sent a letter to be read out in every diocese in Dublin saying the bill I was proposing would be a 'curse upon the country'. That was very heavy for me and it caused me to really wobble. I appreciate much more now that if you want to make changes regarding things like sexual morality, which run very deep in society, you have to take time to bring people with you. You have to educate, persuade, talk to people and have patience. We did eventually get the bill through, but it took nine years. It was an important lesson I took with me when I became UN High Commissioner for Human Rights in 1997 and had to tackle harmful traditional

48 Robinson's cartoonist husband, Nick Robinson

practices in other continents, such as early child marriage and female genital mutilation.

If I could have one last conversation with anyone, it would be with Nelson Mandela. He was the most extraordinary person I ever met, and I was so proud when he chose me as one of his elders. I wish I'd had more time with him and learned from his incredible humanity, his gentleness and his ability to forgive. His humour too – he was a terrible tease. He used humour to stop you from putting him on a pedestal, but you couldn't help doing it anyway because he was so impressive.

I remember my father more than once coming back from delivering a baby, and telling my mother he'd been asked, 'Doctor, is it a boy or a child?' He said, 'I'm so furious.' That convinced me that my father thought I was equal to my brothers. But the school didn't and wider society didn't – I couldn't be an altar boy or a priest. I learned very early in my life as a lawyer life about the Magdalene laundry women. I heard a lot of stories about mothers literally having their babies grabbed from them by priests in the hospital. I also learned how single mothers had been treated, because I was asked to be president of Cherish, the single mothers' organisation. I so admired those women. They were treated as criminals, as fallen women, but they had plenty of fight in them.

It was always important to me that my children knew they were the most important thing in my life. I remember the night I was elected president. There'd been a huge party and when we got home, I got the three of them together and told them, 'Even though I'll now be president, you are more important.' I had no doubt that, as a mother, I had to say that to them, and I meant it. There were times it was hard. I remember a long trip to India, an important state visit for Ireland, and my daughter had her birthday when I was there – I felt very far away from her. I still have a very busy life, but I was very happy to become a granny. I have six grandchildren now. It gives me energy when I'm fighting to tackle the future effects of climate change, thinking about the kind of world my grandchildren will grow up in.

CHAPTER 8:

Courage

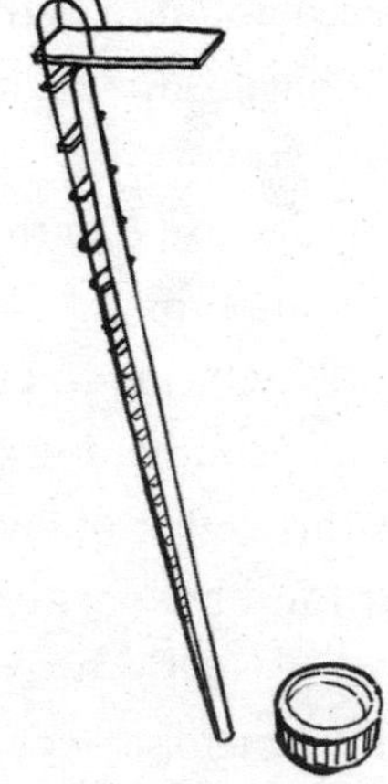

Jane Lynch

Actor

7 January 2013

At 16 I'd assessed that I was gay, but I didn't have a word for it. Growing up in the suburbs in Chicago, I didn't know anyone who was gay – I just knew it was something people whispered about, a bad thing. So it was a scary time. I hung out in a big group of friends and we were all very fun-loving, but deep down I had my secret, so I always felt kind of like a double agent. I had this sense that if people really knew me they wouldn't think I was so fabulous, so I over-compensated at school by trying to be the most fun and the kindest. Some of it was genuine, but I was over-compensating for what I saw as this deficit of character.

I felt for a big part of my life like I was hiding something. I had this secret – my God, I didn't even say it out loud to myself. I remember when I was 16, I was keeping this journal, and I wrote, 'I think I might be gay'. Then I took the journal and walked as far away from my school as I could, found a garbage can behind a grocery store and threw the journal in.

I wish I'd had a *Glee* when I was 16. I wish I could tell the younger me, 'Hey, there are more people like you. It feels frightening now, but times will change and people will become more accepting and they'll not just be tolerant, but loving. In 20 years, this aspect of you will be about as important as being right-handed and tall and blonde.' I have a Twitter account now, and at least half my followers seem to be kids in high school and they say things like, 'I wish you were my mom.' The younger me would find that very ironic – I so wanted someone to be my saviour when I was 16.

I think I was always funny – you're either born funny or you're not. I was good at it, so I grabbed at it and was the class clown. I remember setting out to get people to like me, and that was how I went about it. But my kind of humour is not so obvious, so it took some people a while to understand that I was funny. But that was a good test – if there was one person in the room who laughed, I'd focus on that person. Operation crack 'em up.

If I met the younger me now, I think I'd find her funny, self-deprecating and sweet. I was very careful not to hurt people's feelings – though I'm sure there were days when I wasn't as cute as I thought I was. I had a bit of a temper and got frustrated – I wanted so badly to be understood and when I wasn't, or when my mother just rolled her eyes or shook her head at me, I got angry. If I told young Jane that she was going to grow up to be a role model for other gay kids, she'd be so proud – on the other hand that would be uncomfortable for her, 'cause what did any other kid do for her?

Getting a part in the movie *Best in Show* was a game

changer for me. Until then I was doing guest slots and commercials and voice-overs, so I was making a living, but it was only after *Best in Show* that casting agents started to consider me for my own particular take on things. When I met Christopher Guest[49] I felt he saw me, and I saw him. That's how he auditions people; they just sit in his office and he's not the best in the world at small talk, but he can tell right away what's going on with a person and if he likes them. If I could have been 16 and met the Christopher Guest from 2000, that would have been awesome.

The teenage Jane would spiral into despair if I told her she'd have to wait till she was 40 to have real success – she wanted it all to happen right away. But now I'm glad it turned out like that; it was the perfect path for me.

I'd tell the younger me, 'Put the cigarettes down now – and you don't need to go drinking every weekend because that's going to turn into drinking every day.' I was drinking pretty heavily when I was 16 and already it was getting old and I was suffering terrible hangovers. I'd tell her, 'Don't even play with it – you have an addictive personality.' I still battle that one.

I never planned or even thought about being a stepmother – like I said, what have kids ever done for me? But now I have this really great kid; I don't think I could have designed her any better. She's 11 and she's funny, but in quite an adult way, not in a kooky-pants way. She's sharp and witty – she's an old soul, but she's still a kid, so I have to be a parent to her. I watch my wife, who's terrific at it, and I'm more and more in love with her every day because she's such a good mother. There's nothing like a kid to bring you out of yourself.

49 Legendary writer, director and star of *Best in Show* and *This Is Spinal Tap*.

Jane Lynch

I had a dream last night about being 53 – because I'll be 53 next year – and it was horrible. But then I think, 'Well what's the alternative? Death.' I think when I'm 70 I'm going to look back at being 53 and think, 'Those were the days.' I only became aware of my age when I turned 40, and it was a real shock when 50 came. You expect to get a little pause for thought after that but no, 51 comes right along. I keep older people around me, so I still feel young.

Harriet Harman

Politician

6 February 2017

I was a fuming teenager. They talk about the 'angry young man' – I was the angry young woman. I looked at my mother cooking my dad's breakfast and then his dinner, not having been able to practise as a lawyer even though she'd qualified because she had to prioritise being a housewife. And I thought, 'No way, that's not going to be me.' I didn't want to accept a world in which the only value of a woman was whether she looked good.

My mother never said to us, 'I want you to have the opportunities that I didn't.' That would have been like complaining and not accepting her role. She just got on with it. But she and my dad were very keen for us all to get an education so that we could make our own living, stand on our own two feet and have our own opinions. And my three sisters and I turned into pretty rebellious teenagers.

I was very driven as a teenager, but it wasn't all politics. There was The Jackson Five. And there were miniskirts,

Mary Quant and vast black plastic eyelashes that you stuck on the top of your eyelids. It's a miracle I didn't blind myself and that I have a single eyelash left! But when I look back, I see myself as being consumed by this strong attitude. And my sisters all thought the same. I was born into the sisterhood! There was a whole generation of women popping up saying, 'Yes, we know it's always been like this, but it isn't going to be like this anymore.'

I think the 16-year-old me was probably quite annoying. I was contrary and non-compliant. 'Stroppy' is probably the word. I do look back and feel a bit sorry for my mum having to cope with me. She bore it with good grace, but I think I must have been a bit of a nightmare. I wouldn't want to go back to that turbulent time, and have all those questions ahead of me. I don't have any nostalgia for being 16 – I think being 66 and having a sense of who I am and what I've done is far preferable.

If I could go back to my younger self, I'd tell her not to feel so tortured by the guilt that came with being a mother and a Labour politician trying to get Labour into government. That anxiety that you're doing neither properly and you're caught between the two. I was very anguished but think now there's no way to get that right, and so many ways you can get it wrong, so all you can do is get on with it. In a perfect world I'd have liked to have given up work entirely until my youngest child was five, work part-time until the youngest was 13 and then return to my political work without the intervening years having had any impact. But it just wasn't possible.

I made a point of doing some things to help my fragile, often non-existent, maternal self-esteem. I always picked the kids up from school on Friday – I wanted to be in the playground, talking to the other mums and getting a sense of what was going on. No high heels, no briefcase, no suit – I'd be in a tracksuit and trainers and carrying a plastic bag. Then we'd all go home and have a takeaway. Those Fridays made me feel that for at least one day a week, I was a proper mum.

The 16-year-old me would be astonished that I'd ever get to be an MP, never mind be in the Cabinet. The Cabinet then was just a load of stuffed shirts and Mrs Thatcher! The idea that I'd find myself in the government one day – my teenage self would say, 'Give over, that will never happen.' But I'd have to warn her that it takes a very long time to make change. We were protesting in the early '80s about men killing their wives and not being charged with murder because they said their wives had provoked them by being unfaithful, and it wasn't until 2009 that we got that abolished. I'd tell my younger self, 'You'll have to stick at it for a long time, but it'll be worth it.'

When I came into the House of Commons, there were hardly any women, and those who were there had this kind of matronly Thatcher style. Tweedy suits, silk shirts with pussycat bows – I wasn't going to wear that! I was a 32-year-old and wanted to come accross as a stylish woman, but turning up in a floral frock in the House of Commons made me look even more ludicrously out of place than I already felt. The average MP was a 54-year-old man and I was a pregnant 32-year-old woman. I wanted to wear something that wouldn't attract criticism and would give my constituents confidence that I would fight their case. I had to look like a professional – that's where the smart trouser suits, heels and shoulder pads came from.

I remember my maiden speech well. I was very anxious and heavily pregnant in a red velvet maternity dress. It was very daunting, but I knew exactly what I wanted to say and felt it was incredibly important to say it. If people realised my knees were knocking, that would be no good for the women I was representing, who were coming up to me in the street and saying, 'Keep going.' I couldn't let them down, and I had to prove that women were just as capable of speaking in the House of Commons as men. Those thoughts made me feel stronger than I really was.

I'm absolutely gutted there's been no Labour woman prime minister or deputy prime minister. We're the party of equality, so it's torturous for the women in our party that the Conservative Party have produced two female prime ministers. But while it's important to see women in power, it's more important what you actually do for ordinary women, and Tory cuts have hit women workers and mothers very badly.

A lot of women I meet, councillors and MPs, say I inspired them to do what they're doing. But I certainly wouldn't want them following in my footsteps – I'd want them to do much better than me. We have new problems now, on top of the old, as-yet-unsolved problems. But it was an amazing thing to be part of the radical progressive women's movement and my great fortune to be there at a time when we felt so determined and empowered, ready to beat the odds. I see a new wave of women now ready to do the same thing, and I'm right behind them.

Sir Max Hastings

Historian and Author

22 March 2010

I hero-worshipped my father when I was 16 and felt that I'd never live up to the life he'd led and the adventurous career he'd made. People were always saying, 'Go on Hastings, go for the ball, get stuck in', and I was a notorious coward. My father parachuted, ran the Cresta Run and was a war correspondent – I was very scared about living up to the family legacy. It was only later that I realised my parents weren't at all important people. They were successful, interesting journalists, but I had an absurdly exaggerated idea of their place in the scheme of things.

I wish I'd realised that it's all complete nonsense, that stuff about your young days being the best of your life. I found that being young was pretty awful, not knowing what you could and couldn't do. The nice thing about getting older is that you know you're not going to be PM or win Wimbledon

– you're resigned to what you are. When you're young, not knowing torments you, or it did me.

I was very bad at getting on with people and didn't understand at all how to relate to others. I blamed my never being invited to parties on my parents, but looking back I realise it was just because I wasn't a very attractive sort. My parents were busy getting on with own lives and my mother took a very tough line, saying it was up to me to find ways to make friends. She was right, I suppose.

The best thing about boarding school was that nothing was ever as bad again afterwards. There's a lot to be said for getting the bad bits of life over quickly. For years afterwards, when I was in war zones like Vietnam or the Falklands and feeling sorry for myself, exhausted, dirty and scared, I'd think, 'At least I'm not in boarding school.' My life just got better and better. We all have failures and disappointments and I used to be jealous of everyone, but now I'd choose my own troubles over anyone else's.

I feel sorry for the people who were terrific successes in school – a lot of prefects and school football captains end up as secretaries of suburban golf clubs. They shone at school because they were conformists; most of life's real successes tend not to do what they're told.

I'd tell myself, 'If a girl's going to go to bed with you, she's just as likely to do so after a hamburger as if you take her out and buy her an expensive dinner.' I think of all the money I wasted taking girls out, and it got me nowhere. My now wife, who I first took out when I was 17, said in those days nice girls didn't do things like that – I wish I'd known.

Would I like the teenage Max? Not for a minute – he'd horrify me. I was what the Victorians used to call a 'hobbledehoy'. I was six foot five and incredibly badly co-ordinated, terribly awkward physically and socially. My wife likes to remind me how awkward I was.

One mistake I made as an editor was that, due to hero-worshipping my father, I valued physical courage too much and spent years forcing myself to do all the brave things he'd done. Nowadays I've realised that moral courage is more important and much rarer, and women are much more likely to have it than men. I picked up all my father's prejudices and ideas, and it was a long time before I realised how silly many of them were. I'm still a Tory of a kind, but one knows so much more about the world now. He was a right-wing Tory who believed that Britain was the greatest country in the world and didn't think much of anywhere else. As I grew older, I learned that an awful lot of what he thought was bonkers.

I was awed by my mother. She was tremendously clever and always so well turned out, and a very witty woman with a very sharp tongue. I was also pretty scared of her. In those days people didn't go in for kissing much – it was the pre-Diana era and there wasn't much physical embracing. Looking back, that was rather sad. As a family we were very nervous of physical contact; I've tried to be different with my own children but while trying to avoid the mistakes of my parents, I've just made new mistakes of my own. My daughter said recently that she didn't remember me being around much when she was young. I said, 'I was never missing for the bucket and spade trip' and she said, 'Yes, but you never looked as if you were enjoying it much.'

I was so wrapped up in my own troubles and my own life as a teenager that I wasn't interested in other people, and that's why I didn't get on with them. It took a long time to learn about that. I was very unhappy – all those nights sitting alone in my flat playing Patience. I was terribly lucky with my career, but part of the reason I worked so hard was because I had no social life. I've learned a lot since then.

Sir Ranulph Fiennes

Explorer

21 November 2011

I was quite a happy-go-lucky 16-year-old, but of course everyone in 1960 was aware of the Cold War situation. If you came from a military family and wanted to join up, as I did, you were even more aware. For some reason, there was this craze to dig nuclear shelters. Me and my friends from the village used to wander around in the woods, fish for tadpoles in the stream and work on digging a nuclear shelter into the cliff. We dug deeply into it and made it our gang headquarters. My girlfriend at the time sometimes came to meet me in the woods and I was very proud of showing her the shelter. Then later on, I married her.

By the time I was 16, the only thing I wanted to do was what my father was doing when he was killed in the war – be Royal Commander of the Royal Scots Greys, Scotland's only cavalry regiment. My dad died before I was born, but I was very conscious of everything he'd done and I knew every story about him by heart. The family had for centuries been involved in the army, so I was brought up on those stories. It was in my DNA – you are to an extent what your blood makes you, so dad's tendency would have partly been reproduced in me.

I knew I needed A-Levels to get into the Royal Scots Greys. I was sent to a special crammer school in Brighton but managed to fail my A-Levels twice, largely because I went there when the miniskirt fashion was at its height, so concentration was very hard. If I could go back to that time, I'd buckle down and pass my exams. I did go to the Scots Greys, but only on a short service commission. I thought they might change the stupid rules about A-Levels while I was there, but they didn't, so I couldn't stay on.

I don't think I'm inclined to take stupid risks; I learned lessons from my father. People didn't get to be Royal Commander, especially in the Second World War, if they were just wild risk-takers. Our expedition group today still avoids bad risks if they possibly can. We like to break world records before our rivals, but we know to avoid risks. But when you're young you do sow your wild oats. I happened to go on an explosives course and unfortunately, egged on by my friends, ended up using army explosives to blow up civilian property. That was a mistake because I was thrown out of the SAS as a result.

Before I did my seven marathons, my late wife Jenny took me to the surgeon in Bristol who'd done my double heart bypass operation, after which I'd been in a coma for three days. I think she thought I might have another heart attack if I did the marathons and was hoping the surgeon would suggest it was a bad idea. He said that he'd done the same operation on 3,000 people, and none of them had come back to him and asked if they could do a marathon, never mind seven. So he said he didn't really have an opinion, but I must never let my heart rate go above 130bpm. We did the marathons, but in the last-minute rush I forgot to pack the monitor, so I was never able to tell if my rate went above 130.

There are many things I'd like to go back and advise my younger self about. Regarding expeditions, when we took off from the Soviet Union to go to the North Pole, that gave us a head start over our Norwegian rivals. When they grabbed the world record, we looked back and asked what we'd done wrong – we'd blown our big chance. When we came to huge chunks of open water we couldn't use our sledges as canoes, so ended up abandoning them about 100 miles from the pole and just carrying on with big rucksacks. Then we ran out of food and had to be evacuated by Soviet helicopters. I'd tell myself to plan that better, and I'd also tell myself to take more care to plan for toe protection in minus 50 degrees – that might avoid me ending up with gangrene. We do everything we can to learn from these mistakes.

I had a dreadful year after my wife Jenny died of cancer. A year after that, I was saved from self-destructive tendencies when I met Louise. She has her own opinions about what I do – she had six years of putting up with me switching from polar exploration to climbing, but after doing Everest in 2009 I said I wouldn't do any more climbing, and I haven't.

I'm quite happy with my achievements, but if I went back and told my 16-year-old self about them, he wouldn't be impressed. He'd say I knew what my dad would have wanted me to do and shouldn't have tried to do anything else. He'd say all those stupid other things I've done were second-best.

Sir Salman Rushdie

Author

30 May 2016

I came from India to Rugby[50] when I was 13, and by 16 I was a pretty conventional public schoolboy. Some of the writing I did around that age was about being at boarding school – fortunately that text has disappeared, but I remember that the boy writing it was a kind of cliched public school conservative, including politically. That reflected my experience – I came from a well-off Indian family, and I'd been put into a school with boys from similar families from other places. So it wasn't surprising that my world view was quite Tory. I was very conformist – I guess I did my rebelling later on.

There was one exception to my conventional student persona; I had no idea when I came to school that I'd be judged as someone who was different to the others because I wasn't English-white. It really was a harsh awakening and gave me a difficult time in those early years. I'd been happy until I came to school in England. I've often thought that if I'd

50 The prestigious independent boarding school in Rugby, Warwickshire.

been good at games my background wouldn't have mattered. There were a few other Indian and Pakistani boys who were outstanding cricketers and they didn't seem to have the same experience, but I was lousy at games.

We weren't religious at all – my father was a non-believer and my mother's level of religion stretched to not wanting us to eat pig. That was typical of all our friends and neighbours. It seems strange now that religion has returned to the centre of the stage, but in those days it just didn't come up and it wasn't a big thing. I did like the stories though – Islam has some good ones, though I think the Old Testament has the best. At Cambridge I did a paper on the life of the Prophet Mohammad and the early history of Islam. It was when I was studying for that that I came across the story of the so-called 'Satanic Verses'. I remember thinking it was a good story. Twenty years later I found out how good a story it was.

I was very worried when I went to university in England that it would be a continuation of the same racist treatment I'd had at school. But my father convinced me it was a very good thing to go to Cambridge. Now I'm glad that he did – it turned out to be a very happy time and undid a lot of the damage of school. I went to Cambridge in the mid-sixties, when it was at the epicentre of that decade's social change. It was a very good time to be 18 to 21. They were very political years, the period of protest against the Vietnam war. That was a political awakening for me. It was also the age of the counterculture. Someone called it the 'youthquake' – young people were having an influence on society for the first time. Being part of that made me see everything – myself, my generation, the sexes and society – in a different way.

I loved the satire and surrealism of the mid-sixties. I had

the record of *Beyond the Fringe* and memorised a lot of the sketches – I can still do quite a few of them. Years later, when I was working in advertising, I actually had lunch with Peter Cook and Dudley Moore – I was trying to get them involved in an advert. Dudley Moore was very interested and super nice, but Peter Cook was an hour late, arrived completely drunk, was quite abusive and dragged Dudley Moore off, refusing to do it. I was disappointed because I was very much looking forward to meeting him. Dudley Moore couldn't have been nicer, and Peter Cook couldn't have been more drunk.

I might point out to my teenage self what a huge sacrifice my parents made for me. I think one of the things about becoming a parent is that you understand all the things your parents did for you, which at the time you took for granted or didn't care about. I can see now that for me to go so far away to school was very painful for them, certainly for my mother. They did the best thing for me, but it wasn't the best thing for them. My father offered me the choice to go away and for reasons I now don't completely understand I said yes, even though I was very happy going to school in Bombay. I think they went to great trouble to send me and to support me, and then afterwards, when their expectation was that I'd come home, I said I wanted to stay in England and become a writer – both parts of that sentence were horrifying for them. To them, being a writer wasn't a real job.

I didn't see it then, but now I recognise how much of the way I see the world came from my father. His interests have become my interests, and even my family name was invented because of my father's philosophical interests.[51] If I could get back some of the time when my father was still

51 His father adopted the name Rushdie, in honour of the philosopher Ibn Rushd.

alive, I'd like to talk to him about how much his ideas came to influence mine, and to express my gratitude. As for my mother, I understand much more clearly now how much she gave up to send me to school and how understanding she was, though the separation was very painful for her.

I'm actually rather proud of my younger self. He had guts and enormous willpower. I left university in 1968 and *Midnight's Children* was published in 1981 – it took me almost 13 years to find my way as a writer. I'd go back and tell my younger self, 'Well done for sticking at it.' Committing 12 years of your life trying to do something without any guarantee you'll be any good or have any success takes tremendous desire and will.

I often wobbled in those 12 years before *Midnight's Children*. I had doubts that whole time. Much of that early writing was completely unsuccessful and much of it wasn't published. My first published novel, *Grimus*, was very poorly received – there are huge chunks of it I'd rather hide behind the sofa when I read them now. I was working part-time in advertising and my colleagues were constantly telling me not to be stupid. They told me if I focused on advertising I'd make an enormous amount of money and who did I think I was kidding? Everybody in advertising has a fantasy of writing a book or a TV show, but most never do it. But something inside me made me keep going.

Obviously if I could go back and talk to the teenage Salman I'd have to tell him there's big trouble ahead. Prepare for ten years of... not the best time of your life*. But I have no regrets about writing *The Satanic Verses*. I think it's one of the very best things I ever did. And I'm glad we were able to fight to defend the book and were successful in doing so. And now that the fuss has died down, that book is being read a lot and it's on a lot of university courses. Most people like it. So the book has survived the attack of those who didn't like it and is now in the hands of those who do. It's finally able to be a novel again.

If I could go back in time and wanted to impress the teenage me, I'd show him the 17 books I've written. Martin Amis has this wonderful phrase – he once said what he wanted to leave behind was a shelf of books. You want to be able to say, 'From here to here, that's all me.' I think the thing about a writerly life is that it's long and you don't see yourself as being contained in any one book. The books are like reports from the journey you're taking. I'm sort of amazed that I've written 17 books, though lots of writers have written more. The 16-year-old me would probably like best the books I wrote for my sons – *Haroun and the Sea of Stories* and *Luka and the Fire of Life*. They have the most remarkable way of being interesting to readers of any age, even though they were aimed at 12-year-olds. I often tell people who are interested in my writing to start with those.

You could ask my ex-wives what they think, but I think I'm a perfectly nice, cheerful person to be around. I do have great regret about the end of my first marriage to the mother of my oldest son, Zafar. She sadly passed away when he was 19 years old and actually, by then we'd managed to rebuild a good friendship. On the last day of her life I was in the hospital holding her hand. The marriage ended, but the relationship didn't. We were incredibly young when we got together and over the course of a decade and a half we grew

---

*The Satanic Verses was banned in numerous countries and in 1989 the Ayatollah of Iran issued a fatwa ordering Muslims to kill Rushdie on the basis of his 'blasphemous' novel. A long period of threats, attempted killings, and bookshop bombings followed.

into different people, but we managed a very amicable break up. I think generally I'm a thoughtful husband, but my wife might not agree. I've just been abused by one of my ex-wives in a book[52] so there's clearly some difference of opinion.

I'm a gregarious and social person, but the media portrait of me as someone who goes to lots of parties is a misapprehension. I prefer small groups of people – ideally one-on-one. I don't like large gatherings – you can't talk to anybody and you can't hear yourself think.

It's very, very important to me to be a good father to my sons, and I think they would both tell you we're very close. In the case of Zafar, it was particularly important, firstly because his mother died when he was so young, and secondly because he had to grow up during the years of the attack on his father. He was nine years old when the fatwa began and his whole childhood was shaped and marked by it. I tried to explain what was happening because I thought the worst thing would be hearing about it and being terrified. Of course I was afraid for his security – his mother and I tried our best to make sure he had a vaguely normal childhood, but it was a very tough time for him. He could have become a very messed-up person, but he has great strength and grace and is very calm and good-natured.

If I could go back and relive any time in my life, I'd start in 1979. I was just finishing *Midnight's Children* and my first son was about to be born. In fact, I remember telling his mother to just sit still and cross her legs while I finished writing. I think that time, when I was 32 years old, between becoming a father and two years later, when the book was published to great success, was probably the best time of my life.

52 Fourth wife Padma Lakshmi's memoir *Love, Loss And What We Ate*.

CHAPTER 9:

Fate

Malcolm McDowell

Actor

2 June 2014

At 16 I was at what Lindsay Anderson[53] liked to call a 'minor public school' – he never forgave me for that. I was doing exams in the summer, doing Shakespeare plays and playing cricket and rugby. School was a great place for me, a safe haven. I'd had years growing up in the chaos of my father's pub in Liverpool, falling asleep to the sound of chinking glass and raucous laughter, and the smell of cigarette smoke billowing from downstairs. Did I like it? Put it this way, I don't often go back.

I would explain to my teenage self that alcoholism is a disease. My father, sadly, was an alcoholic. He was a great, larger-than-life character, but as a child I didn't care about that – I just wanted him to be present, and from that point of view he was always a disappointment. Knowing he had a disease wouldn't have made a huge difference, but it would

53 Legendary film director of *If* and *O Lucky Man!*, both starring McDowell.

have helped me understand him. I think he was quite proud of me because I was a good cricketer – he couldn't care less about the plays, though.

My younger self should thank God for being a Northerner, even though it made him stand out at school in the South. It saved my life, being a Northerner. It grounds you and gives you a great sense of humour. And the humour is tough and sarcastic – sometimes you need that to survive. And also the music of the North – I wandered into The Cavern when I was 17 to see a band called The Silver Beatles. Amazing.

If I met the 16-year-old Malcolm today, we wouldn't have much in common. He's insecure about what he's going to do and how life will treat him, and he's a bit pensive. But we would share an inquisitiveness and a sense of humour. He was a very optimistic teenager and a very curious person who wanted to find out about everything. I still dive into the day, and a good laugh is still very important to me.

I started acting at school when I was 11. The first show I did was *Aladdin*, and I played Aladdin. In Shakespeare I played Petruchio, Bottom, Feste. I was always the leading man, but never heavy stuff and no villains. My headmaster was obsessed with the theatre – he took the boys to Stratford-upon-Avon, the Old Vic, all that. We were so lucky. I got to do Shakespeare plays on a big lawn in the evening, underneath a great cypress tree. Such a treat.

When I look back I think, 'What would I have done if I hadn't met Lindsay Anderson?' I wouldn't have made *If*, which was also the road to making *A Clockwork Orange*. It was amazing to be part of these wonderful, heaven-sent movies that were so 'in the language'. *If*, when it came out, shook everything up – you have no idea what it did to the

English establishment. It was a staggering betrayal of their class. You had this public school boy, Lindsay Anderson, turning against his own; it was almost like the 'Cambridge Five', Burgess and Maclean et al, giving our secrets away to the Russians.

The 16-year-old Malcolm would have loved *If* and *A Clockwork Orange*. I remember sitting in the Odeon on Lime Street in Liverpool, watching Albert Finney in *Saturday Night, Sunday Morning*, and just going, 'I want to do that.' That was the crystallising moment for me.

I was totally exhilarated by the experience of being caught up in *If*, and afterwards I felt confident – I was on my way. And to go from that to working with Kubrick[54] – which is as poignant today as it was when it came out 40-odd years ago – that was amazing to me. It's staggering to me how that film has lived on. I'm always being asked to go to screenings of it – it's never-ending.

I don't think I could give my younger self any advice about his career because I haven't learned anything. If someone came to me saying they want to be an actor I'd say, 'For God's sake, don't. You're going to get burned, they'll eat you up and spit you out.' 95 per cent of actors are out of work at any one time. 90 per cent earn less than £10,000 a year. I'm making these figures up, but I'm not far wrong. Of course, if anyone had told the younger me this stuff, it wouldn't have made any difference. I'd still have become an actor, because I had to do it. I couldn't possibly do anything else. That's the difference.

I really don't know why I became an alcoholic. You'd think I'd have been more aware because of my dad. It happened to

54 in *A Clockwork Orange*.

me in the early '80s, before we really knew that alcoholism can pass from father to son. But I wasn't in a great place within myself – lots of changes were going on in my life, and I guess I took to the bottle to cope. But like cancer or diabetes, alcoholism is an illness and you can treat it – it took me a while to work that out. I was a hard drinker for a couple of years, but then my son Charlie was born and I knew I had to stop. I haven't had a drink in 30 years.

I spend a lot of my time driving my kids wherever they want to go – I'm a chauffeur. That's why I don't do theatre anymore; I don't want to miss my boys' childhoods. I can't do a long theatre run in London or New York, which is a pity because I'd kind of like to, but it's not my decision anymore. I'm fairly tough on my kids, but this is my second time around and I'm more relaxed than I was back then, and being a parent is beautiful.

If I could go back to any time in my life, it would be the night I was told I'd been cast to play the lead in *If*. I was doing *Twelfth Night* at the Royal Court and when the curtain came down, the stage manager told me I had a call. It was Miriam Brickman, the casting director, and she gave me the news. I couldn't believe it and rushed over to the pub to celebrate. I bought champagne and looked around but couldn't see anyone from the show, except one man I vaguely recognised. I told him I'd been cast in a movie and gave him some champagne – he must have wondered what was going on. I knew something life-changing had just happened to me.

Ruby Wax

Comedian

26 April 2010

At 16, I was a young hippie rebel, in love with The Beatles. I worked my way into the inner sanctum at school by making friends with the most beautiful cheerleader, and that meant I could get to the guys. She was great – beautiful, but a secret anarchist. I had genuine love for her, but I used her as a shield because the rest of them were cruel.

I'd advise my younger self to walk out on my parents and get a job as a waitress. I shouldn't have stuck around. My parents were really down on me; they thought I was the biggest failure that had ever been birthed. I wasn't good-looking, I had no talent, I was not good at school and I was a rebel – the worst thing you could have been dealt if you were pushy parents. They were really quite cruel and I enjoyed letting them down – I wanted to really give it to them, and I did.

Looking back, I have no image of my younger self in my mind. Maybe I really was a loser, and it wasn't just my parents that thought so. Or maybe I was beautiful. When I look back at old photos I look really pretty, but I felt like a dog then. I do look angry in a lot of photos from that time.

I wish I hadn't wasted my education, but I couldn't concentrate because my home life was so erratic. My brain was gone and I screwed up university. Now all I do is study – for the last five years I've been studying neuroscience. I didn't understand I was academic, but now I really am and it's so late. I've applied to do a master's and I'm just waiting to find out if I've been accepted.

I went to Europe to get away from my parents, but when I went to study drama in Glasgow I really loved it. I loved Glasgow – the people were hilarious and I felt I'd found my people because they had the same grounded sense of humour. Then I got into the Royal Shakespeare Company so thought acting had become my anchor, but I gradually realised I wasn't a great actor. I was very disappointed.

It was Alan Rickman who said to me, 'You can really write comedy.' He forced me to do it. I didn't enjoy writing, but I knew I could write a good line. It was never the laugh I chased – I wanted to write great lines. If I could write tragedy I'd do that – it was never about the laughter for me.

I screwed up my chance in America. I insisted on doing documentaries and they wanted me to be a talk show host. I know I was wrong – if I'd just shut up, I think I'd be very wealthy now.

The teenage Ruby would be amazed if you told her that one day she'd make it. I didn't see anything ahead of me when I was 16, but if you'd told me by the time I was 35 I'd have my own TV show, three great children and a really stable marriage, I'd never have believed you. Yet somehow, it happened.

James Earl Jones

Actor

22 February 2010

At 16, I'd had a quiet-but-rich life on a farm in Michigan, where I was raised by my grandparents. My grandmother taught me a great deal about hate and my grandfather taught me a great deal about justice.

I read a lot of Jules Verne, and a pal and I drew up plans for an earth-burrowing machine to go to the centre of Earth. My grandfather took this quite seriously and admonished us to stop such nonsense.

Besides my grandfather, my hero in high school was Professor Donald Crouch. There was so much drama in my life that by the time I got to grade school I was stuttering to the point that I couldn't really talk, and by the time I got to high school I was pretty much a mute. Professor Crouch discovered I wrote poetry and challenged me to read out my work. Because they were my own words, I could say them by heart.

I was encouraged to write to President Roosevelt regarding issues around justice and injustice. I would let the young James Earl know that the FBI would find that letter inflammatory when they were checking him out before joining the army. I'd also tell him that he'll be very impressed by President Obama and that America elected him.

I was forbidden to speak about my father, who was estranged from my mother before I was born. When I was at school I went up to a magazine rack and discovered a photograph of him in a production of Lillian Smith's *Strange Fruit on Broadway*, starring Mel Ferrer. My father offered me a trip to New York to meet him; when my mother heard this, she countered with a train ticket to St Louis, where she lived. My father never forgave me for choosing to go to St Louis instead of New York.

I'd advise my 16-year-old self that one day he'll meet his father and he'll take him to see Dame Margot Fonteyn in *Swan Lake* and the great African-American opera singer Leontyne Price perform in *Tosca*. He also took me to see *Pal Joey*, and later Arthur Miller's *The Crucible*, as cold and depressing as that tale was. It was *Pal Joey* that lit the flame in me, and I got a job as a stage carpenter at our little opera house in Michigan.

I don't think the 16-year-old James Earl would be impressed with what he'll achieve as an actor; what would knock his socks off would be a good crop, a good year of squirrel hunting or a good bag of deer.

The role that put me on the cover of magazines was *The Great White Hope*,[55] but the one my teenage self would be

55 Jones won a Tony for his Broadway role as boxer Jack Jefferson and was nominated for an Oscar for the 1970 movie.

most proud of would be *Cry, the Beloved Country*. *Star Wars* was an easy buck out of the blue. I didn't make much more than a dollar, either. If I'd made a bid to be in the Darth Vader costume I'd have been a millionaire, but I chose to work as a special effects person and just recorded the voice. Still, I'm very happy to have been part of the whole thing.

Buzz Aldrin

Astronaut

2 September 2013

When I was a teenager, I knew my academic performance was good. Because of my father's aviation pioneering from 1919 to the Second World War I wanted to fly airplanes, and the best way to do that in 1945 seemed to be through the military academy. I graduated third in my class from West Point during the Korean War, so when I'd completed pilot training, I was sent to Korea for air combat. I flew 66 missions and shot down two aircraft.

I was quite immature socially when I was 16. I wasn't shy, but I wasn't a ladies' man in high school. My father was a role model because of what he had done, but he wasn't good at cultivating a relationship with his son. When he was away during the war, my mother and my two older sisters were dominant in the house. I think I was close to my mother – she went to my football games.

I wasn't immediately taken with the idea of space travel. I was in Germany flying supersonic F-100s in 1957, the year of Sputnik. We were on nuclear alert in case the Soviet Union invaded Europe, and Sputnik going over our heads was not of much interest. But in 1959, *Life* magazine showed pictures of the Mercury spacecraft and talked about selecting the first astronauts. I hadn't trained as a test pilot so I didn't think I'd be eligible, but in 1963 NASA relaxed the requirements and focused more on academic achievements, which put me near the top of the list.

It was a combination of unforeseen changes and tragedies that gave me and Neil Armstrong the opportunity to walk on the moon. I wasn't scheduled to fly at all in the Gemini programme, but an accident that killed two astronauts moved me onto it. I was then involved in a very successful spacewalking mission, so I knew I was in a good position. After the Apollo fire in 1967 that killed three astronauts, including my very good friend Ed White, the shuffling around resulted in me and Neil Armstrong being assigned to the Apollo 11 mission.

Apollo was probably the most intensely trained-for mission – we had an hour-by-hour timeline and I think we felt very confident about it. I'd been in combat in 1953 and dealing with emergencies was common. You learned to accept what may happen, or you got into another business. We knew we might be prevented from successfully landing, but we thought we'd still be able to abort and get back to Earth. We thought we had about a 60 per cent chance of landing but more than a 90 per cent chance of coming back safely, even if we didn't land.

Each flight designs their own symbolic patch. I was interested in finding something symbolic about humans landing on the moon for the first time; I couldn't come up with something individual, but we finally came up with the idea of using the symbol of our country, the Eagle, landing on the Moon with an image of Earth behind it. It was suggested that the eagle carry an olive branch in his beak, an image of peace, but that was rejected because the open claws of the eagle looked too aggressive, so we put the olive branch in its claws and that's how the badge ended up. And of course, Neil and I agreed that we would name the spacecraft 'Eagle'.

I felt that if we landed successfully, I wanted to do something personal and symbolic to give thanks. I was given permission to serve myself communion, with wine and a wafer, on the surface on the Moon, but I was advised not to say anything about it at the time – someone had strongly objected to the Apollo 8 crew reading from the Bible, and we didn't want to get into any more trouble with the religious critics.

If we could do it all again, I think as I came down onto the Moon I should have been in charge of the experiments on the lunar surface. Because Neil was there first, he assumed control of what we did. For some reason, the first thing I did at the bottom of the ladder was urinate into my spacesuit. Then I looked out and I heard Neil use the word 'beautiful', which created in me the feeling that it wasn't beautiful. I called it 'magnificent desolation' and thought about how what I was looking at hadn't changed for thousands of years.

I did do *something* first: I was first back into the cabin, so I became the first alien to climb into a spacecraft on the way back to our home planet. Mind you, if I could go back, I'd remind myself to turn on the camera as we left – I forgot, so we don't have any pictures of the lift-off from the Moon.

I might advise my younger self to plan something to keep me busy after I retired. After the moon landing, I felt there might not be anything as great I could do again. That's why

I decided to become the first astronaut to return to military service. I wanted to be a commandant of cadets at the academy but I didn't get that assignment; I was made commandant of test pilots, which was peculiar because I'd never trained as a test pilot. It wasn't what I wanted to do, so after a year I retired. That's when I became depressed and an alcoholic. I faced a similar thing two years ago, when I got divorced from my third wife, but having gone 34 years without drinking, I knew how to deal with depression a bit better.

I don't particularly want to be a lonely pioneer on another planet. I think we absolutely need to send humans to permanently occupy Mars, but I don't think my inherited characteristics would make me a good volunteer.

I don't really have regrets, but maybe the depression and the alcoholism didn't need to interrupt my first marriage. I loved my first wife and my three children very much, but I've been married three times and I'm divorced now. Maybe I could have been a bit more selective, but I did what I did. I'm very proud of my youngest son, who has a PhD and speaks Russian and is vice president of a rocket company. I'm working through some troubles with my eldest son and am trying to help him make some changes in his life. My daughter is the only one who has a child and thanks to him, I'm a great grandfather. That's a legacy.

Danny DeVito

Actor

16 July 2012

I was living in New Jersey when I was 16, and was into going to movies and hanging out with my friends. If I could go back in time, I'd tell myself to crack open the books a bit more, do more reading and get the history and the geography down. Get used to learning. And I'd tell myself to relax more and not get stressed about having a girlfriend. I'd say, 'Don't be so worried about the fact that there's this big thing on Friday night and you have to get all dolled up to go to it – it's going to be there for a long, long time. Don't get stressed about whether you've got a girlfriend – have a good time with your friends. And don't smoke.' I only did that to be part of the group. In fact, I'd tell myself not to worry about the group so much – they weren't such a smart crowd. And to treat my sister well, and spend more time with my mother and father. Boy, would I do that.

Women were on my mind big time when I was 16. I was semi-popular because I was funny and outgoing, but I wasn't

Brad Pitt – I wasn't chased down the street. I had two older sisters – the eldest was 16 years older than me – so I had a big advantage over some guys who didn't understand the opposite sex, and I was privy to a lot of things that other boys didn't get to see at an early age. I saw the boyfriends and listened to the chatter, and I knew the score. I don't want to sound like I was too worldly, but I think I was more comfortable around women than a lot of my friends. I'd tell my younger self to use that advantage more, actually, to hang around and listen to them – there are nuggets of knowledge you can pick up from an older sister.

I had no idea what I wanted to do with my life when I was a teenager. I worked as a gardener in my summers until I was out of high school, and then my sister sent me to hairdressing school. She had a beauty parlour, and she wanted me to go and work for her. I said, 'Angie, I don't know, I don't have any affinity for it at all.' And she said, 'But what else are you going to do? You're not going to college; you need to do something.' I went along with her because she was always pretty smart. So she gave me my little kit and I went to the hairdressing academy, and the minute I walked in I knew I would be forever indebted to her. There were 40 girls and about three guys. The next six months were seminal in my life.

I'm very in tune with hair. If I see somebody and their hair is red, and the next time I see them it's a little lighter or darker, I remember. And I always know when someone's just had a haircut. It's an icebreaker, believe me. I'll give advice to people, even when I'm not asked for it. I'll tell them, 'With the shape of your face, you shouldn't be wearing that flick – maybe you want to think about cutting a few bangs.' I'm always staring at people's hair and have used my knowledge on some of my colleagues and co-stars. I got into trouble doing it once. We were rehearsing a scene sitting round a table, a group including an actress who was a little older. We hadn't had our hair and make-up finished, and I looked at her and said, 'Hey, you got some string in your hair.' I pulled it and her eyebrows went right back, and she was like, 'Goddammit Danny – that's my face lift.' I didn't know, I'd never seen one before.

My parents are dead now but I'm lucky that they always stuck by me. My mum and dad were a lot older than most kids' parents – my mum was 40 when she had me – so I was aware of their mortality. I was with my father when he passed away, and my mom as well. My father died suddenly of a stroke and a heart attack, but we were all together when it happened. That was very bizarre, because it happened right in front of all our eyes. But because of their ages I'd thought about how long they had left, and never hesitated to tell them how much I loved them. When I had my own kids, I always told them how much I loved them. You never want to go without having had that moment when you tell them how much you love them.

I'm very proud of my performance in *One Flew Over the Cuckoo's Nest*. I'd already done the part off-Broadway, so I had a long time to study it. We visited some institutions for research; we said we were graduate students and they let us in, and it was an eye-opening experience. It was a great film, but my teenage self would be most impressed that I played the Penguin in a Batman movie – he had the comic book on his bed. I'd have to tell him that it'd turn out a bit different from the comic though, because of this crazy thing called Tim Burton.

If I told the young Danny how things were going to go, he'd get very excited about it all. I don't think he'd be frightened. I'd be gentle with him and wouldn't just hit him over the head with it. I'd sit him down and say, 'I'm from the future, and here's what you're going to do.' If I told him he was going to direct and perform in all these movies, have three kids and live the life I've lived, I think he'd smile and say, 'Fantastic'.

I'd say to the teenage me, and I think the Dalai Llama said this, 'If something good happens to you, embrace it and let it go. And if something bad happens to you, embrace it and let it go.' I think that's a good way to live your life, right in the centre of the Yin and the Yang, so you're always ready for everything. I wasn't that kind of person naturally and that lesson came hard to me, but you have to learn to trust that things are going to work out.

Marriage is a two-way street. You both have to want the same things. You have to be considerate and make concessions to be able to live together. If you're going to be compadres and friends forever, it's a give and take world.[56]

I've lived a kind of perfect life, and there isn't much I would change. The moments I've treasured the most have been when I've been with my family. For the past 20 years we've been going on vacation with our three kids every year. There's always that time on vacation when you're unwinding for a couple of days – then, after that, you're all relaxed and feeling good. Those are the times you really want to keep hold of.

---

56 DeVito and his wife, actress Rhea Perlman, separated in 2017, after this interview.

Ewan McGregor

Actor

3 October 2011

Sixteen was a very important year for me. I moved to Kirkcaldy to study drama, and it turned out to be a lot of hard work and responsibility. It was a tough time and there was a lot of growing up that year. I'd wanted to be an actor since I was about nine, and that was absolutely because of my uncle.[57] He'd come up to Crieff and he'd be so different to everyone else. Such a colourful, flamboyant character. Not to say that the people of Crieff aren't, but there are more farmers there than actors. I wanted to be like him before I even knew what an actor really was, and I never really changed my mind.

I've always been an upbeat kind of person. It's not a choice, it's just the way I am. I had a very happy upbringing with good friends and family around me. Crieff was the perfect place to grow up – we were bombing around all day on our bikes,

57 The actor Dennis Lawson.

leaving in the morning and coming back at night. We had a real freedom and an independence that my kids don't have.

I always wanted to go to London and try to make it, mainly because I'd loved going there as a kid to visit my Uncle Dennis. But when I went, at 17, to start my course at the Guildhall School of Music and Drama, leaving Scotland suddenly felt like a very big wrench. I can still remember my dad dropping me off. He left me in this really shabby room. I could see him looking round, and we were both thinking, 'Fuck, this is shocking.' I really felt like I was leaving home in a way that I hadn't when I'd left to go to Kirkcaldy – this was something bigger. I became incredibly Scottish and remember sewing tartan ribbons onto my denim jacket. I was this over-the-top Scot abroad in London.

I'd tell my younger self not to worry when he doesn't get a part in a movie. I was about 19, still at drama school, and was up for two things. One was a movie, a really lovely, sad wartime story, and the other was for a Dennis Potter BBC drama called *Lipstick on Your Collar*. I was hugely excited about them both, but what I wanted most of all was to be in another movie. I wanted it so badly but didn't do well at the final audition and didn't get it. As it turned out, the film collapsed – so if I'd got it, I'd have missed out on the Dennis Potter for a film that would never be made. I think fate was playing a wee hand there.

Drama school can knock your confidence, because they focus on your weaknesses. Getting an agent was a huge thing because it gave me a glimmer that I might be good at what I do. I thought, 'Oh – somebody wants me.' And getting the Dennis Potter series – that was the first time I'd had the feeling that someone wanted to cast me and not someone else. Suddenly my old confidence came back. I went into my agent's office and she sat me down and said, 'You'll be working for six months, and you'll be paid £24,000.' I had to stop her and say, 'Can I phone my dad please?' I wanted to tell him I was going to be alright.

If I met my teenage self now, there are probably some things I've done he wouldn't think were cool, but I'd like to think that we'd share the same drive and the same motivations. As a kid, I wanted to be involved in work that mattered. I think I've done that, but also you live and learn, and understand they can't all be like that. I'm lucky to be able to do big films and small films, and even within those have lots of different kinds of experience. I have a very simple approach – if I like the story, I'll do it.

It's been almost 11 years since I had a drink, and only rarely do I notice not drinking. I find it easy to be outgoing in company without booze now. Before, I used to have to have a few pints before I was me, but now I'm me when I arrive. Drinking the way I used to was making me miserable.

When I made *Trainspotting* I didn't think, 'This is me – this is my moment.' But I did have really amazing feelings about the film. I thought the book was fantastic and really captured the spirit of the country. I knew Danny was the best director to do it. And we had this incredible cast. So I had really, really high expectations, but I couldn't have imagined... I remember seeing it for the first time, in London, with my wife and my Uncle Dennis, and coming out numb and shaky. It was so extraordinary. But I already had very strong self-belief, so I didn't feel it would boost me particularly. Now, of course, I see that it did – it became a global film and put me in the public eye.

I love being in Scotland, whether it's for work or just coming home for a visit, and I loved working in Glasgow on *Perfect Sense*. I've made four films there now and even though I'm not from Glasgow, I've watched it change since we did *Shallow Grave* in 1994. It's a wonderful place and I think it's a real character in that film.

I don't think it matters where you live – you can keep your family life private anywhere if you choose not to indulge in all that. I feel like you have to seek it out and I would never do that. So I have a really nice life, with my family life in Scotland and a bunch of friends in America and four kids. That's quite a lot, and it doesn't leave much time for anything else. I'm busy with my kids, and I love it that way. It's perfect.

Ozzy Osbourne

Musician

27 October 2014

I was a rebellious kid; I didn't like commitment and I couldn't hold a job down. I was always being yelled at by my mother for not bringing any money into the house. I was a bit of a drifter, really. I left home but didn't really have anywhere to go. I used to doss around on people's couches. I was a bit of a social butterfly, in a working-class environment.

I'm extremely dyslexic but they didn't understand what dyslexia was then. I went to school, a secondary modern in Birmingham, where there were 49 kids in a class, all boys. The kids used to mess around, smoking behind the toilets. It wasn't the best if you wanted to be taught anything. I was the crazy guy. I made the big, tough guys like me by making them laugh.

I tried to find things I was good at. I tried a bit of burglary, but I was no good at that. I didn't do any major burglary jobs and it was less than three weeks before I got caught. My dad said to me, 'That was very stupid', and I did feel very stupid. Then I didn't pay my fine and I got put in jail for a few weeks. That was a short, sharp lesson, and it certainly curbed my career in burglary.

Someone recently asked me what the best gift I ever got was, and it dawned on me that if my father hadn't bought me a microphone when I was 18, I wouldn't be here now. He saw that I was really interested in popular music so he bought me a microphone, and it was shortly after that I met the guys who would become Sabbath. It was the fact that I had my own microphone and PA system that got me in the band. If I hadn't had them, I would never have got the gig.

First it was just me and Geezer.[58] We put an ad up in a music shop in Birmingham and Tony and Bill turned up.[59] They'd just been busted for smoking dope in Carlisle with their band Mythology – it all fell apart because back then a drug bust was major news up and down the country. Tony's face fell when he saw me because he didn't like me. He was like, 'Oh no', but we started jamming. Tony had a reputation in Cumberland, as it was called then, so we got some gigs there, and in Inverness, over the Scottish border.

The teenage Ozzy would never in a million years believe that he could have the life I've had. How did that kid get from living in Aston in Birmingham to a house in Beverly Hills? I don't understand it. I'll never forget one Christmas Eve when my dad said I could stay up late for a treat, and I'd see the most beautiful woman in the world. He put on the TV and it was Elizabeth Taylor, reading a poem. Years later, I was invited to some charity do and who was I sitting next

58 Butler, Black Sabbath bassist.

59 Iommi and Ward, guitarist and drummer.

to but Elizabeth Taylor. I just thought, 'If only my dad could see me now.' It was amazing.

What would surprise the younger Ozzy most is that he'd stayed alive this long. I wasn't a violent person, but I did some very stupid things in my life. I could have killed myself a thousand times before I even got a microphone in my hand. I had some crazy years with drugs and alcohol in the '70s and '80s. For about 20 years I was drinking a lot of booze, doing a lot of drugs and living the lifestyle. Then it stopped working for me, so I had to get some help. Now I don't drink, I don't smoke and I don't do drugs. But I'm definitely living on borrowed time.

Looking back, I feel very lucky. I'm 65 and I've had a great life. I still do stupid things, but I don't get in my car drunk anymore. I used to say to Sharon, 'I won't do that.' Then I'd have a few drinks and wake up the next morning and she'd say, 'What did you want to go and do that for?' I'm clear-headed these days, but when I fell off my quad bike about ten years ago I broke my neck. I was going about four miles an hour. Typical. One day I'll be going for a walk and a rare bird will take a dump with a rare virus in it on my shoulder, and I'll disappear.

I wouldn't give anyone any advice about anything, especially my younger self. If you asked me to help you out with something I actually knew about – which isn't much to be perfectly honest – I might give a suggestion. But I'd say, 'If you want to try something, go ahead, but remember every action has a reaction.' It's like gambling. I don't understand gambling addicts, because it doesn't work. I've been to Vegas and have had a few goes on the one-armed bandits, and I just don't get the thrill. Driving at 90 miles an hour when you're drunk – that's a stupid thing to do, though I've done it a thousand times myself.

Do I feel ashamed of things I've done? Every day. The last time I got loaded I came back minus a Ferrari. I'm lucky to have Sharon in my life because she's given me proper telling offs that I sometimes used to resent. I'd think, 'Why is she so down on me? I'm alright now.' But there were times I wasn't alright, and I plagued everybody – I was crazy.

If I could live one day of my life again, it would be the day I got married to Sharon. I was off my face all day and didn't make it to the bedroom suite. In the end, they found me face-down in the hotel corridor, unconscious. I'd like to go back to that day and end it by going to bed with my wife.

Sir Paul McCartney

Musician

13 February 2012

At 16 I was trying to scrape through school, learn the guitar and get a date with a girl, which was impossible at that time – I had a real lack of confidence. It's the reason a lot of guys get into groups in the first place – girls and money. All the girls seemed out of my league and I couldn't figure out how to walk up to someone and say, 'Do you want to go to the pictures?' It's terrifying – what do you do? Do you put your arm around her? Do you sit there and wait for her to talk first, or are you supposed to talk first? Do you buy Maltesers? I think I did manage to make it to the pictures with a girl a couple of times, but even then, it wasn't easy to be as suave as James Bond.

I think I later realised the way I felt about girls when I was 16 was something I could write songs about. So I did. In fact, I looked back to those times to write about other things as well, not just romantic things. For instance, there were a few old ladies around where I lived in Liverpool and I got friendly with one of them. I used to go and get her shopping for her, and then we'd spend a bit of time talking about her life. It was fascinating to speak to someone from a completely different generation and, instead of thinking, 'It's just an old person', you realised they were young once and had amazing experiences you could relate to. Doing that lady's shopping became a very pleasant and educational experience for me. I think that led to 'Eleanor Rigby', which was a song about lonely people.

I'm hopeless with dates – the Beatles experts have got them down much better than I have, but I think I'd already met John and George by the time I was 16. George used to get on my bus. I was already writing songs; I wrote my first one when I was 14. So when I met John, I said, 'I've got a couple of songs and some little bits and pieces' and he said, 'So have I.' It was a good thing for us to bond over. We thought, 'Well if we've written one each, maybe we could write one together.' So we did. The first songs were very simple, but we gradually developed over the next few years and, without realising quite what we were doing, we became a songwriting duo. We became very famous as well.

My dad was a big influence on my songwriting. He played piano at home and I listened to him a lot. He taught me and my brother how to harmonise together, and that gave me my love of harmonies. When we got The Beatles together, we loved to sing in harmony. It's a great bonding thing and it's why people love choirs. I remember that if there was a bit of lively music on the radio, my dad would stick his head round the door and bang along with the beat with his fist. It was just one of his little habits, but it's become a very fond memory for me, just seeing his joy at the rhythm of music. He'd tell me to listen to the very low noise coming out of the speaker and he'd say, 'That's called the bass.' How funny that I turned out to be a bass player.

I hadn't long lost my mother when I was 16. I think that like any tragedy, if you're lucky your mind finds a way to deal with the pain to allow you to get through it. As a 14-year-old boy in Liverpool, I could either go under or get on with it. Music was very helpful for that; it gave me some good feelings to replace the sad feelings. And of course, John also lost his mother when he was young. That helped us to bond, having that in common.

I think I was a pretty driven kid. I wanted to do well at school and thought I was applying myself, but not all my teachers agreed and in the end I didn't do that well. I was definitely a dreamer, but I don't think that's a bad thing. I do remember my music lessons were non-existent; we had a music teacher, but he just used to put on a Beethoven record and walk out of the room. We were a bunch of teenage Liverpool lads and just took the record off and got some playing cards out, and when the teacher was on his way back, we put the record back on, wafted the cigarette smoke away and sat up at our desks. Luckily for me, I discovered music in a different way, and then it became a passion.

If I went back to tell the 16-year-old me how his life would go, he wouldn't believe it. I've thought about this before. Whenever I play 'Back in the USSR' live, I often say to the audience, 'If you'd told me as a kid that one day, I'd meet the President of Russia and he'd come to one of my concerts – well, it's impossible isn't it?' So many things about The Beatles, Wings and my band now are so phenomenal – going back would be like *Back to the Future*. I'd have to say to my younger self, 'I've come from the future and everything I'm saying is real. Hang in there and don't despair – you're not going to believe what happens next.'

I'd also tell my teenage self, 'Don't be so nervous about everything – the world's not as bad as you think it is.' I had a good family so I can't speak for everyone, of course, but in the case of my 16-year-old self, I was always thinking, 'I'll never get a girl and I'll never get a job.' I was nervous about all of it, knowing that I didn't have a good answer to the question, 'What are you going to do with your life?'

The births of my children were euphoric times. I was very lucky because I was from a big Liverpool family, so I was often asked to look after a younger kid of a cousin or an auntie. John was an only child and there weren't any babies around, so when he had his first kid he had to figure out what to do with him – he just didn't have the background. He was like one of those dads who think babies are made of glass and worry about dropping them and breaking them. But fatherhood was quite a natural thing for me, which was a great blessing. Some of the songs on my new album[60] are inspired by the big sing-songs we had, magical times where music brought all the relatives together.

The teenage Paul McCartney would love the idea of fame – that was his dream. But it's funny, life gives you minor premonitions, which you don't think of as premonitions until the dream comes true and then you think, 'I wonder if that was a sign.' I remember when John and I were first hanging out together, I had a dream about digging in the garden with my hands and finding a gold coin. I kept digging and found another, and another. The next day

60 *Kisses on the Bottom* (2012, Hear Music).

I told John about my dream I'd had, and he said, 'That's funny, I had exactly the same dream.' And I suppose you could say it came true. I remember years later saying to him, 'Remember that dream we had?' So the message of the dream was, 'Keep digging, lads.'

CHAPTER 10:

Ageing

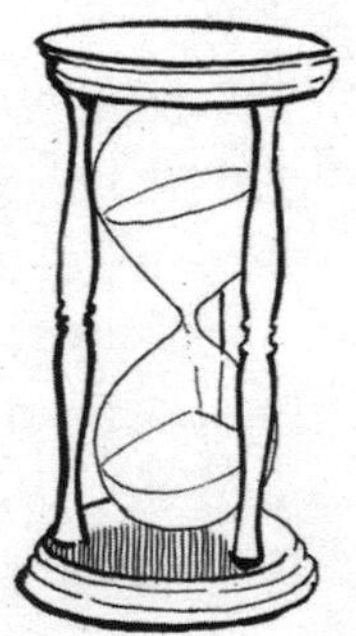

Geoffrey Rush

Actor

9 May 2016

I have a fairly acute memory of my childhood, and there was a big change at around the age of 15. I'd been learning the piano since I was eight. My mum was a working single mum, very resourceful, and wanted my sister and I to learn the piano. But around 15 I fell out with the piano teacher and I also joined the school drama club. To me, it was an oasis of creativity and freedom. I wasn't sporty, and I wasn't keen on the very regimented approach of my teachers, who were mostly men from the Second World War period with short-back-and-sides haircuts. My hair was past my collar, and when I joined the drama group I immediately knew they were my people.

At first we had teachers in the theatre group, who blessed me with their mentorship. But they all got moved on so we decided to run the club ourselves. We did hoary old plays like *The Admirable Crichton* or *Arsenic and Old Lace*. But though I was completely obsessive about being involved in the theatre and being in a rock band, I didn't even entertain the idea of making a career out of it. I felt surrounded by creative activity, but there was nowhere to put it. I thought I might end up a radio announcer or a teacher.

Sometimes I look at old box Brownie photographs of that time and see this pimply skinny kid who looks quite gawky. I don't know if I could give him advice – it's more the reverse, because he still has an impact on me. He taught me how to deal with a life of constant shifts and lots of eclectic influences. He moved schools a lot. He had a mum, two devoted grandmothers and an absent father… Then, when he was 15, he met his stepfather, a shearer who knew about *Beyond the Fringe* and Samuel Beckett, a real old-school rural leftie who listened to late-night radio. I still feel a very strong connection with that teenager – he reminds me to accept new stuff and to always stay on your toes. So I would say, 'Thanks, gawky teenager, for teaching me things that are still guiding my life in my sixties.'

I remember my Year 12 report. Until Year 10 I was very academically sharp, top of the class. I foolishly thought I wanted to be an astronomer – my other great passion – so, under the influence of the wrong kind of teachers, was studying advanced maths and Physics. My school report in Year 12 was full of low marks for effort and industry, and I told the headmaster that I disagreed with them and that he didn't know what I was doing with the theatre group. He threw me out of his office and I shouted out over my shoulder that I'd had a marvellous time at that school and he'd spoiled it. I just felt there was an ignorance about how kids thrive.

One of the most startling things in my life happened right at the end of my university years. The years 1969–71 was a very vibrant time on Queensland state campus. We had a very right-wing state premier, so there were a lot of demonstrations – the university was full of thespians and Trotskyites. At the end of my time there I was spotted by the director of the Queensland Theatre Company and offered a three-year contract. That's still a very strong memory, when I was picked out, because it turned my life around. I did my final exam on the Friday and had my first theatre rehearsal on the Monday. In 1972 I put 'actor' on my first tax form, and I thought, 'This is good, I'm going to try to keep this up.'

I'd tell my younger self it doesn't have to happen when you're 21 or 30. I worked with the Queensland Theatre Company and then went to Europe – including, of course, the theatre mecca that was London. I worked happily in theatre for about 24 years. Then my daughter was born and I thought, 'I'm on a state-subsidised theatre wage – that's not generous. I have to start earning some money.' I did about five auditions for *Miss Saigon* – I love musical theatre – and got down to a shortlist of two. Then I got the letter to say that the film of *Shine* was going ahead. That was just my second feature film and I was 43.

When I read the script of *Shine*, I did think, 'Wow'. I was used to Shakespeare and theatre scripts, but the hero of *Shine* was not the king – he was the aberrant guy on the outer concentric circle. I felt he was like a classical holy fool. There was probably a tinge of autobiography in the way I found my way into that character. I've always been intrigued by the question of how the outsider can claim honourable status in the centre of the story. The film changed my life – I won an

Oscar and was suddenly on the radar. What did Hollywood do? They offered me a film about Liberace, because he also played the piano. I had to say I didn't want to be the new face of the 'keyboard genre'.

The King's Speech was the first time I read an international story that contained a major Australian character. I loved the clash of the Antipodean character and the regal character of the royal family. For me, it was a great experience – sitting at a table reading with actors like Derek Jacobi and Michael Gambon, thinking, 'Wow, this is it!' We all knew it was a great story, but we had no idea how the film would be received. It could have been dismissed as a niche British costume drama, but then we started getting the responses, and people were saying, 'It's not about stuttering – it's about finding your best self.' And then it just rode the wave of the moment. I got a load of mail from people who said it really helped them. That film had some beautiful outcomes.

I'd tell my younger self, 'Don't think you'll be past it when you're 50.' I was 43 when I made a fateful decision and went from my long plod in the theatre and entered a new world, working with heroes in international cinema. I'm in my sixties now and enjoying a period of my life which really only started when I was middle-aged. That's my accidental story. Everyone has one, and they're all different.

Chrissie Hynde

Musician

15 September 2014

At 16, I only had one interest: music. There wasn't anything else. It was 1967, the heyday of music, right when it all kicked off. All the English bands, Jimi Hendrix… I grew up in the suburbs in Ohio and lived by the radio. The Vietnam War was raging and youth culture was taking off. There was a huge generation gap, and we had a motto: 'Don't trust anyone over 30.' For us, it was all about the music and the drugs. I was a kid, so I thought I knew it all.

I'd tell my younger self to be respectful of my parents. My parents were straights – hard-working Americans from the suburbs. They didn't understand what was going on with me, and they weren't too happy about it either. We couldn't really talk – everything would turn into an argument. This big clash of ideologies was when it started to go wrong, but now I can see that my parents were just decent people trying to keep a family together. As a grandmother I see how hard it is and I know I haven't been as successful as my parents at maintaining a family.

I always felt I had to get my skates on. When you feel like a stranger in your own home town, that's not a comfortable feeling – it's much easier to feel like a stranger in a strange land. I'd never seen a passport and didn't know anyone who wanted to leave, but I wanted to bail. I felt very driven. I didn't travel around the States – I went straight to London, because that's where the bands were.

I'd advise my younger self not to get waylaid by drugs. First, I'd tell her to stop smoking rather than think about it for 40 years and then quit. Smoking is the biggest con in our society. Ditto alcohol. I'd tell the younger me to stick to pot – I wasted a lot of time on drugs and alcohol, and no good comes of it. I'm a very private person and have never publicised my shit, but the fact that two of my band died in one year probably tells you quite a lot.

It's hard to be patient with your kids sometimes, when you're trying to pay the bills and keep it together and your relationships are falling apart and you're all over the place emotionally. It's easier when you're a grandparent and you're more relaxed, but I've never allowed a photograph of me with my kids to get out there. The only time was at Joe Strummer's funeral (and they were adults by then) and I said, 'Let's do it for Joe,' because we loved him.

I've had a fantastic time, and I live in the place of my dreams. I love London and always have done. I live a very ordinary life here – I still buy *Viz* magazine, I travel around with my Oyster card and I get the bus. People just assume that it can't be me, so they leave me alone. If you keep your mouth shut and don't talk to the press, you can live normally.

I think staying positive is a discipline; depression is an enemy and will bring you down. You have to fight it, and for me, that means not drinking, smoking or taking drugs. If you live by your principles, it has to be a principle not to descend into the dark night of the soul. I'm older now and think about mortality much more. In your twenties the future looms in front of you and looks endless, though it didn't work out like that for my guitar player, who died when he was 25. But the finiteness of life is in your face when you're my age. But I kind of dig that, to be honest, and it doesn't bother me. I've done what I wanted to do and I'm ready for whatever there is.

Marianne Faithfull

Musician

24 January 2011

I liked school and was a clever little girl. I had a lot of friends – I loved them and they loved me. Everything was good. I was going to go to university and was on the path. I felt quite secure. I did have some doubts about university – would I be equal to it or would I crack up? The idea of competition scared me. I had low self-esteem, which has taken me years to get over.

My parents were both quite difficult. They split up when I was six and it became quite complex. My father was quite distant, but my mother was wonderful and I got a lot of love from her. Later on, when I was in therapy, my shrink used to say, 'The reason you can get better is because you had that early experience of love.'

If I met that girl now, I think I'd like her. We could talk about books and theatre and the ballet. I was always up for life and was interested in everything, but I don't envy her –

I'm much more confident now and I know what I'm doing, which is a great feeling.

I used to think my whole life was a mistake, but now I think the only mistake I made was taking drugs. It was right to leave home and get away from my difficult family, and I was right to come to London, make records and find my own life. I was right to get married and have my son Nicholas, even though I was very young at 17. But I would never have had a baby if I'd waited because life took over, so I don't regret that – my son has been one of the best relationships of my life. But drugs slowed me down and gave me feelings of worthlessness – I lived my life in fear.

It would have helped me then to understand why I had an impulse to run away from men. My mother and my grandmother didn't like men – they thought life would be happier without them. That set me up so that I could love, but I couldn't follow through, because I always wanted to run away before I was kicked out. It took me years to understand that you can be in a relationship and feel free at the same time.

I was a good girlfriend – I was interested in what my partner was doing and think I gave a lot. Mick[61] himself has acknowledged how we worked together – he helped me learn my lines for *Three Sisters*, I helped him with songs, and we had a very interesting time. I don't expect financial rewards for that – I insisted I got the money and credit for *Sister Morphine* but I did a lot more than that, and I'm very proud of it. Mick and I had a real connection in that way and were equals in our relationship, but in the end I had to leave. It was so sad when I walked out on him – I couldn't help it but it wasn't his fault.

61 Mick Jagger, lead singer of The Rolling Stones.

I'd tell myself that getting older really isn't that bad, with acupuncture, exercise, good food and friends. I have a little botox and a little collagen in my lips, and I had some liposuction under my chin to get rid of a double chin – I don't feel at all embarrassed about that. My advice would be not to do it too soon, but I think I look better and younger now than I did 20 years ago. You have to like yourself to take care of yourself; 20 years ago I didn't.

I'd tell my younger self that serious illness needn't mean you live the rest of your life in fear. I got breast cancer, but I never believed that illness was some kind of punishment, like some people do. And I was lucky – they got it very early indeed. I'm a great believer in looking after yourself now. I'm having a physical next year and I'm a little nervous about that, but I feel well and I'm very happy.

Armando Iannucci

Writer and Comedian

19 October 2009

I was a strange teenager – I had two different personalities. At home I was nerdy and bookish – someone who'd been at my school just after me looked up my name in the school library and saw I'd taken out 27 books in one week. But I was also a class clown, doing impressions of teachers. I was a bit of a performer. Maybe I was quiet about that side of me at home, because I felt I couldn't make a living out of it. I aimed to be a doctor instead. At university I was still academic and stayed on to do a PhD on Milton's *Paradise Lost*, because comedy wasn't a job.

I spent a lot of time being under-confident and was constantly amazed I was getting by. I underwent a profound sense of feeling that I was no good, not just academically but in any way, and that I'd managed to bluff my way past a lot of people. I got very nervous, but my friends tell me that outwardly I seemed unflappable and assured. I didn't feel that way internally, but I envy the young me for that ability to make others feel reassured around him.

I would tell my 16-year-old self that exams are not worth the stress. If I could do it again, I'd tell myself that what you do in life tends to be a product of what you're interested in, not what exams you pass. I wish I'd spent more time as a teenager skiving off and enjoying myself, but I got terribly guilty if I wasn't working all the time. At the same time, I was a terrible shirker and very lazy.

I'd tell my young self not to make a to-do-list with 35 things on it – make one that's got three things on it and be happy if you do one of them. Even now, as soon as I finish something, I'm thinking about what's next. I still make my lists and I still tend not to spend a lot of time doing nothing. I envy people who think, 'I've got four days to do my hobby.' I don't have a great desire to climb all the Munros or go skiing – if I'm not working, I just like spending time with people.

I got my phases skew-whiff. I was a middle-aged teenager, and in my thirties I got more youthful and enjoyed myself more. I should have travelled more when I was young, met more people and maybe joined a commune. I maybe should have got more into sport and joined a team somewhere.

I was over-fussy and paranoid when I was younger – I think I had a fear of specialising and making a decision about what road I was going to go down, but now I think I should have concentrated more on certain things. As I've got older, I've accepted that maybe I have an ability to spot a talent in someone else and make the most of it, but my career feels very haphazard. I've certainly been very lucky that I met Steve Coogan and Chris Morris. We came up with *The Day Today* and this minor character, Alan Partridge, came out of it and things snowballed from there. It would have been nice to have done more of *The Day Today.* And I regret that we only did two series of *I'm Alan Partridge*, and they were five years apart.

I'm terribly conscious of the fact that I've never been interested in fashions and trends. Part of me thought that was fine because I wasn't into that, but the other part thinks, 'And therefore you look shit.' But I couldn't quite bring myself to generate an enthusiasm for dressing – part of me likes the idea of just blending in and not really being noticed.

I still go to parties thinking I won't know anyone. I can't bring myself to barge into conversations shouting 'Hi!' One of my big comedy heroes, Billy Connolly, was at the New York premiere of *In the Loop* and came over and said, 'Armando, how are you?' I thought, 'He knows who I am!' and said, 'But you're my hero!' And he said, 'Oh, we should have got together years ago then – I didn't know.' It's stupid, but in my paranoid mind people are saying, 'Who are you? I don't want to talk to you – I want to talk to that person over there.'

I've always felt as if I was in my forties mentally, so when I hit 40 I felt fine and couldn't understand the big fuss. But I didn't expect bits to be hurting and feeling a bit stiff. If I was giving my younger self advice, I'd say, 'Prepare for thinking, "I don't think I can get out of that seat in anything other than an ungainly fashion," and sighing every time you sit down or stand up.'

I still can't quite believe I'm responsible enough to be a father, though my kids don't call me dad – they call me 'the Big D'. But my oldest son is already bigger than me. My eldest is nearly 16, then it's ten and then seven. It's nice to see kids grow up, but what's nice about the older one is that he's become a friend who shares my sense of humour and watches comedy with me. That's a lovely part of my life.

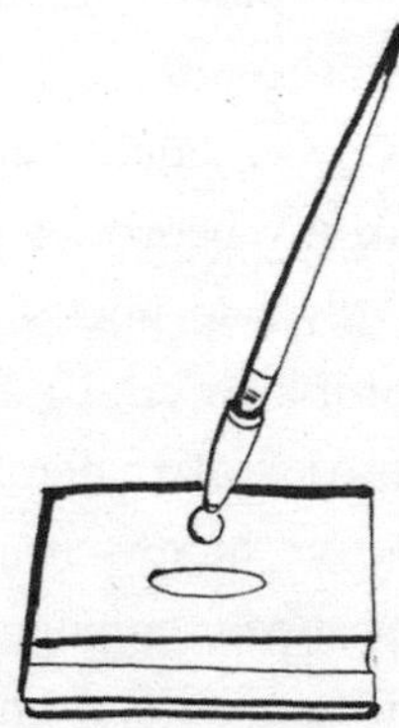

Ian Rankin

Author

5 November 2012

At 16, my life was all about rock music and books – I didn't go out much. I grew up in Cardenden, a very working-class mining village with no private housing. I was surrounded by family – an uncle over the back fence and an aunt two doors along – so every move was monitored and you couldn't get away with anything. Even if you didn't feel like you fitted in, you had to look like you did because you didn't want to get beaten up. I was happiest staying in my bedroom with my hi-fi and my records, writing painfully bad poetry about a lovely young woman who wouldn't look twice at me.

I was painfully shy around girls. I still remember that crippling embarrassment of the two-month run-up to Christmas at school, when you stopped having PE and started having dance lessons. All the boys lined up on one side of the room with the girls on other side, and you had to pick a partner and spend the next 40 minutes dancing the Gay Gordons with them. You had to hang back to let the roughty-toughty kids get their first choice, because if you picked their favourite you'd get a kicking at playtime. It was nightmarish for everyone involved.

I'd tell my younger self to sort out his dress sense. I wore a denim waistcoat with Woolworths patches sewn on the back – peace symbols and the Confederate flag – and big, baggy trousers. Worst of all were my shoes; I convinced my mum that I needed Doc Martens to blend in, but she ordered them from a catalogue and they weren't the real deal: they were oxblood moccasins, with wee tassles. I used to get dragged along to see aunties and uncles, or on holidays in cheap boarding houses in Blackpool and I just vanished into books.

If you met the 16-year-old Ian, you'd see someone shy and a bit of a hanger-on. I think being Scottish, we can have whole conversations with people without looking them in the eye once. I'd be in my bedroom, reading comics and imagining myself in these alternative worlds, or I'd be writing my own stories. I never showed any of them to anyone, obviously – I hid them all in my old bureau drawers.

My parents weren't great readers. I don't know where my reading and writing bug came from, but ever since I could read, I didn't want to stop. We had a tiny library in Cardenden that the miners had chipped in for and I remember the frisson around the age of 12 when I could start taking adult books out. I couldn't see X-certificate films like *The Godfather* and *The Exorcist*, but no one could stop me getting books, so they were a vicarious thrill. They contained taboo knowledge, stuff you weren't supposed to know. I loved that sense of danger and thrill around books.

I've got diaries from my late teens and early twenties, and in them I seem to feel dreadful about the way things are going. I struggled for my first two years at uni, studying the old crusty texts. My mum became ill at the start of my uni career and went into hospital. She spent the next 7 or 8 months deteriorating before she died, so every weekend I was going back to Cardenden, watching her get more ill and my dad going to pieces and then heading back to Edinburgh. The world seemed bleak – I'd like to go back and tell my younger self it will all have a happy ending.

I think my dad loved my writing career. He passed my books around his friends, but he died when I was 29 so I'd only had two or three books published – sadly, he never saw me become a success. I wish he was still around and sometimes I think I've channelled that into my books. My new character, Malcolm Fox, has a dad in a care home which Malcolm pays for, but he doesn't always want to visit him. My dad would be in his nineties now – maybe that's the kind of relationship I'd have with him if he was still around.

I think the teenage Ian would be dumbfounded by how his career has gone. If he dreamed of writing, it was as a literary novelist, not a guy whose books you'd buy in an airport bookshop. He'd want to be studied at university or as a set text in schools. I'm not sure he'd have wanted to be a well-known popular writer, and I'm still not sure I'm used to it now. I might look quite relaxed on TV, but it's taken me 20 years to get there. When I first went on *The Review Show*, I was an absolute bag of nerves.

I feel like I'm part of a generation that just isn't getting older. I'm still listening to the same music as I was when I was 16. I still dress quite similarly, though the trousers aren't so baggy and I've ditched the denim waistcoat. I still spend my money on books, albums and beer, but I'm definitely slowing down – I notice that my son walks faster than me, and I used to sprint everywhere. As Leonard Cohen says, 'I ache in the places where I used to play.' These thoughts probably do make it into my books, but Rebus is worse off than me. He's well into his sixties now – he's always been ten years older than me – and he smokes like a chimney.

I'm aware that longevity doesn't appear to be in my genetic make-up; my mum died in her late fifties and my dad when he was 72. Sometimes I feel I should be trying to pack more exciting stuff into my life, but then I think, 'I don't like exciting stuff. I don't fancy bungee jumping or even a safari. I fancy sitting in my room reading a book.'

Margaret Atwood

Author

31 October 2016

I was 16 in 1955 and living in Canada. This was a time of Elvis Presley, rock'n'roll, circle skirts, penny loafers and formal school dances with strapless dresses – though I never went that far. In twelfth grade, it might surprise you to know, along with my partner Sally, I was our school's entry in the Consumers Gas Miss Homemakers contest. We had to make a baked potato in a gas stove and iron a shirt with a gas iron. We didn't win, but we got some very nice charm bracelets.

One thing I would advise my younger self to do would be to take secretarial studies to learn touch typing. I still can't type. Careers advisers had a short list of possible careers for girls – primary school teacher, nurse, airline stewardess and home economist, which meant something along the lines of a nutritionist or dressmaker. I didn't want to do any of those things but I looked at the salaries, being a mercenary child, and home economists made the most. So I took those classes and learned how to fasten a zipper, but I never learned to type.

I'd tell the 16-year-old Margaret to stop worrying about her hair – it is what it is and there's nothing you can do, so just forget it. In reality, I didn't reach that point of acceptance until I was about 30, after some untoward experiments.

I read a lot as a teenager, but I did a lot of other things too. I made my own clothes, and ran my own puppet show at school. We made the puppets and the stage, and did all the voices. I was quite entrepreneurial, and made money doing that. We ended up getting an agent and putting on our shows at children's Christmas parties. I also wrote and sang in a home economics-based opera and was on the basketball team; you didn't have to be as tall then. I was very participatory.

I became a more anxious teenager when the serious exams arrived, but not terribly so. I wasn't that anxious about boys – there always seemed to be a plentiful supply. This was the stage of going steady and serial monogamy, and it was before the pill. You didn't have to worry about having sex because you weren't going to have it – that was understood.

Sixteen was the age at which I started to write. My friend remembers me announcing this in the school cafeteria. She said to me later, 'You were so brave, saying you were going to be a writer right out loud', but that's because I didn't know you weren't supposed to say that. I don't know where the inspiration came from. There were no role models and I knew zero about it, but I was reading Hemingway and Orwell and lots of science fiction, as well as nineteenth-century classics at school. I went out and bought a book called *Writer's Market* that told you where you could sell your writing. It said true romances made the most money so my plan was to write those to make money and write my masterpieces in the evening. I was no good at first, but I thought I was, so I kept going.

If I met the 16-year-old me now I'd think, 'What planet did you come from?' I was not the same as my cohorts because I grew up in the woods and wasn't too concerned about what other people thought. I was quite sarcastic and full of smart talk and quips, making fun of things – my friends and I would probably be considered quite harsh these days, but we got that attitude from the movies.

I think some of my independent thinking came from my parents. My mother hadn't followed the pattern either, and she never told me there were things I couldn't do because I was a girl. My parents weren't happy about the writing idea, because how was I going to make money? I considered being a journalist, but my parents brought home a male journalist friend who told me I'd end up writing the ladies' pages and the obituaries. So they successfully diverted me from that course. But not into science, which was where they wanted me to go.

If I was to give the younger Margaret advice, I'd tell her to stop overloading her schedule with too many things. But I've been saying that for 50 years. And I'd tell her to do something about being a compulsive helpaholic – I need to find a way of not doing that because it eats up a lot of time, and you can't help everybody in the world. It would be hard for me to go back and show off to the young Margaret about my subsequent career – she wasn't very easy to impress. If I told her about my success she'd say, 'Yeah, so you did it.' Of all my novels she'd probably like *The Handmaid's Tale* best – she was reading dark science fiction like *Fahrenheit 451* and *1984*.

I'd tell the younger me, 'Forget the melodrama – it'll be okay. It gets better up until you're 30. Then it gets even better after you're 40.' When I was 20, I didn't know what the plot was going to be so I was full of anxieties – will I meet Mr Right, will my career work out, will I be happy? By the time I got to 40, at least I knew about half of the plot. And you're more likely to be listened to as a 40-year-old woman, if you've made any headway in your career, than you are in your twenties.

When you get to 76, there's a whole load of people who have died, and who you never got to say everything you wanted to. By the time my parents died they weren't really capable of those kind of conversations but I'd already had them earlier in our lives, because you just never know.

If I could go back in time, I might revisit one of our trips to the Arctic – it's actually a fantastic place. We also lived in France for a while in 1991; maybe I'd go back and relive one of those very nice fall days. Or a summer in Northern Canada – very beautiful. But what really gets me up in the morning is looking forward to what comes next. Too much time looking at the past and you're in the rocking chair.

Sir Roger Moore

Actor

29 September 2014

At 16, I'd been working for six months already, for a company which made instructional animated films for the army and air force. My job was tracing illustrations on a lightbox. I loved it, but due to a misunderstanding when I was collecting film from a laboratory, my services were no longer required. Then I was unemployed, so I went to the swimming pool a lot.

The war was still going on when I was a teenager, which was absolutely terrible. I remember coming home one day and my mum had just found out that her brother, one of her favourite people in her life, had been killed in Italy. He was a regular soldier who had been blown up when one of his platoon stood on a mine. But apart from that, I was a very happy and carefree teenager – I had no responsibilities.

I had a wonderful relationship with my parents. I was an only child and was terribly spoiled. I didn't have to share

– I used to laughingly say they only had one child because they reached perfection on their first try, so didn't have to try again. But actually, I must have been a large baby who kicked a lot because after I was born my mother was advised not to carry another child.

I never thought about acting, but I did always enjoy clowning around. I was often chosen to read poetry and stories aloud in class. My father was in the police, and his job was to draw the accident scenes for court evidence. He worked mainly at home and if the sun was shining he'd take me swimming instead of working. If anyone ever asked me about my career plans, I said I wanted to be a policeman like my father.

If I could talk to the 16-year-old Roger I'd say, 'Be prepared to put up with criticism. Be prepared to be part of an industry where the vast majority are out of work. Save your money. Continue to smile. Be well mannered. And just love it.'

The teenage me would be surprised that I was successful; of course he dreamed of it, but he wouldn't have worried if it hadn't happened. I remember when I had enough money for either five cigarettes, or to get the bus. I'd have to walk all the way to London, or I'd be sitting on the bus regretting that I didn't have a cigarette. So when it finally came to a time when I could afford both, I'd sit on the top deck wafting a cigarette around and making a great show of reading my lines so that everyone could see I was an actor.

Looking back, I've been very lucky. I remember being in New York – I'd gone there without a permit – and in less than a week I had a job on a live television play. Then Hollywood beckoned and I had to decide which film studio in America to go under contract to. It was sort of ridiculous – I was only about 26.

I wasn't an Albert Finney or a Tom Courtenay – I didn't have their natural talent, so had to work quite hard at acting. My life's been alright, but people like that get to play wonderful parts. I spent my life playing heroes because I looked like one – practically everything I've been offered didn't require much beyond looking like me. I would have loved to play a real baddie.

Ageing has never bothered me. My wife and my children love me, so that's alright. I count my remaining hairs and say, 'Oh, they're still here.' I'm getting like the guy in Michael Caine's story about the man with three hairs who goes to the barber's, and when the barber asks which side he parts it on, he says the left. But then a hair falls out and the barber says, 'What shall I do?' and the man says, 'Part it in the middle.' Then another hair falls out and when the barber asks what he should do now, the man says, 'Just leave it ruffled.'

I don't like watching my old films. I have a big ego and don't like to be reminded that I'm not as good as I think I am. And I think 'damn' when I see myself doing something active in a film that I can't do anymore, like running upstairs. I've never sat down and watched a whole James Bond film.

My lovely wife, who's Swedish, didn't see a lot of my films before she met me. She'd seen a James Bond film because the American ambassador's wife in Copenhagen invited her to a private screening, but that was *Dr No*. So she knew Sean Connery was James Bond, but not me. Her favourite Bond with me in it? She's never said. She's across the room, I'll ask her... She says the one where I have the karate thing – I think she means *The Man with the Golden Gun*. Yes, I thoroughly enjoyed doing that. The two ladies – Maud Adams and Britt Ekland – I found very sweet.

I think there are times when good luck comes along and things just start to happen – you have to recognise those moments when they come, and use them. I do go into my shell sometimes, and I loathe arguments – when you lose your temper, you've lost the argument. I always tell people, 'Listen to others, weigh things up, take good advice and reject that which you don't think will do you any good whatsoever.' Have I been good at following that advice? Not really, but I just keep going. How does the song go? 'Keep right on till the end of the road'.

CHAPTER 11:

Hindsight

Ian McEwan

Author

15 April 2019

At 16, I was a very slim, pale fellow with Buddy Holly glasses and a very thick pile of dark hair. I'd been at boarding school 2000 miles from home since I was 11 and had been mildly depressed, though I didn't have the analytical tools to recognise it, or even to say it to myself. But around the age of 16 I realised that although it was school, I was in the most extraordinarily lovely place, in a beautiful stretch of Suffolk on the River Orwell. I was waking up to literature and reading a lot of poetry and music. I was listening to Bach for the first time, and a lot of jazz and the electric blues. I became wildly excited about life, roaring on all fronts. I was embarking on an amazing awakening.

The great lack in my life of course, at my all-boys school, was the opposite sex. So a lot of longing was channelled into this love of music and books – it was slightly unnatural. At 16, a very charismatic English teacher told me I was clever, and I suddenly felt clever for the first time in my life. He introduced me to Graham Greene, Iris Murdoch, Brian Aldiss, William Golding. I became very earnest and serious; I began to get the idea that the study of English literature was like the priesthood and I was going to dedicate myself to it and probably get a job teaching English one day.

I used to look forward to going home for the holidays, but within a week I'd be restless and bored because there were no kids around. My father, a military man, was stationed in Germany, so since I'd been about 12 I'd made the journey from Suffolk to Germany – boat, then train. All by myself. I was very fond of my parents – they were very kindly and had a lovely commitment to my education. But the things that education gave me, that love of literature and the arts, didn't mean much to them, which gave me a bit of arrogance that I condemn myself utterly for now. I went through a five-year stretch of thinking anyone who hadn't read *The Wasteland* wasn't worth talking to. How unbearable of me.

Much later on I saw the full humanity of my parents, and I saw that they were shaped by two great forces I'd been very lucky to avoid: the Great Depression and the Second World War. I realised that a lot of my generation's parents had stared into the abyss and seen death on a scale that was unimaginable to our generation. And so when it all ended and the country began to get a little more prosperous, they clung to ordinariness, stability and regularity. I later saw how things that seemed boring to me, like polishing a car, were soothing for a man who'd been through slaughter. So I'd love to send that message back to my younger self: 'You are in a life with no danger and you must appreciate that people who have been in real danger find comfort in routine.' What did we do? Grow our hair and walk around with no shoes on, smoking a bit of dope and thinking we were on the cutting edge of experience. Nonsense.

I think my younger self would have been amazed that in 1972, just after my university days, I'd see the cover of a literary magazine – *New American Review* – and it would have four names, all in the same size – Philip Roth, Günter Grass, Susan Sontag and Ian McEwan. I was 22 and almost fainted – to see my name among these legendary writers who I had such admiration for.

Around 1973 or 1974 Martin[62] introduced me to Christopher[63] and they ran through some of their routines together, which were very obscene and made my ribs ache. Whenever I came into a room, Chris would go into third-person mode and say, 'Here comes the slim, ironic figure of Ian McEwan.' During that time I met all the young men, or mainly men, who became lifelong friends – James Fenton, Craig Raine, Clive James, Julian Barnes. And we had a lot of fun running around town together, having our first books and articles published.

I didn't rack up scores of girlfriends the way Martin was famous for – I quite liked focusing on one relationship. And I loved fatherhood from the start, absolutely adored it. I got married in 1982 and we moved to Oxford and had two sons, and I had two stepdaughters as well. We had a big household in Oxford and it was a lovely time, actually. I see my children a lot – they've been a source of immense pleasure in my life.

62 Novelist Martin Amis.

63 Journalist and author Christopher Hitchens.

If I could go back and have a final conversation with anyone, I think I'd choose my first love. Her name was Polly Bide and we fell in love at university and stayed friends for the rest of our lives. Then around 2001 she began to get ill, and she died of cancer in 2003. I did see her, but in all the busyness and the narrative of her illness – its moments of depression and hope – we never sat down and had the kind of deep conversation in which we acknowledged she was dying. She was a lovely, lovely person and I still miss her.

Death is always there, like a distant mountain range you're always approaching. I think you just have to try to live your life to the full. You've had the gift of this consciousness for 70 or 80 years and hope you've made the most of it. I feel a sadness about it, really. I feel that life is good. Then you have these moments when you think, 'This all has to end – not even in nothing, but beyond nothing.' And the fact that everyone else is going to end too doesn't make it any better. There's a line in Larkin's poem 'Aubade': 'Not to be here, Not to be anywhere.' People who believe in an afterlife will never know they were wrong, so it must be a great comfort to them. But not to me.

If I could relive one day, it would be in 1976 when I was with a couple of friends and we went for a huge hike in Big Sur in California. I must have been about 27. We had this wonderful afternoon, with the ocean crashing around us and unbelievable vegetation around us. There came a point when we were heading back to our tents and we felt so happy, so good in our bodies, that we decided to run the last five or six miles along the path. It was that wonderful easy running you can do when you're young, and as we went through that landscape I just thought, 'I'm in heaven.

This is beautiful.' I felt the delight in it all – the physical act of running, the extraordinary landscape around me, good friends and the thought of the evening ahead of me just as the sun was setting. I thought, 'I've got a cove in paradise.' I knew it at the time and that moment has remained with me ever since.

Slash

Musician

10 March 2008

I was pretty reclusive at 16. I didn't like school – I didn't mind the concept, but I didn't fit in with anyone there. I didn't see school as a priority – that was my guitar. I was ditching school, doing a lot of drinking on my own and playing guitar on the high-school bleachers instead. I took my guitar everywhere. I was a complete sponge for Led Zeppelin, Hendrix, AC/DC, Aerosmith…

I had a good sex life at 16. I had an on-off girlfriend, and she was my sexual partner. It wasn't as easy then as it is now for a 16-year-old to get laid by lots of people, but I did alright. If I'd known then that I'd make a living out of playing guitar – and about the limousines and the screaming girls and the drugs that would come with it – I'd have been very happy about the future.

I'd tell my younger self that success isn't always what it

looks like. Often when you're at the top of your career[64] you don't always feel so up on the inside – a lot of it is just survival and struggle. When that changed for me[65] I was really relieved to get out of it. It was a huge high to escape it and to get away from the internal wrangling – I liked the struggling part more than I liked cruising.

I'd reassure my 16-year-old self that I wasn't going to change much. There were definitely periods when I started falling into the abyss,[66] but I think my sense of reality and my dedication to the music got me out of that. I don't think I ever became a prima donna. I was always pretty easy-going and quite nice to people. As long as I could get my cigarettes and booze, I was fine.

I'd be freaked at 16 to think of myself as a father, but I have two little boys of three and five now, so my life has a whole different dynamic. More than anything, I got bored with the drunken, smacked-out Slash thing and eventually got jaded with it in Guns N' Roses, so I felt fine about leaving it behind. I certainly enjoyed it at the time though.

64 In 1987, Guns N' Roses' debut album *Appetite for Destruction* sold 15 million copies in the US

65 Slash left the band in 1996.

66 Slash's autobiography is called *Smack, Crack, Groupies and Firearms.*

Alistair Campbell

Journalist and Former Downing Street Press Secretary

30 January 2012

I felt like a pretty happy teenager; I must have been angst-ridden on one level because 12 years later I ended up in hospital with a massive nervous breakdown, but day-to-day I felt good. I worked very hard at school and had various part-time jobs. I have a big extended family in Scotland and spent all my holidays working on my uncle's farm there, which I loved. He used to pay what I thought was ridiculous money, so I lived with him and had a great time going out on the lash with one of the other workers. I played the bagpipes and loved football, cricket and Burnley FC, of course. By the time I was 16 I spent a lot of my time and money at Burnley matches, and when I was at school I never took off my Burnley scarf. The teachers tried to make me, but I wouldn't take it off.

I didn't have a really serious relationship until I was older, though I had a few girlfriends. I was quite confident and never worried about being attractive or getting off with girls – I always felt that girls came to me quite a lot. Getting hooked up for a serious relationship wasn't a big priority at the time.

The 16-year-old me would be relieved to hear that he finally sorted his drinking out – he was already beginning to drink too much and was worried about it. I never had a problem getting served in pubs and liked drinking from when I first started. My other half Fiona recalls that I never seemed to get drunk. I did have a ridiculous capacity for drink. Sometimes I got violent when I was drunk, and I was very lucky that no one was badly hurt. I don't drink much now, and I notice that people who do drink a lot get boring really quickly.

I wasn't politicised in the sense of being a member of a political party, but I was quite opinionated and I was definitely anti-establishment. I wanted most of all to be a footballer, but I wasn't very good at it so that was never a runner. But one of the great things about leading the life I do now is getting asked to do things like play a charity match with Diego Maradona – back then that was the kind of thing I dreamed of doing. At the same time, if you told me I'd end up doing something to do with words and language, I wouldn't be surprised. I always wrote a lot – poems, songs and short stories. There weren't journalists in the family, but my dad used to get the *Sunday Post* every week and I remember reading it from cover to cover. That was maybe an early indication that I might be interested in journalism.

I don't want to sound arrogant, but I always felt I'd lead a different life to most people. But if you told the teenage me he'd become a journalist who went to Malta for a summit between Bush and Gorbachev at the end of the Cold War, that he'd become friendly with a guy who'd become prime minister, that he'd travel the world meeting presidents, kings and queens, and would make friends with people like Clive Woodward and Alex Ferguson – I think he'd say, 'Nah, I think you're pushing it a bit.'

I think the younger me might worry that the adult me became too sucked into the establishment. But he'd be pleased I turned down becoming part of the House of Lords and didn't take a knighthood. I don't go to Yorkshire much anymore, but I think he'd feel I've kept in touch with my roots and my family. Britain hangs on to a class structure that I don't like. When I worked for the Labour Party we had to deal with the fact that the British media is so bloody biased – we did that by setting the agenda in a very strategic way and I'm proud that we did that and won three general elections, changing the country along the way.

I don't think I was aware of having depression until my breakdown. I think most people would have said I was quite happy-go-lucky, though who knows what people really think? I'm obsessed with sport now, but I didn't do that much when I was young – I played a bit of football and cricket but didn't have exercise as part of my daily routine. If I could live my life again I'd make playing sport a much bigger part of my life. I smoked too, and that's another thing I wish I'd never done. I haven't smoked for 20 years, but I still get asthma. I think it's a horrible habit now, but at the time it was a big part of who I was.

I remember saying to a senior civil servant that I didn't understand why some of the civil servants didn't work with us better, and she said, 'You have to understand – some of them are bloody terrified of you.' I said, 'But I'm one of the easiest people you could work with – I'm a team person.' She said, 'When your office phoned to say you wanted to speak to me, it sent a panic throughout the floor.' I said, 'Well, that's about them, not me.' And she said, 'Yes – but it's also about your reputation.'

I'm not sure if I'd go back and do anything differently, not the really big decisions. Ireland[67] could have gone wrong, but it went right. The conventional wisdom is that Iraq went wrong, but I still think we did the right thing. Do I wish fewer people had died? Of course, but would I rewrite the dossier? Not at all – the people who later said it was the basis on which we went to war were the same people who said at the time it was irrelevant. Tony and I took enormous care over it.

I'm very ambivalent about having a high profile. Part of me to this day doesn't like the idea of being filmed. I can be paid a lot of money to make a speech to a bank, a building society or a construction firm, because I'm well-known for my work with Tony Blair. I have a very interesting and varied life – part of it I like, and part I don't.

I always found *The Thick of It* funny. It's a caricature, but if you actually analyse the character of Malcolm Tucker, he's someone who's at the interface between power and the media and wants to control the political message and the media, which is what I did. Every day on Twitter there's someone who'll say something like, 'I've just been told I'm the Alastair Campbell of the organisation.' That might mean they're the press person, it might mean they're the spin doctor, or it might mean they're the ultimate team player. But if you're still being talked about a decade on, you must have done something right. When I was a journalist, I hated a lot of what the Thatcher government did and I thought the Labour Party represented ordinary British people.

67 Campbell was part of Tony Blair's team that negotiated the Good Friday Agreement.

We changed the terms of political debate. Along the way, myself and Peter Mandelson became identified with this whole media thing, but I'm proud of what we did because we were anti-establishment*.

I've been thinking about happiness a lot, and part of it is having a sense of belonging. I feel British first, then Scottish, then Yorkshire. English is quite a long way down. Part of what I'm interested in politically is pursuing happiness – I think it's a really good way of looking at government policy. When we look at say, education, are we helping our children to be more happy? That doesn't just mean having fun – it's also about fulfilment. One of the best things we did when we came into power was to give children free access to museums. I like the idea that every policy maker shouldn't just think about the economy, society and equality – they're all important, but we should also ask what makes the country more happy. How can a country be happy when two million people a day fork out their hard-earned cash to buy the *Daily Mail*? I've learned not to listen to the *Today* programme – why start your day by giving yourself a headache?

If I could go back and relive a day, I'd go back to the birth of my kids. The three general election wins should have been the greatest days of my life, but I felt depressed on all of them and couldn't enjoy them. The Royal Festival Hall[68] and all that – I said to Tony, 'I just want to get home' and he said, 'I feel exactly the same.' I think it was the sense of the pressure. Everyone else was euphoric and you just thought, 'Oh my God – what's next?'

---

* Campbell left the Labour Party in July 2019 saying it 'no longer truly represents my values'.

68 The location of Labour's victory party on the night of the 1997 General Election.

Benjamin Zephaniah

Poet

23 March 2009

At 16, I'd just left borstal in Birmingham. I was a very angry young man who hated Babylon and anything in a uniform. I was sleeping in various girlfriends' places and every now and again I'd visit my mum – she was very worried about me. I was a bit of a renegade and was robbing houses for a living and partying every night – at the time it felt like a great life.

Deep inside me even then, part of me already wanted to be a poet – but I kept it quiet. The word 'poet' conjured up images of dead white men, but when I heard poetry, I loved it and thought, 'That's what I want to do.' When guns started appearing on the streets, I decided to move to London to try to be a poet.

I would say to that 16-year-old kid, 'I know you're dyslexic and it's hard, but try to read more.' I'd say, 'Don't be ashamed and don't be shy of it – bring poetry into your life.' I remember going to rob houses and stopping to look at what books were on the shelves – and thinking, 'Wow, they read Shelley!' When I moved to London, I lied to people and said I was a novelist – I didn't feel prepared for the poetry scene.

I ended up getting my real education at a bookshop in London. Page One Books had a grant to publish new voices and agreed to publish me if I joined their co-op. A collection of lesbian feminists, straight feminists, Marxists and Irish Republicans were my teachers, and they introduced me to many writers and new ways of thinking and asking questions. They made me self-aware.

I tell you what I like about the teenage Benjamin – his life is so spontaneous and he could move around the country easily. I don't have that freedom now – though I don't have a mortgage, I have a house, a recording studio and six computers. I remember when I stayed with my girlfriends, I always slept nearest the exit so that when the police came in I could be straight out of there. And that did happen!

I used to be very violent towards women, just like my dad was to my mum, but I could never do that now. If I saw a man lay a hand on a woman, I'd go for him. I once deliberately dragged a girl a few yards along the road, after trapping her hair in the car door. Many years later I met up with her and apologised. She said she could never fancy me now because I wasn't a real man anymore – I'd listened to too many white liberals. It made me realise how far I'd come and how much confidence some women still lack in their own gender.

I'd tell my younger self that he should prepare for living much longer than he expects – I'd assumed I wouldn't make my thirties because of my lifestyle and the people around me. When I was younger I went around with much older people, but now I spend time with much younger people. It might be because I've never had children and have never adopted the conservative concerns of parents that I somehow connect with young people. I'm honest with them, I don't cover up my own past and I don't preach to them.

I think I made one big mistake with my marriage. My wife was very young and I gave her an ultimatum – either marry me now or I won't mention it for five years. It was probably a mistake, putting on that pressure. We hardly ever argued – I just came home one day and she was gone. Maybe if we'd argued I would have seen things coming a bit better.

My biggest fear is growing old alone, and it's happening to me now. I think it's unnatural – it's not good for your mental health. We're pack animals and we like to groom and protect each other. And at least once or twice a year I like to have sex. I get groupies and they say they love you, but they don't really care about you. That can feel lonely.

Benny Andersson

Musician

4 December 2017

I was an ordinary 16-year-old with no real clue what to do with my life. I didn't know that I should be a musician or a composer. I'm a self-taught guy, but I could already find my way around the piano. Then I got an offer from a rock band, The Hep Stars, who had lost their organ player, so I just slipped into it. I would tell my younger self, 'Just keep on doing what you are doing. You don't have to worry so much. Take it as it comes and everything will sort itself out.'

The early '60s was a great time to be 16. I was listening to all the music from the UK: The Beatles, The Rolling Stones, The Kinks, The Who – those were the days! Brian Wilson is one of my heroes, but it was definitely Lennon and McCartney who inspired me to write music. I was 19 when I wrote my first number one. It was called 'Funny Girl' and I still think it's a good song – a rubbish lyric but a good melody. I thought,

'Maybe this is something I should spend my life trying to do', and I haven't had a reason to regret that yet.

In the '60s, being in a rock band was not considered a real job. We were the biggest band in Sweden from 1965 to 1969 but my parents would still say, 'What are you going to do after the Hep Stars?' There were a couple of years before ABBA where all four of us needed to work to put food on the table and pay the rent, and I come from circumstances where we didn't have much money. Music has been good to me, but I know what it's like to struggle.

I was very young when I became a father. Even if I thought I was a mature 16-year-old and was ahead of my friends at school, it wasn't an ideal situation. It wasn't great when I was away touring, but it works now and has done for many years. Now my son is 53 and my daughter is 51. They say, 'We're happy you did what you did, because it means being able to live a decent life'. They don't complain, but I don't know. My younger son, Ludvig, is 35 and I was with him the whole time he was growing up – I loved being hands-on. We do everything together, and now we are working on the next *Mamma Mia!* movie. My wife gets envious, because she doesn't see him as much as I do.

ABBA came together organically. Björn met Agnetha and got engaged, and at almost the same time I met Frida. Frida and Agetha were solo artists, I had my band and Björn had his. Then Björn and I made a record called *Lycka*, which means 'happiness'. For one song, we asked our wives to come in for backing vocals and all of a sudden, wow – they sounded good! Björn said we should try to write pop music and sing in English. That was 1972 and we wrote 'People Need Love' and it became a hit. After that, to make people realise that us guys from the North Pole exist, we decided to enter the Eurovision Song Contest. All of a sudden, we had an audience that was not just in Sweden.

I've known Björn for 51 years and it's like having a brother. That friendship has been very important and we still talk every week. We are not very much alike, which is one of the reasons we're still such good friends. Relations within ABBA have always been good – we're all good friends and have met through the years to talk about things.

If you drink too much, too often, for too long, you get into trouble. I decided 16 years ago that I had to give it up, and I think it was probably the best decision I've made in my life. All of a sudden, you're fighting fit every hour of the day. It's the best thing I've done.

I was never political as a teenager, but I am now – that comes with age. You realise that everything is important. I am engaged, I have opinions and I support people who share them. I think *The Big Issue* is a great initiative, for example. Top of my list is gender equality,[69] but it is pretty messy today with Brexit, Catalonia and Donald Trump at the wheel in America. The UK leaving the EU is like your friend turning around and saying, 'I don't like you anymore.' It feels bad for us, but let's wait and see if it actually happens.

There are a lot of things that my younger self could look forward to. I don't understand why ABBA's music is still so popular, but I should hope it has to do with the quality of the songs. None of us would have thought when we quit in 1982 that our music would still be around 35 years on, but there's still as much life in the records as there was then. We were lucky. The music was kept alive by *Muriel's Wedding*,

69 Andersson has donated to the Feminist Initiative Party in Sweden.

which was a really good film, then Erasure recorded a few tracks and had a big success. Then *ABBA Gold* was released. There must be millions of kids out there that don't know about ABBA but know the songs from *Mamma Mia!* I'm very proud of what we achieved with ABBA, the music of *Chess* and a musical in Sweden called *Kristina*, about Swedish immigration to North America in the nineteenth century. That was a huge success here – it's more of an opera, really.

There's going to be a digital version of ABBA. I don't know if we're going to be holograms, but it's a huge project and a huge honour. We have a year and a half to work on it. It is exciting because we are at the forefront of what technology can do. We have to make it worth coming to as an audience – they need to understand that we are there, even if we are not there physically.

Ending ABBA didn't feel any different – I just kept on doing what I liked to do. I wanted to try to write music for the theatre and then Tim Rice showed up with an idea for a musical about chess – I said that was boring enough to get our teeth into! I formed a little band because I wanted to go back to my roots in Swedish folk music. We're now a 16-piece band called Benny Anderssons Orkester. We tour every two years, bring a dancefloor and play for four hours. I still get the buzz.

Boy George

Musician

3 February 2014

At 16, in my head, I was very advanced for my years. I wanted to be an adult, not a kid. I was a punk, wearing the punk uniform and adopting the pose. I had spiky hair, black lips, eyeliner and bondage trousers. Then, in the blink of an eye, I switched to New Romantic: skyscraper hair, make-up – another really outrageous look. At first my mum was very against me going out like that and tried to stop me. My dad would just be reading a newspaper and he'd take a look and say, 'If he wants to go out and get beaten up, let him.' Gradually my mum realised I wasn't going to change and she gave up and became an enabler. She was great on the sewing machine. She made lots of stuff for me, because I couldn't afford things.

My teens were a time of freedom, music and excitement. I had a job as a runner in a printing place, so I could wear whatever I wanted. I used the London Tube as my catwalk, and everyone stared at me – it was great. I met people on the Tube and had affairs with them. I remember I was over in Bank delivering mail, and this very handsome Italian man was staring at me. He asked me if I was a girl, which I liked, and then he asked if I had a girlfriend or boyfriend. I ended up going to a party with him that night.

When I was a teenager I did everything to be the opposite of my dad, but now I see I'm just like him. My dad wasn't the cliché. He was Irish and had been a boxer – he could be unbelievably unreasonable, but he wasn't stupid. He had beautiful handwriting and he was very handsome. When I came out, he was kind of amazing. He put his arms around me and said, 'You're still my son and I love you.' A total contradiction. I have his better qualities. He was incredibly generous and kind. He would do anything for a stranger or the woman down the road. But when it came to the people who really loved him, that was more difficult.

My mum was so graceful and stylish when my dad left her after 43 years of marriage – she forgave him. She was so respectful of his memory when he died, and that made me love her so much. In my late twenties I had some long conversations with my dad and I said to him, 'The way you treat mum, why don't you just divorce? You could be great friends.' He said, 'You don't understand, son.' It was all about 'family loyalty'. Then, after 43 years, he left her for a younger woman! He did some awful things, but we laugh about them now. We say, 'Oh my God, remember when dad chased the driving instructor down the street because mum had put her best coat on for her lesson and dad decided she was having an affair?' The whole cul-de-sac was out watching. We were all mortified at the time, but we laugh about it now.

My advice to my younger self would be that jealousy doesn't make you more attractive – if you go and smash a guy's windows, he's not going to like you more. I was thinking about one of my last relationships recently. I'd got a taxi to this boy's house and managed to get myself past his security gates. How awful I must have seemed. Why did I think he would say, 'Yes, now that you've broken into my flat and tried to kill me, I really want to be with you.' When I look back at how I dealt with heartbreak – I'd never behave like that now. It was undignified. I'm a Buddhist now, so anyone I've ever hurt goes into my prayers. And my last relationship, when it went wrong, I just let it go. I said to myself, 'Come on kid, don't make a fool of yourself – you're too old now.'

I would tell my younger self not to do drugs.[70] If only I'd known the kind of misery I would cause myself, all the drama, the pain I brought my mother and the waste of money and time – and it doesn't make you feel better. I'd also tell myself to talk less and listen more. I've met some amazing spiritual people who told me I needed to listen. I remember doing this therapy course, and I was playing up and being the centre of attention. And the teacher said, 'Will you shut the fuck up?'

I'd have been indifferent to the idea of fame when I was 16. My whole career was an accident – the only reason I started a band was that everyone else was doing it. I had no ambition – I just wanted the bohemian lifestyle. Then I met Jon Moss and he joined my band, and I was in a relationship with him and I really got into the whole thing. But it's only in the last six years that I've come to look at what I do as a job and I do it with more respect. But it's not 'all or nothing' anymore,

70 George was an on/off cocaine and heroin user in the late '80s.

like it was when I was younger. I can't imagine living my life feeling like that ever again. I had no 'off' button.

You often make sense of your life in hindsight. When I was in prison[71] it didn't feel like it was teaching me anything – I was just getting through this unpredictable day-to-day, dealing with people who were unhinged. Afterwards I realised how much I need my own company, time on my own just to think. And I read a lot – everything I'd lied about reading in the past: Oscar Wilde, Dickens, *Wuthering Heights*, *Catch-22*. I got friends of mine to send me classics. I found so much I loved, and now I read loads.

As an older man, I understand why some people take a long time to come out. I'm reading Morrissey's autobiography now – I love him – and I understand why he never came out all guns blazing. I think he wanted to avoid defining himself as anything clear-cut. Unfortunately, when you come out people define you by what you do in bed. Lots of people get nagged to come out and when they do the press say, 'All you ever do is talk about being gay.' I keep telling people that being gay is about three hours a week. I met Morrissey when Culture Club were massive and he knew I was a massive fan, but he was horrible to me. He wouldn't speak, and afterwards he called me unbearable. Then again, I probably was.

71 He was jailed for four months in 2009 for falsely imprisoning a male escort in his flat.

Dylan Moran

Comedian and Actor

26 January 2015

I'd tell my 16-year-old self not to take everything so seriously. I'm stunned when I look back at how monumentally important I thought everything was. I was incredibly intense, ridiculously up myself. It was all about me, and books and poetry. Not that those things aren't important to me anymore, but in those days it felt like do or die. Now I want to say to my younger self, 'If you think of life as a play, you're the bumbling, forgetful character who appears in scene seven, looking for his keys.'

I had a terrible time at school. I wasn't academic and I just didn't get on there. But I read a lot – post-war American fiction, like John Cheever, Philip Roth and Saul Bellow, those big names who had the status of demigods then – and a lot of theatre, Chekhov and Kenneth Tynan. I also wrote a lot and thought a lot about what I might go on to do, because it didn't seem like I'd end up being a dentist or an accountant like a lot of the people around me had planned.

Was I an angsty teenager? Yeah, I'll accept angsty. Fatalistic, doomy – you get to 40 and you're a million shades of grey, but as a teenager it's all in black and white. That's the adolescent condition. I didn't grow up in a city – we were out in the sticks, 30 miles from Dublin. I was desperate to get to the city, and my friends and I spent our time in the acres of dullness around us, making each other laugh. In retrospect it feels very innocent – I knew nothing really, but I had a bunch of decent friends and we did have fun. I was always drawn to people who were good at telling funny stories.

Being an Irish Catholic – that stuff enters your bloodstream when you're very young, no matter how you feel about it. When I was growing up we were the only family I knew who didn't go to church. It wasn't a passive rejection – it was a passionate, violent rejection. I loathe the church and am always amazed when people go on about what a progressive, forward-looking guy Pope Francis is – he's just another 500-year-old man in a dress talking about other people's business and issuing edicts from a system based on the sayings of a political revolutionary from 2000 years ago. In the last few years I've been obsessed with East Germany, because I think that was the parallel experience in Europe. I think East Germany under Honecker and the rest of the gang was very similar to Ireland under the church.

When I was about 19, I went to a comedy club and asked if I could go onstage for five minutes, and that was it. There was a lot of anxiety – 'Sure I hope this works, what if I make a fool of myself?' But there's obviously something attractive about taking that chance. It's adrenaline junkie-ism really –

it's not courage. There's a typical story arc for stand-ups – they tend to have a lot of self-pity, whether they're tragic or not. There's generally a mix of high self-regard and feeling sorry for themselves, because constantly trying to cause laughter is a suspect activity really, like constantly trying to defuse bombs other people don't even see. I wonder more and more what that's about. You sometimes see very sad situations with people who are always 'on', always joking, and that person is basically a fucking disaster. They're full of tension, and they use laughter as a kind of a hiccup.

I think if the teenage me met the 43-year-old me, the first thing he'd think would be, 'How did you get so fat? What happened to you?' But he'd be pleased that he got out and did something he really wanted to do. I really didn't cope well with the idea of trying to make a living doing something I didn't want to do – I didn't think I would last. Put me in an office and I'd end up in jail. I spent my whole time thinking about writing, and I draw parallels between people who do that kind of thing and people who do sports. The same obsession. My eyes open first thing in the morning and my first thought, every day, is about work.

I would tell my teenage self, don't bother smoking – just get a little tray, put a bonfire on it and walk around with it. And see how you feel about that.

I'm on the road now, back to doing stand-up, and I'm getting used to it again. Your material depends completely on where you are in your life. I was talking last night about how I've reached that point in my life when I see something lying around the house, something like a burnt-out candle or a piece of rope, and I put it in my pocket and think, 'That might come in handy.' What sort of apocalyptic scene am I awaiting the arrival of, in which this old piece of candle will become essential? What is going on in my brain?

I'm still having the shock moment of realising I'm not young anymore – I'm living in a tsunami of those shock moments. The second half of your life just feels like a huge conspiracy theory – all this stuff happens to you that no one told you about. It makes me glad I didn't value athleticism and good looks when I was growing up, because you search in vain for it when you get older, that's for sure. In my day, we used to wake up with a pie in our hand, and then we'd smoke a cigarette – now everyone is suddenly Jane Fonda. I don't worry about my health, but I do worry about dying.

When I look back, there's never been a time when I was standing on a mountain of gold screaming joyfully at the sky. I'm a very ordinary person who hangs out with his wife and children. But there were nights, early on, when I walked off stage, and I'd just done something I didn't know I could do, like the comedy equivalent of a triple salchow. The first time that happens, you think, 'Oh right, so I am a God. I should adjust. I'd better get myself some really nice trousers.'

Meat Loaf

Musician

11 March 2013

At the age of 16, I was preoccupied with American football, because I got to hit people. I took my anger out. That's what I took on the stage in the late '70s. In fact, I still take it on the stage. I was always a performer – I had a folk trio in college and bands in the '60s, but I didn't take entertainment seriously until I came to Broadway to do *Hair* in 1970. People could see I was a bit carefree about acting and they told me if I took it more seriously I could be really good.

Basically, in the music business I've always been on the outside looking in because I'm an actor. People always said, 'Well if you're an actor you can't possibly mean what you sing – you can't feel the songs.' I say, 'Go and tell that to Marlon Brando in *A Streetcar Named Desire* or de Niro or Johnny Depp.' Sometimes music critics are not very smart. It's like telling an actor, 'Here's your script – we need your real person to deliver the message.' Some guy on my Facebook said, ‘I prefer guys who write their own songs.’ So I say, ‘Okay, I’ve written songs – I just don’t like them.’ Not many people know I wrote Bucks Fizz’s ‘Magical’.

I never wanted to play by the rules, and I still feel that way. I don’t agree with most of the things any government does. I’d never outwardly done anything for a presidential candidate until I sat down with say Mitt Romney, but we talked one-on-one about China, unemployment in America and defence issues. There was no one else in the room. People on my Facebook were amazed and said, ‘We didn’t know you were so smart’ – because my name is Meat Loaf, people think I’m a blithering idiot. I read Shakespeare and Tennessee Williams – I read constantly. I’m always trying to read about my craft.

My dad was an alcoholic who would disappear for three or four days at a time. I don’t remember him every hitting my mother, though that might be blocked out, but he would hit me and throw me around. But alcoholism is a disease – I don’t hold a grudge and I love my father. There are too many people who go, ‘Oh, I got beat up as a kid and now I do this’ and don’t take responsibility for their own problems, but I don’t go there. As far as I’m concerned, my dad has no part in my personality. When I get mad, it’s not my dad’s fault – it’s mine. I have an addictive personality, but that’s my deal.

I’d want to smack the teenage me if I met him now – he didn’t have his head on straight. My mother was ill with breast cancer for so long, there’s a lot of my childhood that I’ve just blocked out. My mother died when I was 18 – maybe a psychologist would help me deal with that, but I’m perfectly okay and don’t want to deal with it. If I could go back to my teenage self, I’d tell him not to yell at his mother.

Her last words to me were, 'Where were you?'. I'd run away to California – I couldn't deal with it. It took me ten years to deal with her death.

My younger self wouldn't be happy about the fame that's coming. When they were promoting *Bat Out of Hell*, they kept showing me these ads with me as 'the new star', and I kept taking the word star out. I don't see myself in those terms. I guess I'm a celebrity, but that's not my goal. I'm not like Madonna – she did remarkable work and was very smart, but her goal was to be a star. My goal was to work.

Each of my songs has a different character and I have little triggers I do to bring them to life, tapping my hand or whatever. It's like a spirit coming into your body. I have a wildness onstage, and if you push the right buttons, it comes out offstage, too – like when I was on *Celebrity Apprentice* and yelled at Gary Busey. They didn't edit it like it went down though, and I was very apologetic afterwards.

I don't regret anything, because you can't change it. My career has gone on for 47 years and I've made mistakes, but only because I didn't know any better at the time. I'm rebellious, but when someone asks me to do something I find it hard to say no – I can't let people down. When my doctor told me not to use my voice, I said, 'Well I'm singing for three hours tonight.'

I didn't know it then but when I lost my voice back in the '80s it was psychosomatic. I was singing fine then I had a thing with Todd Rundgren[72]. I said something about an arrangement of his and he said, 'If you can't speak to me in musical terms, don't speak to me at all.' So I just went, 'Fuck you.' Then the record company pushed us to make a new

72 Musician and record producer.

record really quickly and I thought that was stupid – *Bat Out of Hell* took a long time, which is why it was good. I had no way of getting out of the situation other than losing my voice. So I did.

I wish I could go back to the day in 1975 I sat down in a New York coffee shop, got my coffee and asked the guy next to me, 'Could you pass the Sweet'N Low?' The minute I heard him answer, I knew it was John Lennon. If I had an idol in the music business it was him, and I wanted to talk to him so bad, but everything I thought to say, I decided, 'No, that's stupid.' So the only thing I ever said to him was, 'Thanks for passing the Sweet'N Low.'

Mick Fleetwood

Musician

18 May 2015

At 16, the young Michael Fleetwood was dreaming his life away. School, conformity, the rules of the game – I was very confused by all that. I left school when I was 15 and immediately felt liberated. I was happy. I was excited. I was an adventurer. I became Dick Whittington, off to see what was happening. I had dreamed up this fantasy that might actually come true – to go to London and play the drums.

I was hugely inspired by my sisters, Sally and Susan. Susan was a fine actress and Sally was already in London, a sculptress in the world of the arts that I was fascinated by. She took me to all these coffee bars in Chelsea when I was on the way to boarding school, and I'm sure I romanticised them. I saw students smoking and playing folk guitar, with a Lenny Bruce record on in the corner, and I wanted to be in that club. The only thing I really knew was how to play drums. I had no great talent or technical ability, but I could play, and that could be my way in.

I knew my father – he was me and I was him. As a young chap he went on adventures and canoed down the Rhine. He saw things and wrote about them – he was a dreamer. He went into the army and the RAF and didn't like it, but flying fascinated him. He was an aviator more than a war pilot – he liked being between the earth and the sky. He wasn't a huff-and-puff guy with a moustache, aggrandising the game of war. He was one of many who did what he had to do, but he was revolted by the fact that he had to go and hack people to pieces. He thought deeply about things and probably aspired to be a writer his whole life. So he was overjoyed that I wanted to do something non-conformist. He would have loved to do that himself.

I've had a funny and crazy life, but I've never felt that I'd crashed and burned. I'd always dreamed of doing this, being a drummer in a band. I honestly don't think I ever lost sight of that vision, but probably there were times when it got close, when the band got very big and my life got very complicated. In many ways it still is, but the saving grace is that I'm still doing that one thing I can do – I've always kept on playing. Yes, I've got distracted at times, but even when I was in and out of financial problems and family problems, I kept playing.

My ability to play the drums was like having a safety net when I was failing exams at school. I have a better sense of what went wrong now, but I always had this sense of wellbeing, even at the worst times – my music got me through when the shit hit the fan. And my parents were always saying, 'You're okay. Who gives a shit how much you have in the bank?'

If I could go back, I'd find a way not to turn my back on the wave I was riding. I'd have liked not to have been so detached from my elder children, Amelia and Lucy, and my first wife Jenny – I'm aware that they got burned in the bonfire. There was never any malice from me to her or her to me, but there is a quiet sadness – if I'd had the tools, I like to think I'd have done a better job. I'd have been more present for them.

I don't think you can live with regrets. I think that's a losing game. But you need to have grace and admit to being vulnerable, especially as the years tick by and you think about what was going on. I'd say to my younger, narcissistic, self, 'You were like a fool putting his arse in a bonfire and pretending that he's not going to get burnt.' No doubt my behaviour hurt my family – I was full of love, but my life was on a track I couldn't get off.

I have moments of great sadness when I think of Peter Green.[73] He was crying out. Listen to 'Man of the World' and 'The Green Manalishi' – that song was like the temptation of the devil, eating him alive.[74] He's spoken about taking LSD, and he was already sensitive and on a journey of questioning everything. He came from a hard, working-class background and I had no concept of that. My family weren't wealthy, but the world I was in was very different and I had a great childhood – I had no excuse. Peter had memories he wanted to get away from. I think he got away and then felt guilty that he was attaining everything he had ever wanted.

If I knew then what I know now about mental illness and danger signals, I would have been a better friend to Peter.

73 The founder member of Fleetwood Mac suffered long periods of mental illness which led to him leaving the band in 1970.

74 Green says the song, written after a drug-induced dream, is about money, represented by the devil.

But I didn't know, and then it was too late – I was selfish. I spent years just wanting the old Peter back, and he never came back. He's changed, but he's alive. I had to let go of the relationships I once had, but I owe everything to that man and the faith he had in me from the start.

I'd tell the teenage Mick that he's going to be very lucky. He finds academic work very hard, but I'd tell him, 'Don't worry – just hang on to what you feel, Michael. That's the most important thing. Don't ever let go of it.' I'd like to say to him – and this is something I'm still not always successful at – 'You don't need to feel insecure about not being able to verbalise well – you're panicking, and that's getting in the way of you expressing yourself.' I know I can express myself now, but back then, I just wanted to make sure people knew I wasn't a fucking idiot.

Miriam Margolyes

Actor

3 November 2014

When I was 16 I wanted to be popular. I was popular with girls but not with boys, because I was fat, and I was quite angry inside that they couldn't see how fabulous I was. I wasn't academic. I wish I had been, but I was lazy and naughty.

I had a hothouse relationship with my parents. My family was like an impregnable fortress that only daddy and mummy and I were allowed in. It was a while before I realised that other children didn't have that. I used to get a bit fed up that I wasn't allowed to have a bicycle because my parents were afraid I'd get killed.

I was a performer from the minute I danced out of the womb, no question about it. If I didn't have an audience, I'd go and find one. I didn't know I'd be an actress though – I don't think I knew how good I was until after I left university. I deliberately went to Cambridge to move away from my parents, which was very distressing to them. But I'm glad I did it.

I didn't use to think I was like my mother, but now I see I'm very like her. When soldiers march, I cry. When I hear an opera singer, I cry. She was just like that, very emotional. My dad was the complete opposite – she was an extrovert and he was an introvert. She was confident and loud, but he was rather shy and nervous in all social encounters, except in his surgery. He was a GP and in his surgery he was paramount, but outside of it, he just sort of dwindled. I think he hid behind her. Whenever there was a problem and he had to speak to someone on the telephone he used to say, 'You speak, Ruth.' I was furious about that. He should have stood up to things, but he never did.

I would advise my younger self not to tell my mother I was gay. Some people can handle that kind of information and some can't, and she couldn't – it was too much for her. I think it's an indulgence of people who are gay to think that everyone's got to put up with their gayness. If it's a burden, we should be privileged to carry it and not insist on vomiting it over everybody else.

I've always felt a kind of guilt over my mother's stroke; she had it soon after I told her I was gay. People tell me I shouldn't think like that, but I do. We never lost our closeness, but when I met my partner I never told my mother she was my partner. I'm glad I didn't because she liked her, even though she couldn't speak to her. It's a funny thing, but I feel that if my mother hadn't had the stroke she would have stopped me being with my partner, and that would have destroyed my life. So maybe it was meant to be. But my mother was the victim and had to suffer, and that doesn't make me feel good.

My father made me swear on the Bible that I'd never sleep with a woman again. He took me into the lounge, a room we only ever used for solemn and social occasions, and I held the Bible and swore on it. And I suppose I meant it, but I also knew as I was saying the words that I wouldn't be able to keep them. Because sex is a powerful thing.

If I could go back, I wouldn't play around so much. I was not faithful to my partner; we didn't live together, so a lot of the time she wasn't physically there. And because I was never confident of being attractive, the fact that someone was prepared to go to bed with me was such a fabulous surprise that I went along with it. Now, of course, I'm old and I'm not able to play around. Nobody wants to fuck me now.

There are lots of things I wish I'd done. I wish I'd learned a foreign language. I wish I could type properly. I'd love to be able to ice skate and to tap dance. I can't even swim the crawl. I think it's a bit embarrassing to be 73 and not able to swim front crawl.

The younger me would be surprised that I didn't get married. Or maybe deep down she knew she'd never get married. I always knew I'd never have children. I think she'd be very disappointed to know she was still fat. If there's one thing I would change about my life, it would be my shape. I've been lazy and greedy, and that's why I'm fat – it's absolutely disgraceful. I'm quite healthy but I have gallstones and kidney stones I have to drink masses of water, so I keep pissing all day, which is a real nuisance.

If I was trying to impress my teenage self her, I'd tell her I toured a show which I wrote myself. *Dickens' Women* toured on and off for almost 25 years around the world. The teenage

Miriam read a lot of Dickens – *Great Expectations* was her favourite, though now it's *Little Dorrit*. She'd be impressed that I'd been invited to Sandringham for the weekend, and she'd be impressed that I got the OBE and a BAFTA.

I hear the voices of my parents in my head every day. They're always with me. Sometimes it's a bit irksome, wondering what they'd think of me. They wouldn't have approved of my criticism of Israel's behaviour regarding Gaza – they'd have thought I should shut up. I know that's what Maureen Lipman thinks, she tells me often enough.

If I could go back in time, it would be to when my headmistress told me that I'd been awarded a place at Cambridge. I remember the moment well. We were all called to the headmistress' study, and she read out the telegram, which my mother had sent to the school. She could have waited until I got home and had the pleasure of telling me, but she knew I'd get an incredible buzz from hearing it from the headmistress in front of all my compatriots. I think that shows what an utterly amazing woman she was. I knew right then that my life would change forever; I would join the company of the exalted. And I did.

CHAPTER 12:

Fulfilment

Sir Roger Bannister

Athlete

5 May 2014

At 16 I was focused on getting to Oxford. No member of my family had studied there and it was quite difficult to get in then. I was impatient to leave school for reasons I'm not sure of now, but I was keen to get on with my medical career.

I'd tell my younger self that he could and should learn more from his parents. I was rather independent then, though my parents did encourage me. I was always very active and involved in things. I threw myself into everything when I was at school, then when I was at university – I was president of the sporting club and the students' union. I always felt I must exploit the opportunities my parents hadn't enjoyed to the full. And Oxford is a wonderful place.

It seemed to be the fashion in Oxford to have a sport, so I went along to the track, paid my guinea and joined the athletics club. I didn't run very fast at first – I was included in the team because I'd been seen diligently shovelling snow. In my first big race I was the third-string runner and I was told to just keep out of the way. But with 200 yards to go I felt I could still run faster, so I proceeded to overtake everyone and won by 10 or 15 yards.

It was a windy day on 6 May 1954 in Vancouver, when I went to run in the Empire Games. The conditions weren't good. I only decided I was going to go for it half an hour before the race. My coach said to me, 'If you don't take the chance when you get offered it, you might regret it for the rest of your life.' In the end I ran in three minutes 59 seconds. I heard the announcement of the times over the tannoy by Norris McWhirter, founder of *The Guinness Book of Records*. When he got to 'a new world record, at three...' the crowd roared and nobody heard the seconds.

I think the world record was important to Britain. There was a feeling after the war that Britain was finished. We'd borrowed extensively from America and had to pay huge debts. We'd lost an empire. So we did things. We had the Festival of Britain in 1951. We had the climbing of Everest in 1953. We won nothing at the Helsinki Olympics in 1952, so everyone was very disappointed in me and the others. I knew I couldn't retire on such a disappointing note, so I had to stick with the running just a little longer.

For the first ten years of my medical career, it was an uphill battle to prove to others that I was dedicated to medicine and would not be moving into sport. For me there was never any doubt that medicine, ideally neurology, would be my career. My big dream was to add a small contribution to the knowledge we had about the brain. It was only after I'd been a consultant for many years that I considered offers like being chairman on the first independent Sports Council.

My wife has always been with me, helping in everything I've done. We have four children – my daughters, a painter and an Anglican priest; and my sons, a banker in America and CEO of the Phoenix Insurance Group. They're high achievers, but they all put family first. I have 14 grandchildren. My eldest grandson is the British champion motor glider.

I'd rather be remembered for my work in neurology than my running*. If you offered me the chance to make a great breakthrough in the study of the autonomic nerve system, I'd take that over the four-minute mile right away. I worked in medicine for 60 years; I ran for about eight. I enjoy my life now, but I'm not very mobile. I have something called Parkinson's Disease and unfortunately that restricts me, but I make the most of my life despite my hindrances.

* Roger Bannister died in March 2018 aged 88.

Dame Mary Beard

Classicist and Author

21 July 2014

When I was 16 I was a mixture of a terrible little swot and someone who fancied themselves as cool and radical – I couldn't make up my mind as to which I was. I was doing Latin, Greek and ancient history at school, but I desperately wanted to be where it was at. I was living in Shrewsbury and lusting after the big city and politics.

I wanted to be an archaeologist and had already been on some archaeological digs. It was fantastic to be able to tell your parents you were off doing something earnest and fine, but actually you were living on a campsite with other young people and had a ball of a time. It was like an archaeological Glastonbury – and sometimes just as muddy.

I wore loads of make-up at 16 and invested a lot in my appearance, but I think people always do. I think saying, 'So and so doesn't care about their appearance' is always wrong. For example, not dyeing my hair is a sign that I care about my hair in a different way.

Boys were on the radar. There was nothing more sexy than having a bloke. Our school was close to Shrewsbury School, so there were a lot of try-outs with blokes, which were usually not very satisfactory – just snogging and a few steamy letters, really. I'd tell my 16-year-old self that those snogging sessions won't come to anything.

Even in Shrewsbury there were attempts to experiment with mildly illegal substances, and that's difficult if you don't smoke, so smoking was not a vice. There was a little bit of pot going around but you couldn't inhale.

I certainly drank, because I used to go to the pub. I remember my mother would drink Guinness – which seems odd – or my parents would have sherry at home and I drank that with them. You didn't have a bottle of wine as you do now, it wasn't something you kept in the fridge.

I went to an all-girls school so I was cloistered. I would tell the 16-year-old Mary that there will be people who think you should give up your job when you have kids, and that there were jobs women would naturally not do. When I got to Cambridge I discovered there were these people and I felt ambivalent. I'd already formed ambitions without realising it was meant to be a struggle.

The one category the Romans and Greeks didn't have was 'teenager' – you went directly from childhood to adulthood, without a tortured, elongated process of becoming an adult in between. It's always interesting to think how different the ancients were from us. We think it's very natural that teenagers are difficult, but to some extent we must have created them like that. You don't hear much in the classical world about rebellious teens.

For a teenage girl in Shrewsbury, Angela Davis was really

quite exciting. I had a poster of her up at home and she was everything you wanted from a radical revolutionary – a woman, black and beautiful! I loved Janis Joplin and thought Bob Dylan was very cool, but Angela Davis was my hero. I can't remember how I got interested in the Black Power movement, but I did.

If someone had said to me at 16 that I'd be a professor of classics and on the telly, I would never have believed them. You can never quite remember what your ambitions were, as you always alter them. But I know the younger me would be very pleased with what I've done.

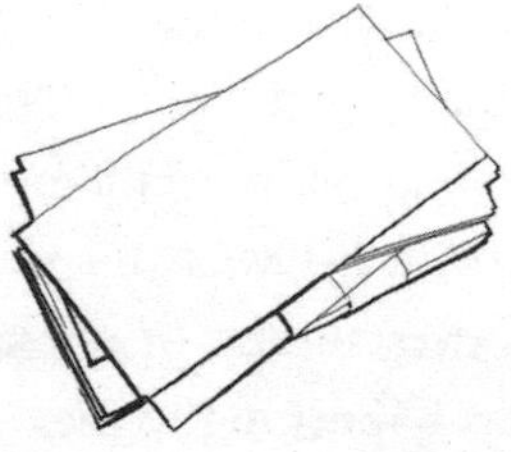

Colm Tóibín

Author

2 April 2018

My father died when I was 12, and for the first three years of secondary school I was in the school where he'd just been teaching. It was only years later, when I had to go into therapy, that I realised that as a schoolboy I always chose to sit in seats where no one could sit beside me. I went right to the back of the class and sat on my own, and I stopped seeing my old friends. Basically, I cut myself off for a couple of years. No teacher noticed that this boy, who'd just lost his dad, was sitting alone and walking home alone every day. But no one then had a real understanding of what an 11-year-old could feel. Or more to the point maybe, what an 11-year-old could not feel. I wish I – or anyone around me – had had some understanding of unexplored grief. I just had no idea what was happening to me.

My older sister went off to school after my dad died, so it was just me, my younger brother and my mother. We simply didn't talk about it. It wasn't to be mentioned. The house was briefly full of people, then they all left. I missed him, but even more than that, I just didn't know what to do with such a huge feeling of loss. None of us managed very well. If I could go back in time, I'd say to my mother, 'Look, we have to deal with this.' Instead, I became obsessed with poetry. Yeats, Heaney, Sylvia Plath – I must have been the only boy in Ireland reading 'You stand at the blackboard, daddy, In the picture I have of you'.[75] I started filling notebook after notebook with poems. Perhaps I'd have done that anyway, but the poetry held me together emotionally. And it still does.

By the time I was 16 I was outwardly quite a gregarious boy with lots of friends. A lot of my friends liked girls, and I enjoyed talking to girls too. I must have known that some of my friends were *really* interested in girls and thought, 'Well, I will be too when I meet the right one.' It took me a while to work that one out. You see, the whole thing about gay desire is that if you don't know about it, you don't understand what's going on at first. I must have been aware that I enjoyed any chance to see other boys without their clothes on, but I still didn't quite realise – I was just compartmentalising my thoughts and not handling them. I had no reference points. I mean, you heard the word 'queer', but there weren't any actual queers. It was like the word 'ghost'.

When I was in college I did meet a boy who really flaunted his sexuality. I avoided him like the plague until one day I found myself sitting next to him, and he turned out to be very funny. He turned to me and said, 'You're one too, aren't you?' We started to go round together, but I still really didn't know. Then I went to Barcelona and these two very good-

75 From 'Daddy' by Sylvia Plath.

looking boys started following me. I had many words in my lexicon but 'cruise' wasn't one of them, so I just thought, 'These lads couldn't be nicer.' Then I went back to theirs, and that was very exciting.

When I got to university, there were a lot of people writing poems and short stories, and they were all much better than me. It's been like that all along, really. I sent poems to the local newspaper and they never printed them. I read my friends' poems and could see something about my own just wasn't working. When I came back from Spain I started working as a journalist, but I still had this urge. I thought, 'God, I'm one of those sad people who has the urge but not the talent.' I started writing short stories but they got rejected too – they were no good. I tried to write a novel, but it took years for it to be accepted. The moment I found out it had been was a great moment. Eighteen months later, the first published copy arrived in the post. And then I was a new man.

I wouldn't bring the 16-year-old to accompany me to the Oscars, because it would be a let-down. He wouldn't see much showbiz. Have you ever seen a novelist at the Oscars? You're at the very, very back. You don't go through the main entrance. There's no red carpet. I found it all very funny. I went in the side door, but I wanted to say hello to the people I knew on the film, like Nick Hornby and Saoirse Ronan, so I waited in the foyer. But a man got on my case, saying, 'You sir, are going inside now – you're blocking the way.' I left but then sneaked back and he was right on me again. Afterwards I went to the *Vanity Fair* party, and as I was going in, Elton John was coming out. I nearly said something to him but thought, 'I know all about him, but I'm sure the last thing he needs is to know all about me.' When I went in everyone seemed to be making a fuss over some woman so I asked who she was and it was Lady Gaga. Oscar night is not a big night for the guy who wrote the novel.

If I could have one last conversation with anyone, it would be my father. I'd want to tell him everything that's happened. I didn't get to have any of those grown-up conversations and arguments, about the church – my father was a Catholic – or about politics – he was a Nationalist. I'd like to tell him how much Ireland's changed.

I drifted into journalism. I drifted to Spain. I drifted to America. And I drifted back home. I never had a career plan. Right now I teach at Columbia University in New York one semester a year. My boyfriend lives in Los Angeles; he's a very good swimmer, but I can beat him at tennis and he's younger than me. You can't know what this means to me – if he only knew the amount of work I've put into my forehand. The amount of pain and lost matches. Honestly, what a thing to tell that boy who sat alone at the back of that Christian Brothers classroom in 1967: 'In 51 years' time, life will be wonderful: you'll wake up in the morning in California with pomegranate trees outside your window. You'll get your breakfast juice straight from the orange tree in the garden. You'll go and play tennis with a younger, athletic man. And you'll win.'

Dominic West

Actor

27 December 2018

At 16, my main preoccupation was with getting drunk. Oh, and I played Hamlet in the school play. So I was quite focused on that, and the rest of the time I was trying to get illegal drinks in pubs. Did I have a privileged upbringing? Well, I grew up near the moors, just outside Sheffield, with six brothers and sisters. We had a couple of dogs and various other pets – hamsters, fish and all that crap. I spent most of my time on my bike going up and down the road. We were quite self-sufficient because there were so many brothers and sisters. We did have friends, but I don't remember leaving the house much because I just played with my siblings. So yes, it was a privileged childhood, spending all that time on the moors with my big, raucous family.

I didn't go through a big rebellious stage in my teens and I don't regret that. I was sent away to school when I was 13 and I was very unhappy, because I missed home so much.

But by 16 I'd got over that and I'd discovered acting, and that took up most of my thoughts. It helped me navigate this huge, amazing school I was at, and find my place. So I was a pretty happy 16-year-old.

I have five sisters, so even though I went to an all-boys school, I didn't have any fear of the opposite sex. Maybe I missed having girls around me, but we did have quite a lot of girlfriends coming down to visit us all at school… Actually, I didn't really have any girlfriends – I just wished I had. I had crushes that were unrequited. But when I was about 17 I started getting involved in plays and going to the Edinburgh Festival, and then it all kicked off.

I think as a teenager I was closer to my mum. I got to know my dad much better in my twenties and had a lovely time with him after they got divorced actually. So I ended up pretty close to them both. My mum was quite romantic and I'm also quite romantic in my ideas about things like Ireland, music and poetry. I'm quite a softie in that way. And I have romantic ideas about childhood, the simple life and living in the country. From my dad, I think I get my sense of humour; he was a very funny guy. And also my fairly Victorian idea of fatherhood – I'm pretty strict. I heavily limit my kids' screen time and insist they're in bed on time, mainly because we have five kids and I'm always knackered, so I get them out the way before we can start the drinking. But I'm also very affectionate with them.

I think deep down that when I started acting, it was probably the only thing I could do. And I thought I was good at it. Whether I thought I would ever make any money from it, I don't know. I enjoyed it so much that I thought it was a bit ludicrous that I'd ever be paid for it. I didn't think much about the future, but I did try to travel as much as I could. I hitchhiked across Europe when I was 18 and then went to South America, where I worked on a cattle farm in Argentina.

At Eton they identified what I was good at – acting – and gave me the facilities and opportunities to pursue that. I think very few schools do that because they don't have the resources, and a lot of talented actors don't get their chance. I was incredibly lucky to go to a school that could. It's true that Eton also gives people confidence, but that's a double-edged sword because often that confidence is misplaced. As is some people's assumption that they're the best people to run things. That's quite annoying and often quite offensive to people.

Of everything I've done, I think the teenage Dominic would be most impressed by *The Wire*. He'd be amazed that I actually managed to get into it and he'd have loved watching it. My mum loved theatre and couldn't understand why I'd ever want to do anything else. She came to see everything I did in the theatre and used to say, 'Why on earth are you doing American TV? What a complete waste of time.' I think because her mother-in-law was American she didn't like America very much. The teenage me would also not have expected to have five kids, and I certainly didn't think one of my kids would get a trial for Southampton FC. He's only 10 and it's just for the academy, but I was so bad at football that I couldn't have imagined that. The young me would be very impressed by him.

When I look back at my life, I might say to my younger self, 'Don't be so lazy – be bolder and shoot for the stars.' I don't know if it was through self-doubt or just laziness, but I feel I took the easy option a lot. In terms of work, and taking my job and my talent seriously, I let other people make decisions for me and allowed other people's ideas to cloud my own. I wish I hadn't always gone for the job my agent wanted me to take, which was often work that wasn't very interesting. What I wanted to do in my early twenties was experimental and radical theatre, but I didn't do it because I went off and got high instead. Maybe I did a bit too much partying and I should have... actually no, I enjoyed partying, fuck it.

I've been away working while my kids have been growing up and I have some regrets about that. It's only been for work I've really fought for, and I think I've usually put my family first. I haven't been careless – I've flown home every weekend. I was away a lot when I was making *The Wire* and that was pretty painful at times because of my daughter.[76] I regret that absence, but I did the best I could.

There was a wonderful woman in my life called Kay Eaton who very much looked after me when I was ill as a young child. She was my great-granddad's secretary and she helped me a lot. We had this joke that we were girlfriend and boyfriend – I was four years old. She never married. I really regret not being with her when she was dying. I was on a job away, and I think she didn't have a very nice death in a home in Sheffield. I wish I'd got to her and thanked her. She brought me great comfort when I was ill, and I wish I'd been able to do the same for her when she was dying.

I've just turned 49 and I've thought a lot about the time that's left. In terms of my career, I do regret not doing all the great Shakespeare roles when I was young because I do love Shakespeare. Though I don't wish I was still young. I

76 Martha, with then girlfriend Polly Astor.

don't feel guilty about much and I've done my best in the way I've treated people. God, this sounds like I'm just about to die! I don't know… I've always been a bit frightened of death. I suppose what I'm really frightened of, apart from the moment of death and the actual condition you're in when you die, is the regret that you didn't do as much as you might have. But really, it's all about my kids. I'm very conscious I'm at that stage when it's my last chance to be a big thing in their lives. I'm taking a lot of next year off to do that, so we can stay closely involved and be happy. Actually, when I think about it, I couldn't really give a rat's arse about my work.

I've never been so happy in my life as I have been in the last ten years. And it just seems to get better and better, because my kids and I are at a time when we give each other great joy. Last Christmas we went to see the giant trees in South California. I remember the whole day, from getting everyone out of the RV and walking up to the wood. There weren't many people around, the mist was lifting in the forest, the sun was coming up and we were in the presence of these astonishing 3,000-year-old giants. And I did get a sense of immense happiness and peace.

I have a strong sense of wishing my time would slow down so it could just be like this for a bit longer. I don't have a great foreboding about the future, but I do feel I'm in the summer of my life. And it can't last forever.

Eddie Izzard

Comedian

31 July 2017

When I was 16 I made a definite pact with myself to make a go of acting. I'd decided this at seven, but I reconfirmed it at 16, the way people renew their marriage vows. There was pressure to go to university – I'd got 12 O-Levels, so people kept asking what I was going to do. In my head the answer was be a performer. I'd made some headway with a decent part in a school play. I played a servant hand-cuffed to one of the main characters, a duke. I had this huge helmet on, with a visor that I could make go up and down as if by magic. So I kept doing this, while sitting with the duke in a pub, trying to drink a beer through this intermittently rising and falling visor. My teacher said, 'That's not really Shakespeare is it?' But it got a huge reaction, big laughs. And that was my first experience of comedy.

My mother died when I was six, and I got my first role in a Christopher Fry play when I was seven. I think, looking back, that I started performing to get affection from the audience. That seems like a swap I did. My mum liked amateur theatre and dad had a good sense of humour, so maybe I was merging their identities. I don't want to think about whether I might have been a different person if my mum hadn't died, because the way my brain works I'd spend hours going through different scenarios with her in them, and it would be too painful.

I have some very vivid memories of my early childhood. I think that's because my mum died – in the immediate years after, I would bathe myself in these memories. I didn't talk about it with my brother, but I went over them; 'And then we came back from school and she was there… And then that Christmas we wrote those letters and she put them up the chimney… Then we went to Sweden on holiday…' And I just kept re-painting them and locked them all in, and they stayed with me. Lots of people tell me they don't have any memories from before they were six, but I do. I have them painted brightly in.

I started using chemistry classes as a comedy practice tool. The teacher had a slow, methodical way of speaking and I started finishing his sentences. 'We have sodium and we have chloride and we put it...' 'In a bag?' 'No, not in a bag. We put it...' 'In your hat?' 'Not a hat – just shut up.' So I was getting the laughs. I only recently found out that my brother did exactly the same thing, with the same teacher. I wasn't an obvious romantic lead, but I did think that comedically, I was punching above my weight.

Even though I'm transgender, I am one of the lesbians, so when girls came back to school after three years I was quite excited. But I didn't impress them at all. 'Hey, I'm not in the team and I don't do much except the occasional bit of acting – do you want to go out with me?' I tried looking like a cool rebel by not doing any work, but that didn't impress them as they were all working very hard. There was nothing interesting going on with my looks. I couldn't master clothes and I was just about getting my acne together. I was discovering hairdryers and brushes, so you could stop your hair all going in one direction.

I describe myself as being emotionally dead when I was 16. I could function, I could hang out and I could pass some exams, but I was never brave enough to step in if someone was being bullied. I'd stand aside and hope someone else would come along and stop it. And then I'd feel ashamed. If someone bullied me though, I never cried – I just didn't feel anything.

I'd love to tell my teenage self that not only will he get to perform, he'll do it in multiple languages. He wanted to be in the forces, so I'd have to tell him, 'You won't be in the forces, but you'll do more marathons than anyone can count. And you know there's something different about you, though you wouldn't call it transgender yet – not only will you be able to come out with that, you'll actually stand for parliament. And most people will be okey-dokey with it. You'll go on the campaign trail and most people won't ask why you're wearing lipstick or a dress. They'll ask about schools and hospitals. Not everyone – some people are just full of hatred – but other people will tell them to shut up.' I'll be standing in the first general election after 2020.

There have been certain markers in my career when I thought I'd turned a corner. My brother was always very honest with me. He came to see my college shows and he wasn't very impressed. Then one day he came to see me at the

Town and Country Club 2 in Highbury and he said, 'Wow, you're really doing it now.' Then in around 1988 I went solo and started doing street performance. I'd go to Edinburgh and do my thing on the Mound. One day when I was setting up my little stage a man came up and said, 'Oh', and then ran off. Then he came back, dragging his whole family, and they all sat down to watch me. He was obviously saying, 'This is going to be good.' I suddenly realised I had the 'it' thing – I just had to get it indoors. Then in 1991 I was nominated for the Perrier Award.

In stand-up I don't think you play a character – I think it's you in brighter colours. It was a risky move coming out as what we used to call a transvestite, and I felt quite proud of myself. Back in the '80s I said I was TV and I had to explain to people that this didn't mean I was a television. I reclaimed the word transvestite, because then it was a very negative thing. I talked about 'boy-mode' and 'girl-mode', but I avoided telly. I still don't do sketch shows, sitcoms or panel shows – only interviews. I didn't want to get put in a box.

If I could go back to any time in my life it would be when we lived in Bangor in Northern Ireland, or Wonderland as I used to call it. It would have been just before the Troubles kicked in. Mum would be alive and I'd be in my gang in Ballyholme Primary School. I'd have a sugary breakfast then mum would hand me my satchel and she'd walk us to school. I'd paint a picture, then play in the playground and then we'd have one of those little cartons of milk that Margaret Thatcher eventually took away – obviously a horrible person. Those were just good days followed by more good days, and we didn't think it would ever change.

Harry Shearer

Actor

22 November 2010

I worked as a child actor, but by 16 I'd just started university and planned to be a very serious person. I was studying political science with a minor in Russian. I used to be fluent in it – my wife is tired of me pointing out that I read *The Brothers Karamazov*[77] in Russian. I was a bit of a smarty at school and had jumped two years ahead, which meant I was two years younger than everyone else at university. So socially I was retarded, a complete fish out of water.

I wasn't an easy-going child. I have a quick temper and was probably even more prone to act on it back then. If I met that kid now, I'd think he was callow, but I'd see he was a smart kid and I'd probably like him. He was far more orthodox in his beliefs than I am – he believed that one side had a monopoly on political wisdom and the truth. I haven't changed that much though, except – and people who know

77 Dostoevsky's infamously complex 1,000-page masterpiece.

me will be shocked to hear me say this – I'm probably a tad more mellow.

I tried doing a bunch of serious things when I came out of university, and along the way some friends were managing a Hollywood emporium-come-movieplex in Hollywood and I got involved in doing their radio advertising, making funny commercials. I met someone there who was involved in a new topical comedy show on the radio; I sent them a tape and by the time I got home, there was a message on my phone asking if I could come into work the next day. So I didn't have to think about it. It was a very exciting thing to be part of – a commercial rock'n'roll radio station with a show doing satire on very serious news. It was the perfect marriage of my interests. We did three ten-minute shows a day, with a deadline every three hours – ridiculous, but lots of fun.

I've always had a couple of guidelines I've tried to follow, 'don't do shit' being the main one. I tried to stay away from crappy stuff, so that if people saw my name attached to stuff they might have faith it would be good. On that basis, I'd tell myself not to make what was probably the worst basketball movie ever made – *The Fish that Saved Pittsburgh*. It had an excellent cast and a decent idea, but it was cursed by the hedonistic after-hours practices of the production team and turned out to be a total bunch of crap.

I like to do lots of characters, so I tried not to get stuck on just one character or one tone. I knew quickly that I wanted to be in showbiz for life, so I made choices to enhance my longevity and not get typecast. The only character I wouldn't have minded getting stuck with was Derek Smalls. I wouldn't have minded Spinal Tap taking a little less time to catch on, but it worked out pretty well. We didn't tell ourselves we'd made the funniest film of all time, but we knew we'd made exactly the film we wanted. I thought it had a good chance of succeeding because I thought the story we told was on the money. But though the box office was good, the distribution of that film was not. I've always chosen not to be in violent films, and I'm still proud that the only untoward incident inspired by one of my characters was when a former pro basketball player was arrested going through an airport metal detector with some marijuana wrapped in silver foil down his trousers.

I usually say what I think, but with *The Simpsons* I've learned through the years to let the audience decide how the show is going.[78] Am I saying that I've learned to shut up? Kind of...

The 16-year-old me would be amazed to find out that he'd be playing loud, stupid rock'n'roll shows in places like the Royal Albert Hall, Wembley, Glastonbury... That would really knock him back. But he'd have no idea what an amazing transaction you can get between a live audience and a performer, the sheer energy levels compared to performing on a comedy programme. It's like being hit by a force of nature, it's like the greatest wave you've ever ridden.

78 He was quoted in 2004 as saying he thought the show was declining in quality.

John Lydon

Musician

5 July 2010

My main concern at 16 was septic spots. Teenage acne – a living nightmare. I always felt unattractive, and thought no one would ever speak to me again. It's amazing at 16 how self-involved you are in an incredibly negative way. You eat yourself up with worries that aren't really important at all.

I was kicked out of school at 15. I was seen as a problem child because I would continually ask questions and had a way of forming a sentence that sounded like an incredible insult. I learned the art of implication and disguised aggression, but really, I just wanted to know things. The day I got expelled, I turned up late on my bicycle and in my long leather coat, as I often did, and the teacher refused to let me into the class. I refused to leave because it was an English literature class, which I loved, and we were studying Shakespeare. I was accused of being a Hells Angel – yeah, I was pretty damn tough on that bicycle – so then I had to go to a school for problem children.

I didn't speak much to my father around that time – he never much understood me. But after school I wanted to continue my education at college, so to raise the money I asked my dad to get me a job on the building sites where he worked. We were kind of alright after that because I was a hard worker and he liked that. But he couldn't understand me saving money to go off and read books – that made no sense to him.

If I could go back now, I'd be kinder to my parents. They went through an awful lot for me. I had some serious childhood illnesses and one left me in a coma, then I lost my memory. The years from about seven to 11 were spent trying to remember a lot of things, including who my parents were. They put up with all of that and I made life very difficult for them. By the time I was 17, I was running around with the Pistols. I wasn't a thief or a liar, but they didn't know where my mind and my imagination would take me next and I suppose that scared them.

I had problems adapting to the Sex Pistols – I didn't find too many like-minded souls. They didn't understand my concept of what a song was, or the topics I would pick. I mean, I raised a few eyebrows there. They had their little friendships and all knew each other really well, Sid and Paul, Malcolm and Glen. They picked me up when they saw me on the Kings Road in an 'I Hate Pink Floyd' T-shirt – Malcolm found that intriguing, but the others didn't understand.

I had Irish parents and grew up in England – I was naturally anti-establishment. I was always aware of that right-wing thing creeping around us, especially as I lived in a real melting pot of cultures and races in Finsbury Park. The place I was brought up in was freer, far less hateful and far more open-minded than any other part of the country I could imagine. The Pistols all came from a trendy, arty part of west London and were very narrow-minded in comparison. They were obsessed with impressing, wearing the right clothes and knowing the right people. Load of nonsense.

I wrote the songs because none of the others had any know-how with the written word. I took to it really well and will always appreciate them chaps because they gave me the chance to become a songwriter. I've always felt attached to the disenfranchised, being one myself, so when I wrote I put myself in the role of defending people with no defence strategy of their own. Any institution that expects you to be cannon fodder on their behalf is naturally my enemy. I had no personal animosity towards the royal family themselves. I felt sorry for them because they're born into an institution they can hardly understand. But there's a simple way out – just denounce the title.

The songs I wrote led to me being openly discussed in parliament under the Treason Act, which at that time carried a death penalty. I was making enemies in all the right places. I loved all that, but my manager[79] didn't. So he tried, through various acts of skulduggery, to create various silly scandals to try and take the attention away from the situation by forming red herrings in another direction. But I wanted the political slam of it. Being well-adjusted mentally, I felt I could handle a debate on that. I don't think I've ever written a song that was wrong. I believe that freedom of expression is a most excellent thing.

79 Malcolm McLaren.

With PiL[80] I got to pick the members, unlike with the Pistols – it was more rewarding in an artistic and humanistic way. Rather than attacking social issues, which I thought I'd done quite well in one album, I thought I'd analyse my own internal thought processes and try to come to grips with myself. In a weird way, the Pistols robbed me of the tail end of my childhood. You can't sort yourself out under that stress, and the alleged managers and adults that were supposedly trying to help us really weren't. So with PiL I went into self-analysis.

You can't always be the angry youth, and why would you want to be? You grow up. I'm looking forward to being 100. I'd love to be an old bugger in an old people's home driving them crazy – 'My nappy's wet! Where are my incontinence pants?' The old folks that shout all the time are letting you know they're alive! And you should rally around them for that, not reject them. They're trying to tell you something.

It's a shame that when I think of everything I've done, I'd trade it all to have brought a new life into the world. That's the most amazing, wonderful thing. I'd have loved to be a dad, but Nora and I couldn't have kids. I'm kind of well-known where I live for running really good parties for kids – Halloween, Guy Fawkes, I love doing it. I'm always up for looking after things. If I take a walk in the country, I find about five or six things I want to take home and look after. It's just the way I am – I can find a bird with a broken wing under a bush like no one's business.

80 Lydon's more experimental post-punk band Public Image Ltd.

Sir Rod Stewart

Musician

17 September 2018

I'd left school by the time I was 16. My dad got me a job in Kentish Town working as a screen printer, printing wallpapers. But I was a very unhappy screen printer. Around the same time, I lost my virginity, hence the song 'Maggie May', which is all about that. At 16 I was finding myself. I was quite shy with women, believe it or not – I still am. I think that was sort of a plus. I actually have a song about this on my new album called 'Look in Her Eyes'; it's about the kind of guys who just push themselves onto women and get the look in those women's eyes wrong, especially when there's alcohol involved. When I was 16, it was a different time, but I've never pushed myself on a woman. I know it's corny, but I've always enjoyed the romance of the chase and the general romance of the whole thing.

It was when I was about 16 that I had trials for Brentford. I was trying to be a footballer, but that all went pear-shaped.

If you'd asked me then what I wanted to be, I'd probably have said a footballer, but deep down I knew I wasn't that good at it. I was keeping my dad happy – he was a big Hibs fan and he really wanted one of his sons to make it. I had the basic skill but I didn't have the commitment. It wasn't a burning desire. Not like music was.

We didn't have much money; in fact we had no bloody money, but we were a tight clan. And we still are, the Stewarts. I had an extremely loving family. My dad wasn't very demonstrative with his love but I always knew it was there. I was sort of brought up by my sister Mary, who turned 90 on Boxing Day this year, bless her. I think my mum was getting tired of children and I was a little bit of a mistake. I wasn't meant to come along. As my brothers said, I was the most expensive mistake ever.

I was a happy kid, I didn't want for anything. Occasionally I'd get a new pair of football boots, but mostly it was hand-me-downs from my brothers. We had one football that was beaten to shit because we played in the street with it. We were just like any kids, playing football in the street. I try to teach my sons now to play on my pitch at home – I have a half-size AstroTurf pitch and it's beautiful. But they always want me to go out and play with them. I can most of the time, but I tell them, 'Listen, when your dad was young he used to play outside the pub waiting for his mum and dad.' My dad painted a tennis ball white so I could see it at night, and I used to just kick it about outside the pub while I was waiting for them to come out.

It was around the age of 16 that I first heard Sam Cooke, on a little transistor radio that I'd put against my ear when I travelled from Highgate to Kentish Town to go to work.

Then I suddenly turned into a Jack Kerouac rambling beatnik – I grew my hair long and started listening to all the great folk singers of the time. I think Woody Guthrie had just died and Bob Dylan had just made his first album, which was a huge influence on me. America seemed like such a romantic, distant place, and I remember listening to that album and it painted this picture for me of the US, of New York.

I didn't know I was much of a singer. I had a teacher at school called Mr Wainwright – I can still remember his fucking name – and he used to pick on me all the time and make me come to the front of the class and sing. I didn't have a clue how to sing but he kept making me, and in the end I used to make excuses to get out of his class. Then one year my dad bought me a guitar – he must have seen there was money in it. And that was it. It all took off. I always had this singing voice. There was a TV show made about me back in 1965 called 'Rod the Mod', and it shows me about the age of 18 singing at all the old clubs there were back in the day. And my voice was amazing, I must admit. I invited all my family round to watch it, about 40 or 50 people, and they all said my voice was amazing.

I love going to see Celtic play. I always watch the Celtic–Rangers match. For the last one, I'd just finished a gig in Seattle and I flew all the way to LA, heading straight to the Celtic Supporters' Club at quarter to four in the morning. It was packed. I walked in and said, 'Right, I'll have a double Cosmopolitan please.' knocked it back in one and had a hangover for the rest of the day. Ha!

I love my cars but I never actually passed my driving test. When we were in the Jeff Beck Group, we had a road manager called Pete Saunders, and he used to have to drop us off after gigs. Woody lived near the airport, I lived in Highgate and

Jeff lived in the south. The drive was killing him, so he said, 'I tell you what we'll do – I'll go and take your driving tests for you.' These were the days before you had to have your picture on them. So he did – then we had driving licenses and could take ourselves about.

The one thing that hasn't changed since I was 16 is my love of the blues. I did a show on Smooth FM and told them, 'Listen, I'm not going to play The Carpenters or Donovan. I'm not even going to play Adele, though I think she's brilliant. I'm here to pay homage to the guys that got me started – Muddy Waters and Sam Cooke. I owe that culture a great deal.' I used to laugh at my son Sean, because he always wanted to dress up like he was a black guy – tonnes of jewellery and his trousers hanging halfway down his arse. I said to him, 'You're the wrong colour, mate!' And he said, 'Dad, you used to try and sound like Otis Redding and Sam Cooke.' That shut me right up.

If you met the teenage Rod now, you'd probably think he was a cocky bastard and that he liked himself too much. But that's sort of attractive in a way. Then you'd think, 'Shit, he can sing.' The 16-year-old Rod wouldn't believe I'm still doing this at 73, and he'd be totally surprised that I'm still enjoying it as much as I did back then. He'd also be impressed that I still love football as much too, that I teach my four boys everything I know about the game. He would be impressed that the passion still exists in a 73-year-old to get out on the field and have a kickabout with his boys. He'd think, 'I hope I end up exactly like that.'

The idea of being splashed all over the tabloids for years – that wouldn't bother the young Rod. He'd love the thought of all that attention. He was born to be a show-off. With a nose and haircut like that, there was nothing he could have been but a rock star. I always say to Ronnie Wood, 'What else could we have been?' We weren't going to work in Sainsbury's, that's for sure. There's nothing wrong with working in Sainsbury's by the way.

Those years from the end of the '60s to the mid-70s, with six solo albums and three Faces albums, they were hectic. The only thing I didn't like was having to write lyrics. I remember Ronnie Lane and Ian McLagan[81] locking me in a hotel room and they wouldn't let me out till I'd written some lyrics. But the love of the music got me through. My favourite Faces song is 'Ooh La La', though I didn't sing on that – it was Ronnie Lane or Woody. Those were good old days, great fun. I wouldn't have missed them for the world. Was it as good on the inside as it looked from the outside? It was better! Being with the Faces was like Christmas Eve every night.

The break-up of my marriage to Rachel[82] – you don't know how you'll feel until it happens to you. You never have the right tools to handle it. Until that point in my life I thought I was Jack the Lad. Then she left me. I remember my older sister Mary saying, 'You know one day she won't be with you?' And I said, 'Of course she will!' But Rachel was only 21 when I married her and I was fortysomething. It knocked me. If I was giving advice to my younger self I'd say, 'Look mate, there's no way round it, there's no way over it and there's no way through it. Just remember what King Solomon said: all things pass.' And they do pass, and in time you do get over it. And life goes on.

---

81 Ronnie and Ian were in the Small Faces and Faces as the bass guitarist and keyboard player respectively.

82 Hunter, who left him in 1999, after nine years together.

I stepped up the pace of work again with *The Great American Songbook*. I did that as a labour of love, and it's sold nearly 30 million copies now. Then I did another album, and then I did my autobiography, which opened up the floodgates. I just thought, 'Jesus Christ, my mum and dad have already passed' and it made me realise how much I wanted to know about my family and my past. My brother and sister were telling me stories about the war, all my mates were telling me stories and so were all the guys I'd been in bands with, and I thought, 'I've got so much to write about.' I started writing songs again. And I thoroughly enjoy it now.

I've never written a song and thought it was a classic. Never ever. 'Maggie May' wasn't even supposed to go on the album. We had nine tracks and the record company came to me and said, 'Look, we can't put an album out with just nine tracks – do you have anything else?' And I said, 'Well, I've got this one song. It doesn't really have a title yet, but I could give it one.' And if that song hadn't been on the album, I wouldn't be here talking to you today. Well, maybe not.

If I could go back to one moment in my life, it would probably be when I was in The Faces. I was driving an old Rolls-Royce and heading to Swiss Cottage in London, and the BBC came on and told me 'Maggie May' was number one. I turned the car round, went to my mum and dad's council house in Highgate, walked through the door and told them. We all had a big hug and we all cried. Then I said, 'Well, I've got to go now, I'm meeting some friends', and off I went. That was probably the most joyous moment I've ever had. But trust me, I've had many, many others.

CHAPTER 13:

Love

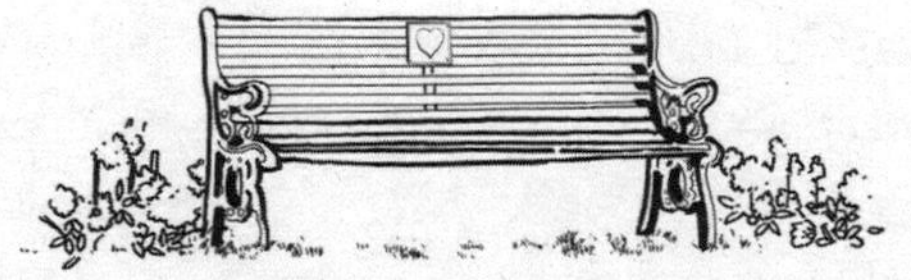

E. L. James

Author

10 December 2012

Even at 16 I was quite successful with boys, actually. I don't think I was especially attractive – I was a bit of a hippie with my beads, desert boots and Indian dresses – but there were boys 'hanging around', shall we say.

When I was 16 I'd started rebelling a bit, but I don't think I was an angsty teen. The mother-daughter thing was challenging, but I think it is at that age. Otherwise I was very happy at school, I had lots of friends and I was working part-time for Sainsbury's, so I had a bit of money. At the time I might have thought I was angsty, but looking back I think I was just an anxious teenager, who's turned into an equally anxious adult. I definitely thought of myself as overweight, but really I wasn't. I'd say to my younger self, 'For God's sake, don't worry about your weight now – you can worry about it later.'

If I went back and met the younger me now I'd find her a bit reticent, but funny. We'd both be nervous, anxious people trying to talk to each other. She'd be mostly fretting about boys and exam results. If I told her what was in store, on the one hand she'd be very proud about getting published – she'd been writing stories since primary school. But she'd be completely freaked out by the thought of fame. If I gave her a hint of the scale of the success, she'd be giddy and scared. And to be honest, that's how I still feel.

I'd tell my 16-year-old self, 'Value your privacy.' I don't feel like a public persona, but people make assumptions about you based on nothing. It's frightening. Going through the process since *50 Shades* began to take off, I've realised that I don't want celebrity. I'm not interested in doing lots of interviews, going on TV, any of that. I want to be able to go on the Tube and listen to my iPod and no one knows who I am. I've had a very successful career in TV, which I really enjoyed, so to have all this suddenly happen to me in my middle age has been a huge bonus and it's been great fun, but I almost feel it's happening to somebody else. Visiting Hollywood, that was a hell of a week. I'd like to go back in time and live that again more slowly and take it in. I met the most interesting, talented people. It was a bit of a whirlwind, though a bit stressful too. But the real me comes home at night and does the laundry and chats to my children. All the other stuff is kind of unreal.

I wouldn't change the books – I wrote them for myself and it would be disingenuous to change anything about them. But if I'd known how successful they'd be, I might go back and tell myself, 'Don't talk to anyone in the media about them, ever.' I try very hard when dealing with the media to just be myself, but I've become a lot more guarded lately because so many things get taken out of context. People are obsessed with my sex life, which is completely bizarre – it's a work of fiction!

My sons just take the piss out of me all the time, as teenage sons do with their mother. But they've been so cool about it all, so supportive and proud of me. They're also faintly embarrassed and also not that interested because they're getting on with their own lives, which is fantastic. I know they haven't read the books. They're not that keen on reading at all – they're boys and they have Play Station 3s. It's a huge shame and an irony that Niall and I are both writers and our children won't read. My father died in 2002, but my mum's read the books a couple of times and she loves them. She's very proud of me.

I believe my readers are mostly interested in the love story – that's the overwhelming response. The press seem to navel-gaze about the sex, but what the readers want is the love story. Women love to read a passionate love story and that's fundamentally what it is. I've had loads of letters from male readers too – one great one from a guy who's 71 and said, 'Thank you so much for reminding me what it's like to fall in love.' That's so sweet.

My favourite books are the ones that capture that feeling of falling in love. *Twilight*, definitely. *50 Shades* started as a piece of *Twilight* fan fiction. I think it's an absolutely fantastic, beautiful love story. I like *Jane Eyre* as well, and *Emma* – Mr Knightley! That's just lovely. Emma not realising she's in love is just like Christian in *50 Shades* – he doesn't realise he's in love, either.

My husband's great, and very family-orientated. Advice to my younger self about men: find one that makes you laugh, above everything else. A sense of humour can get you through so many things. And you need a man who lets you breathe.

I always wanted to be a mother, though when it happened I wasn't prepared for all the hard work. But I feel incredibly lucky. There's a whole other story there that I won't go into, but it wasn't easy for us to have children and when we finally did... I do not take my children for granted. I adore them – they're fabulous. The birth of my first son was so incredible and such a gift, having a little tiny baby. I was just beside myself with happiness.

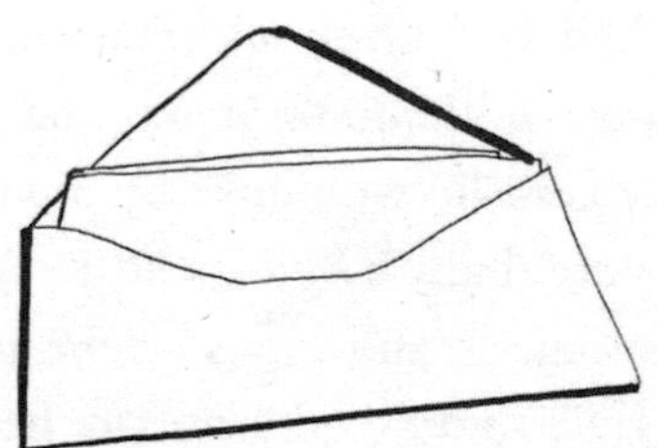

50 Cent

Musician

26 October 2015

At 16 I had already been involved in street life for years.[83] I was aggressive enough to get by on the street, but then I'd go home and be my grandmother's baby. I was outside hustling, but I still had to talk my grandmother into letting me walk home from school myself. I said to her, 'Look, I'm bigger than you now.'

I came to live in my grandmother's house when some of my mother's eight siblings were still there.[84] My Aunt Sylvie, she hated me being there. She'd been the baby, then suddenly it was me. My grandmother would look at me and there would be a little moment when she wouldn't say anything, then she'd say, 'Come on here, baby.' And I said to Sylvie, 'Do you notice she always pauses and looks at me before she speaks to me?' And Sylvie said she did notice, because

83 50 Cent, born Curtis Jackson started dealing drugs at 12.

84 His mother, a cocaine dealer, was murdered when he was eight.

everyone noticed. And I said, 'I think she sees my mother's face on top of mine.'

I think shock is the best way to describe how I felt when my mother died. I didn't understand it. When you have a single parent as your guardian – they're your whole life. I was eight and I was just like, 'What do you mean?' She'd spent a lot of time away from me – she was always hustling. She had to be very tough, to be around a lot of men – she had to adapt. At that time, they didn't have teen programmes helping teen mothers. My mother was 15 when she had me and she wanted to give me what I needed, so she couldn't rely on welfare.

It scared me half to death when my grandmother was diagnosed with cancer. My aunt would call me with updates all the time and she always said, 'Don't worry, she's fine.' I've never told anyone this, but two years ago, the day she called to tell me... It was early in the morning and I was on a treadmill in the gym. I got to the hospital and the whole family was there. My aunt told me the doctor said she'd had a stroke and there was nothing they could do. They took me to see her and she was the smallest I ever saw her. I said 'Hello?' and I saw her eyes jump when she heard my voice, like she was trying to see where I was at. Everyone else left and I talked to her for a little bit, then they all came back in and her heart rate started to drop. My aunt said, 'Shit, she was waiting for you.' I've seen a lot of people pass in the neighbourhood – I've lost them to motorcycles or altercations or drugs. But none of them impacted me like when my grandmother died. She was the love of my life.

I felt I had to do whatever it took to get by. The stuff that came out of my mouth when I was outside the house – wow, that kid was crazy. I was the youngest in the pack; everyone else was at least 16. People told my grandmother stuff I'd done and she'd say, 'Nope, not my baby.' We all wanted nice things and nice clothes because we wanted to attract girls. So we had to hustle to afford them.

When you get hurt as badly as I did[85] you become afraid of everything, because you know anything can happen at any time. I got shot in the afternoon, in broad daylight, so I got scared, and that made me harder than I was before. The only time I was comfortable was when I didn't care. So I just said, 'Fuck it.' When you have the pistol and you're looking for them, your attention is shifted. You're not afraid anymore. You're like, 'I hope that *is* them coming up the block now.'

I started writing lyrics full time in 1997. I met Jam Master Jay from Run DMC and he had a label which would take people on and develop them until they were ready to go to a major. Jay taught me how to count bars and when the chorus should start and stop, and I kept practising. Sometimes hard work beats talent. I wrote all the time, so I got better and better.

I think Jay liked me because I looked like the lyrics. I had all the jewellery and I looked like a hustler. I'd been on the street so long that people respected me. The honest truth is at that point, the drug dealers were the leaders of the neighbourhood and had more money than the rappers. The things LL Cool J and Run DMC wanted were the things guys hustling already had. Now, of course, the artists are way richer than the dealers – hip-hop culture has grown so much.

Eminem had this competitive energy that made him the

85 50 Cent was shot nine times at close range in 2000.

guy all the other rappers worried about.[86] From the early days, he was this great battle artist. The guys who were up against him would think of everything you could say about him and he'd say those things about himself first, so he took away everything they had against him. He was writing all this personal stuff. I was never anything like that – I came into music with songwriting intentions, because that's where the money was.

If I could talk to my teenage self, I'd tell him to focus on music with a stronger intensity. He could still have this career without going through all the things I went through. And thinking about relationships – I think back to when I was with someone and that person could have been the person I was with for the rest of my life, but I didn't have the references to know there was something special there. It's like the clarity I got about my grandmother after she was gone. Some people have been better at that than me; if I look at Jay-Z, I'd point out that he capitalised on people better than I did.

If I could go back to any time, I'd go back to when the sales figures for the first week of *Get Rich or Die Tryin*'[*] came out. I went to sit at the back of the tour bus and just thought, 'Wow.' I couldn't believe it. When I got those sales, I knew that from then on I didn't have to wait for someone else to say it was okay – I could say it was okay myself. But I also knew that feeling, that confirmation, of finally having the momentum – you only feel it once. I knew I'd never have that feeling again. Because everything was about to change.

86 Eminem signed 50 Cent to Shady Records in 2002.

* The album debuted at Number one on the Billboard charts on 2003, selling over 870,000 copies in the first week. It went on to sell around 13 million copies.

John Cleese

Comedian and Actor

5 January 2015

I was rather a simple teenager because sport mattered so much to me. I was at a rugby-playing school, but I was not the right shape for it and it didn't appeal to me – it was too much about brawn and not about brain. But I did adore soccer and cricket, and if I could have played for Bristol City or Somerset I'd have died a happy man. One of my happiest ever times was during my last year at prep school. I was about 13 and it was a glorious summer. I had my little group of friends and I was captain of the cricket team. I began to feel confident, that I might be good at things.

Shortly after I was confirmed, I decided religion was a load of rubbish. I was expecting some sort of gold haze to descend on me, and when it didn't I gave it up in anger. When I studied for confirmation, the process of taking me through the spiritual issues was pathetic. I would have liked someone to ask me if I thought there was an afterlife and what might it be like, instead of just being given a doctrine about what I had to believe.

If I met the young John now, I'd try to bring out his interest in wider subjects and I'd recommend books for him to read. One of the disappointments of my life is the lack of intellectual stimulation there was in my younger life. I was vaguely interested in the meaning of life, that kind of thing, but those interests weren't stimulated in any way by school, nor by my parents. Mother read the *Daily Express* and books about doctors and nurses falling in love, and dad read things like Nevil Shute, but books on history or philosophy weren't on their radar screen. I didn't have very good models in my parents. But one thing I did get from my mother was that she had a great sense of humour and there was no question when we communicated best – we were at our closest when we laughed.

I think I spent too much of my life doing what I thought I ought to do and didn't have enough fun. The problem when I got to Cambridge was that I was too dutiful. I very much admired people like Stephen Fry who just said, 'Well, I'm not going to go to lectures,' and spent the time doing what they wanted to. I might have seemed a bit strange to people because I was relatively introverted and often used to sit in my room at Cambridge and just read a book by the light of my Anglepoise. There was a group at Cambridge called the Eggheads, and I was never approached to join because I was never regarded as serious. But I was happy there, until I fell in love for the first time and the heartbreak began, and it didn't really go away for many years.

I was famously late in developing my romantic life. And because I didn't always choose wisely, I brought into my life stresses that weren't there before I started dating. I made a series of mistakes with women who, let's just say made a lot of demands of me which I often was not able to fulfil. I found it difficult to speak to women because I'd been to single-sex schools, and my relationship with my mother, tip-toeing around her, made it more difficult. I behaved very similarly in relationships. I had a tendency to placate women, and if I was unhappy about something I'd be most likely to sweep it under the carpet. Over time I got better at that. There was a bit of my dad in me. I would meet someone and think, 'It would be lovely to make this person happy.' Unfortunately, unhappy people tend to stay unhappy.

As my time went on at Cambridge, I began to develop a much wilder, more inventive kind of humour. After I did *The Frost Report*, which was actually a pretty conventional show, I did *At Last the 1948 Show*, and that was when my humour became wilder and sillier. And of course, that was the perfect introduction to Monty Python. Python was a risk but we felt safety in numbers. We all thought it was funny, and though we had no idea if anyone else would, that gave us much more confidence than if we'd been on our own. If I hadn't met them, I might have just stayed a writer. I needed to be in a group to perform. There's a reason I've never done *The John Cleese Show*.

By accident, I got into a business where I was given a lot of attention. If I'd been a lawyer, which it looked like I would when I left Cambridge, I wouldn't have been under the scrutiny of newspapers. That stuff isn't easy to handle, especially when you're so young. I remember my dentist said my jawline had changed because, since I'd had all that attention I'd started grinding my teeth.

Romantic relationships, alongside my relationships with my daughters, have always been far more important to me than my work. I remember Terry Gilliam once said to me, 'You're always saying the work isn't particularly important to you, but look how happy you are now that *Wanda*'s a hit.' But that was because my relationship with a woman was good at the time. It took me a very long time to find a good relationship, but I'm very happy now. If you asked me what I would like most right now, I'd like someone to leave me £2 million so I could buy a house in London with a garden, and Jenny and I could have another cat and a dog and I could do nothing but read for the next nine months.

Ambition has had a very limited importance for me; 'The paths of glory lead but to the grave', as Thomas Gray's great poem says. I learned that poem when I was 19 and I've carried it with me ever since. What does it all add up to in the end? You might be a king or have pots of money, but how significant is that, how happy does it make you? The saddest things the Americans have misinformed us about is that it's all about public success; that's why they're such a miserable, neurotic, competitive bunch.

I don't need much to make me happy: cats, books, nice food and good weather. I get offered a fair amount of honours – 'Would you come here, do this?' – and I think, 'There may have been a time when I would have been flattered by this, but now I just don't need it.' It's unimportant to me what my professional legacy is. It's much more important to me that when I die, people I've been close to think I was a decent, kind chap.

Neil Gaiman

Author

30 January 2017

At 16 it was 1977 and I was a punk. I talked three school friends into forming a band called XXX – I was the singer and songwriter. I was... 'blossoming' is the wrong word, but I was moving out of geeky. Many years later I went to a recording of a BBC Radio 4 comedy and I ran into Steve Punt afterwards. He said, 'Oh, you're Neil Gaiman!' I waited for him to say his kids loved *Coraline* and instead he said, 'I was at your gig.' I saw this little moment of his starry eyes. I wish I could go back and give that moment to the teenage Neil doing his first gig in the school hall. And I wish I could also tell the young Neil, who eventually gave up all fantasies of rock stardom, that there will be a weird time in the future when he'll be onstage in Tasmania reading his poetry to an audience with a backing bank that includes David Byrne. Or that he'll sell out Carnegie Hall for a gig in which, after a reading, he'll sing the country song 'Psycho' with a string quartet. So he'll get to fulfil those rock star fantasies after all.

The punk thing has always been a driving force – the idea that you do something by doing it. You don't need to know what you're doing because you can learn on the job. It meant than when I did start out as a writer, I put a Muddy Waters quote on my typewriter: 'Don't let your mouth write no cheque your tail can't cash.' I knew it was fine that I could talk my way into things but then I had to do the work. When I was 16 I thought everything would happen by magic. I'd been a freelance writer for six months and had advances for two books. I had no idea if I could write a book – I just said yes when people asked.

It's been really interesting recently talking to friends I've had since I was a teenager. My friend recently drew a comic that shows all this monstrous chaos going on all around the young me, and I'm just calmly walking down corridors reading *Stranger in a Strange Land* or *The Left Hand of Darkness*, happy to be living in the land of books. I definitely didn't feel I fitted in. I was awkward, uncomfortable and not terribly happy in the real world but incredibly happy in books. I used them as a survival guide and also as an escape. I dreamed of becoming a writer but it seemed impossible, like dreaming of having invisibility or super-speed.

If I really wanted to show off to teenage Neil, I'd show him my five Hugo Awards. Those awards for science fiction would matter more to him than the Carnegie Medal or any other award. The fact that I've collaborated with Harlan Ellison or had dinner with Lou Reed, that would be cool to him, but the idea that grown-up Neil has Hugo Awards, the younger me would think, 'Wow, yeah, I came through.' And if could tell the 12-year-old Neil that one day he'll write a *Doctor Who* episode... wow. Especially as 'The Doctor's Wife' came from an idea I had watching it when I was about eight.

In 2009, my father died in the middle of a business meeting when I was on my way to New York to do a book signing. I got a phone call from a sister when I was in the taxi, saying that dad just had a heart attack and died. I stopped, walked around a bit, then went on to the signing. There were about 12,000 people there and I started signing at about one o'clock and finished about nine at night. Then I went home. And there was a message from my dad on the answer machine. It was just a cheerful message, saying, 'It was mine and your mother's fiftieth wedding anniversary yesterday – beautiful weather and you know, it was a lovely sunny day 50 years ago, too. Anyway, just calling to say hello. And you're not there.' And that was the first time I cried. I just heard his voice and fell apart. If I'd known it was going to happen like that... there are so many things where I look back and think, 'I wish I'd asked you that, I wish I'd written that down, I wish I'd taped that conversation.'

There are friends I thought would be around forever who just went, like Douglas Adams. I loved Douglas – he was big and complicated and irritating and wonderful in equal measure. When he died I was being interviewed on the phone. Suddenly it flashed across my computer screen: 'Douglas Adams is dead.' The journalist called me up about a month later and said he was transcribing the interview but there was nothing he could use after I read that Douglas was dead, because I wasn't even there anymore. So many people who were part of my life and my landscape – I wish I could go back and encourage myself to spend more time with those people, learn more from them. Whenever somebody dies I feel I'm kicked up the arse by the universe.

Time is a beef, and I wish I'd known how fast it goes. I wish I'd enjoyed it more. Stephen King – and again, I wish 16-year-old Neil had been able to be there, he'd have been in complete joy – showed up at a book signing of mine in Boston in 1992 and afterwards we went to his hotel. He gave me the best bit of advice. He said, 'You know, you've got to enjoy this. This is magic. You do a signing and hundreds come. You're one of the most beloved comics writers in the world. Enjoy it.' But I never did. I worried it would all go away. I worried I'd break it. And it wasn't until I was 48 and met my wife Amanda[87] that I thought, 'Oh, you run your life completely differently to mine. You fill it with doing the things you like, and meeting the people you like and eating the things you like. I suppose I could try that too.'

I still worry. I suspect it's how I'm built. The fear that I can't do it is probably the driving force that keeps me writing. That part of me is actually in my books, too – I do really good 'menace is just around the corner'. My novel, *The Ocean at the End of the Lane* is not actually autobiographical, but that kid is me. I was going back to the seven-year-old me and giving myself a peculiar kind of love that I didn't have. That book was me saying to him, 'It's okay, everything's going to be fine.' I never feel the past is dead or young Neil isn't around anymore. He's still there, hiding in a library somewhere, looking for a doorway that will lead him to somewhere safe where everything works.

If I could live one day again, I'd take my fiftieth party in

87 American artist Amanda Palmer.

New Orleans. In the morning my wife, who was still my fiancée then, inveigled me into a hat shop and bought me a top hat. Then she said she was off to find a tea shop and she'd text me when she found one. Ten minutes later I headed off to meet her, crossing a big square on the way. And there was Amanda, dressed as a bride, posing as a human statue. And then a load of our friends stepped out of the crowd and my friend Jason performed a non-binding marriage ceremony between an author in a top hat and a human statue dressed as a bride. The whole thing was wonderful. I looked around at all my loved ones and thought, 'Okay, this is what you get for being alive for fifty years.'

Amanda is amazing. There was this point where I thought, 'I think I want to marry you because I'm never going be bored again.' She's enough like me – well, we're from the same planet. But she does these amazing, surprising, peculiar things that I would never think of doing. These things where you think, 'Really? You're really going to do that? Okay. I'll stand here and hold your clothes and if you get arrested I'll bail you out. I love you.'

Olivia Colman

Actor

15 April 2013

Boys were my main preoccupation when I was 16. I was fairly successful with them, against the odds. In a room full of girls I'm not sure they would have pointed me out, but I always got on well with them and think they thought I was fun to be with. I was low-maintenance and low-drama.

I was never very good at school and used to dread going. It never came easy for me; I always felt there must be something else. I started to like school a little more as I got older because the teachers began to treat us more like grown-ups. Then at 16 I had my first school play – I was Jean Brodie in *The Prime of Miss Jean Brodie* – and I immediately thought, 'This is what want to do. I don't want to do anything else.' And that was lucky, because I'm not qualified to do anything else.

As a teenager I worried in private about lots of things, but I was good at faking it. I worried about school work, what I looked like, whether my hair was a bit too this or that. But I was never one of those surly teenagers who doesn't smile. My lovely godfather said it was always lovely to see me, because I was the only teenager who smiled. And I was so in awe of him that I thought it was one of the best things anyone had ever said to me. So it made me want to live up to what he said. He was adored by everyone, a bit like Ollie Reed with less booze. He was funny and witty and handsome and gorgeous. When I did Miss Jean Brodie he said I was 'Amazing, amazing – fucking brilliant.'

I was a fairly jolly teenager but even the most sane people go slightly nuts when their hormones are flying about. There was a time when I had a problem with not eating and was struggling with body confidence. But I kept smiling at everyone. I had black clouds, and I still do. As I've grown up, I know when there's a black fug coming and that it'll pass. My friends and my dear husband know, and they know that with some tea and cuddles it'll eventually go. I had postnatal depression after my first baby, but I knew I loved my baby and have always been able to see what I have in my life. It would be nice to go back to those early fugs and tell my younger self, 'You'll be okay. This will pass. And you will be loved. Don't make any rash decisions in this moment. You can make the world work and have a brilliant time. And if you're not skinny, fuck it.' I'm basically a pretty upbeat person.

I wish I'd worn fewer clothes at 16. I'd say to myself, 'If you don't like your body now, just wait till you get older.' My body has changed as I've had children, but I feel much more confident now. I'd like to tell young Olivia, 'You're lovely, you're loveable. Life is not bad for you.'

I wouldn't tell my younger self about anything that will happen to her – if I told her she was going to achieve her dream, she'd stop trying. You need that fire up your arse, you really do. And I still feel it. I know what it's like not to work, to struggle, because I had a whole year of not working, when I had a few auditions and failed every one. I still feel that today, that anxiety. I don't want to be there again. It's much nicer not worrying.

Of all the things I've done, I think my teenage self would be most excited about Paddy Considine's film *Tyrannosaur*. All I ever wanted to do was act in something great. My younger self wouldn't be surprised that I've been best known as a comic actress – my 'in' with people was always to be funny. I loved every second of *Peep Show*, *Rev* and *Twenty Twelve*, and Robert Webb and David Mitchell are two of my favourite people in the world.

I always desperately wanted to be a mum. I've always been in touch with my emotions – I'd be the one left sobbing in the cinema. But when I had children it took away my skin completely. So now, at the hint of feeling something, I'll be crying on the bus. I have no armour at all. My husband is a bit the same. We sit watching *One Born Every Minute*, clutching each other in tears every time a new baby comes out. Making *Broadchurch*, I couldn't stop crying. It's just awful, the idea that your children could go before you. I'd have a scene and they'd say, 'You're not crying in this scene,' and I'd think, 'Yeah right – good luck with that.'

I'd love to go back and relive the first time I ever saw my husband. And the first time we said we loved each other. It was at the rehearsals of a play. I immediately thought, 'That's the person I'm going to marry.' I absolutely threw myself in – I didn't play it cool. And at first he just couldn't see it. He can be very slow on the uptake. I had to work on him. I remember one day, about three months later, him saying, 'What are you thinking?' And I said, 'I love you'. I knew I had him by then. We married seven years later and we've been together 19 years. He's the best person in the world.

Simon Callow

Actor

23 November 2009

At 16 I was short, fat and very uncomfortable in my own skin, but that might not have been apparent to anyone else because I was very articulate and very noisy and extroverted. Mine was a depressingly bad school from an academic point of view, though I had one wonderful teacher who introduced me to Baudelaire, Flaubert, Mozart and sherry. It would have been so much better if I could have found a way of enjoying games, but it was such a macho culture and full of aggression, that I just loathed it.

I think my teenage unhappiness was partly due to sexuality – I thought I was gay but didn't know what to do about that and I thought no one I knew would understand. More generally, I just hated being 16. I hated childhood, in fact – detested it. I thought of it as an unbelievably tedious period you had to get through, like being in hospital. You're beholden to adults, you have no money of your own. I was aching to get out into the world. I felt imprisoned.

I wish I'd spent more of my adolescence making love. I'd love to go back and put the teenage Simon into public school, only because he might have met someone and had a nice love affair. As it was, it wasn't until I was 21 that I had one.

I lived alone with my mother – she and my father broke up when I was 18 months old. We lived in a small, cramped flat together and we didn't get on brilliantly, because we had such different temperaments. She was very quirky, full of theories – she favoured Swedish reform cooking, which meant a lot of salads, which children hate, of course. She was a very experimental cook, but had no gift for cooking. She was very strict, and liked laws and rules, as well as corporal punishment. If I wasn't doing homework I had to be completing a household duty. But one thing, we did laugh together a lot.

Counterbalancing my mother, I had two excellent grandmothers. Father's was a very tough, hard-working woman who adored me and took me to the theatre and the cinema. My mother's mother was probably the most formative influence on my whole life. She had an extraordinarily generous, rich, big personality, very embracing, loved partying. She didn't have much of a formal education, but she believed in the supremacy of human personality. She was always shovelling jelly babies, cigarettes and antibiotics at me – she had no sense of boundaries at all. She thought if she liked those things, why wouldn't a 13-year-old boy?

If I met the younger Simon now, I'd think he was a noisy, hyperactive, opinionated show off, though not unintelligent. I might be surprised how well read he was. And I might be surprised that he was quite a kind person. The 16-year-old me would be shocked to find out I'd become an actor; he wanted to be a writer, and wrote constantly. But when I left school, I was going to the theatre a lot and I wrote a letter to Laurence Olivier. He wrote back and said that if I liked theatre so much, why didn't I get a job in it? So I took his advice and went to work in the box office at the Old Vic, until I eventually went off to study acting.

I do wonder what would have happened if I'd gone with *Amadeus* when it went to Broadway. Paul Scofield, who played Salieri to my Mozart[88] didn't want to go so I didn't go either, but I would have loved to have gone. And it might have changed my life, because it was the most amazing success of the decade. When I started acting I expected to be a classical actor and play all the great Shakespeare roles. I haven't remotely done that, but I'd done so many other things; directed, written, done sitcoms and films. I've had some great cameos, like *Amadeus* and *A Room with a View*. But I'd have loved to have done more films and bigger parts.

My mother always kept me mentally stimulated, and I thank her for that because I've never been bored. I don't think I had it ingrained into me that I was entitled to happiness – I can't really relax and have fun, because I always want to work. If I had to choose between being happy and having my mind engaged, I'd always choose being engaged.

I'm immensely proud of *Four Weddings*. It was the height of the AIDS epidemic and it was so great to play a gay man who wasn't dying of AIDS. That film possibly changed a lot of people's ideas about homosexuality. It was so cleverly written; some people might not have even noticed that John Hannah and I were lovers until the funeral. It came as such a bombshell and it was so loving and witty and celebratory, and

88 In the 1979 National Theatre production.

I don't think anything like that had ever been done before. Hugh Grant says in the film, 'We never noticed we already had a perfect marriage in our lives,' and he's referring, of course, to us. We were the great love story.

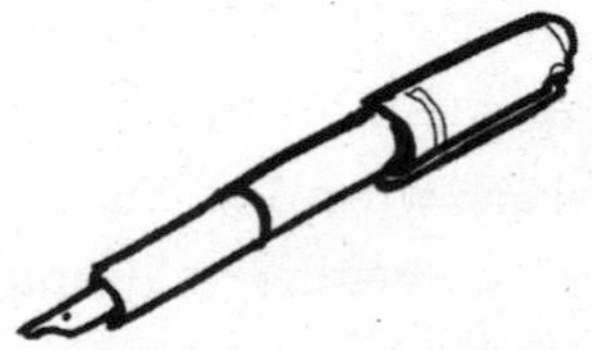

Wilko Johnson

Musician

6 July 2015

I kept a diary when I was a teenager. It's excruciating to read it now – me getting really uptight about stuff that's going down. I'd love to get in a time machine and go to that teenager and slap him round the head. 'You absolute twat! You have no idea. None of this matters.' But then again, every now and again you find this tiny hint of something that will become really significant, like a record you've bought.

I hated school. Oh dear, I hated it. School's horrible, isn't it? There you are, being dictated to by mediocrities with leather patches on their elbows – you're actually oppressed. You always get these celebrities telling you about these teachers who changed their lives. It amazes me. I can't think of a single one of those people I have anything but contempt for.

I knew very little about music, but when I was about 15 I fancied playing the guitar and getting all the girls. Through learning the guitar I started to find out about music. I heard

The Rolling Stones, and I thought, 'Wow'. Then I looked into what influenced them. So I discovered American blues music. I never had any ambition to be a rock star. It was just fun. I'd never have believed I was going to have decades living the dream in the world of rock'n'roll.

Everybody must have asked themselves, 'What would my reaction be if the doctor told me I was going to die?' When I was told in 2013 that I had terminal, inoperable cancer, the way it struck me – I was immediately calm. I resolutely set myself against ever indulging in false hopes or looking for miracle cures. Although this tumour, which ended up at three and a half kilos, the size of a baby, was growing inside me, I still felt healthy. I wasn't losing weight or in any pain, so I didn't want to waste the little time I had left.

I spent the whole year after I was diagnosed believing life was at an end. I moved into this strange intense consciousness. It was very interesting – I saw everything differently. I was thinking so intensely, having real insights about life that I can't even put into words. I believed completely that I was going to die and I accepted it absolutely. And I started to feel alive.

Just over a year after my diagnosis, I met this top surgeon who told me he could operate. I had been misdiagnosed. I remember this very impressive man sitting by my bed, telling me what this big, complicated operation involved, and I was just looking at him thinking, 'Is this guy telling me he can actually cure me? After a year of accepting there's no cure? Is this just another mad thing that's going to happen this year?' Before I knew where I was, I was waking up in hospital. Then a couple of days later the surgeon came to see me on the ward to say that he had the lab reports and they'd 'got it all'. I was sitting with my brother and we started applauding!

If I could go back and whisper in my ear at the moment of my terminal diagnosis that I was actually going to live, would I? No, I don't think I would. During that year, so many amazing things happened. My farewell tour, making the album – everything was so emotionally charged. People came up to me in the street and shook my hand. I remember a gig in Kyoto, it was absolutely rammed. Oh man, at the end of this song, 'Bye Bye Johnny', I looked down and just saw a sea of faces with tears in their eyes, looking up at me and singing, 'Bye-bye'. It didn't make me sad. I thought it was amazing to feel such affection. I came home with sackfuls of letters from these people who really cared about me, written in broken English, which made them all the more touching. None of that would have happened if I hadn't been facing death. There were times onstage when it was so overwhelming that I thought, 'You know what? It's almost worth it.'

I'm parachuting back into the land of the living now. For a while I was actually afraid to say out loud that they'd got all the cancer out, that I'm cured. But I can say it now. When I look back at that year, it's almost like a fading dream. And now I'm back to being like everyone else, dreading going to the doctor in case they tell me I've got cancer. I don't think, 'Oh that's alright – I've done that before. I'll just have a groovy insightful time.' All the old fears have come back, and I know I'm really getting better now because misery has descended upon me again. I'm back to the old me, moping about the place.

If I could go back and live one time in my life over again, I'd go to the mid-'70s. Things were good for me then. I had everything I ever wanted: money, sex, drugs and rock'n'roll. Dr Feelgood were doing great. I had my little family. I always had a video camera, and I have hours and hours of home video footage. When I watch them I see my wife Irene – it doesn't upset me, she's there, that's great. Then I see my son, a little toddler, in the back garden and oh dear, he breaks my heart. You have kids and you love them so much. What can you love more than a three-year-old kid? But time is constantly taking them away from you. That three-year-old kid, you're never going to see him again.

I never worried about getting a girlfriend, because I was very happily married by the time I was 19. And I remained so. Me and my missus, we were together until she died ten years ago of cancer, and I, well man... I'm in love with her still. I still really miss her. I first saw her down Canvey Island youth club when I was 16. I can still picture her standing there. Then my band played the school leavers' party and I danced with her, and her friend told me I'd been dancing with Irene. That was the first time I heard her name. A few weeks later I got to walk her home and I kissed her outside her gate. It knocked me off my feet. I just went Blammo! And I remember when she died, I went to see her in the morgue. She was lying on this table. God, Jesus man... she looked like a saint. And I kissed her. And she was cold. I remember that last kiss and I remember the first kiss and there were 40 beautiful years in between.

Bonus Material

Billie Piper

Actress and Filmmaker

2 March 2021

In my early teens, I was already at a theatre school in London – Sylvia Young – with the intention of becoming an actor. I became the face of the *Smash Hits* magazine relaunch in the mid-nineties and had a series of commercials running in tandem. Hugh Goldsmith (managing director of Innocent Records, who launched his Virgin-affiliate label with Billie's 1998 hit 'Because We Want To') asked me to make a demo, which went well because I loved singing. I didn't think I was a great singer but I could definitely hold a tune. Then, I don't know how long after that – it felt like overnight, I have no concept of time frame around those years of my life – he signed me. And I started just doing live shows.

By the time I was 16, I had left Swindon and was living in London on my own. I was in a hotel in Maida Vale at first, then I got together with this guy who had a flat in Kilburn and I wanted to move in with him because I was lonely.

I was working every day for up to 18 hours, living on a diet of garage food and takeaways. I was obsessed with music so I was living for MTV or The Box, they were constantly on a loop on my TV. I wasn't fully reclusive by that stage, I still had energy and a desire to be part of the world. I'd been working for two solid years, but I was still in a slightly more positive place than I'd be two years later. I think, in my own small person's head, I felt equipped to live that life at 16. And maybe I was practically. But not emotionally.

Those teenage years are a period of my life that I'm reflecting on now for the first time in my adult life. And there's a lot of missing pieces, to be honest, which I think speaks for itself. Those first few years were totally thrilling, and I just felt like I was living a dream of mine, but I was often in very strange, very adult situations that I wouldn't subject my own kids to at 16. Actually, my real takeaway from my 16th year is just how exhausted I was, because I was a teenager going through everything a teenager goes through but very publicly, with a schedule that would rival a high-flying businessperson. It must have looked peculiar from the outside, but I was having fun at that point, so I couldn't feel what that really meant. And I certainly normalised it very quickly.

It wasn't too long before that pop star life just stopped sitting well. I was absolutely burnt out and my love of performing was non-existent. I wanted to have a normal life. And I missed acting. There were a few things happening. One of the things I'd got so used to was having number one records and a high level of success. Then I had a single that didn't chart well and I remember thinking that it was the biggest failure ever. At the same time, I was sort of unravelling personally. That combination led me to think I needed some time off to re-evaluate what I wanted to do. I was so sick of doing what people wanted me to do. All of this thinking was subconscious, I'm not sure how aware of those moods I was, but that's what I ended up doing. Thank God!

I got into a meaningful relationship at that difficult time, where there was encouragement to prioritise myself for a while. So that was very helpful. Yes, my time with Chris Evans was partly parties and pubs, but it was also another education in many ways. It felt like my uni years, in the sense that I was meeting all these different people. I was living my life without a schedule and I was learning a lot from it. Also, I was with someone who was incredibly optimistic and wilful and definitely operating in a way that was very aspirational. Someone who knew what he wanted. And that felt very new to me, to be honest. I'd always seen people working for other people. He seemed to be working for himself, on his own path, with big intentions. That was quite inspiring.

Always in my head, the whole time throughout my singing career, was my hope to be an actor. In fact, that's why I decided to go with the singing career, because I felt like it would open doors for me in the future. Also, I got to perform, which I loved. So, the acting ambition was always there, it was just a question of when there would be confidence to rebuild. I had to go and do lots of lessons and training again. And then it was just a case of getting an agent and going to castings and being horribly rejected over and over. Having to prove myself twice as hard because people felt like they already knew everything about me as a person. And I think at that point I had quite a reckless reputation so there was a lot of fucking legwork!

I felt really, really emotional when I got the job as Rose (Tyler) in *Doctor Who*. I took my nan out for high tea in London, and I told her, and then it felt really real, because we had a very close relationship and she knew I had this passion for acting. So, yeah, it was super-thrilling, really exciting, and very moving for me because I wasn't sure which way my life would go. I didn't know if I was going to go back to normal life after my singing career, a life where I wasn't pursuing the things I wanted to pursue.

If I'm at a convention, they often show 'Doomsday' (the *Doctor Who* episode which saw the final parting between Rose and The Doctor) before they introduce me on stage and I find it so upsetting. I remember what it meant to me. It all felt very big. On a personal level, I had become very close to David (Tennant) and we'd been through something very big together. I was sad about losing a sort of everyday friendship. Also, I think Russell (T. Davies) writes in such a way that you can't help but be moved by his writing. There's this sort of 'life will out' spirit coursing through all of his work, which is very moving. Also, that episode marks me choosing to walk away from something that had been really significant and integral in my life and I was quite nervous about that. And as well as leaving the show, I was moving back to London into my own flat, Chris and I had separated – what was I going to do next?

I would love to go back to my former self and say, 'None of this matters. You're amazing, you're going to do just fine.' Therapy has been crucial to my getting better, so I'd tell my younger self to get a therapist. I just don't know how young kids cope anymore, I really don't. I think everyone's super-anxious, or at least that's how it feels to me. If you can get your kids any sort of mental health support or family therapy, just get it. There's no shame in it whatsoever. When I think of characters like Suzie and Mandy (from the TV show *I Hate Suzie* and the Piper-directed film *Rare Beasts*), they might have had quite different lives if they'd had therapy.

If I could go back and have one more conversation in my younger days, I think I'd go back to pre-fame years with my mum and dad. Because I think everyone's relationship really took a hit during those years and it would be nice to go back and reflect on that in a way that was much more focused. We had little contact and a strange sort of arm's-length relationship which is fine now, but if I could, I would go back and prepare us all more for that.

If I could go back and relive any time in my life, I would go back to my very, very early teens, just out of Year 7, going into Year 8, when I had full anonymity. No paranoia about everyone knowing who you are. I'd just hold onto those moments with my mates, driving around in boy racer cars, Oasis or The Prodigy playing on the radio. Smoking fags. Kissing everyone. Those feelings of freedom and abundance. Living a life full of things that are so inconsequential. That is my idea of heaven.

Dave Grohl

Musician, Singer-Songwriter and Filmmaker

31 March 2020

At 16, I was already fully immersed in music and learning to write and record and perform. I was a music junkie. So, I was amassing this crazy record collection, most of it underground independent Punk Rock bands. But I wasn't only listening to the albums for personal enjoyment, I was learning to play my instruments from them. I never took drum lessons, I just learned from listening to Led Zeppelin and Bad Brains and The Police and Sex Pistols records. I didn't have a teacher to show me how to write songs, I just had a Beatles' songbook. I would sit and play along to Beatles' songs and I started understanding composition and arrangement and harmony and melody and dissonance. And riff and core and rhythm. So, I was pretty locked into my bedroom at that age. If I wasn't on the bus to and from school, I was in my bedroom, just studying these albums.

I was a terrible student in school, which unfortunately made for an uncomfortable adolescence because my mother was a high school English teacher at the fucking school I knew I was failing in. I really had little interest in what most people thought was the conventional route to take in life. I just thought, 'When I'm free, I'm just going to play music and find a way to pay the rent, because there's no way I could become a professional musician. I'm just going to work at the Furniture Warehouse, or at the local gardening nursery, or at best, an independent record label, but as long as I have a bed, a lamp and an apartment, I'll make the rest work.' I was a romantic, idealistic 16-year-old, I really was. I just thought, 'Okay, the world is mine.' I don't think I knew right from wrong, I thought I'd figure out life just as I figured out these songs.

It's funny that Nirvana became so famous for this Gen X darker side of life thing, because I truly had a very happy childhood. My parents divorced when I was six or seven years old, so my mother raised me. I think because she was a public school teacher, she understood people, especially kids. She really gave me freedoms that a lot of other kids didn't have. As an English teacher, a brilliant writer and a teacher of public speaking, she understood the importance of having some sort of creative outlet in your life. I would sit in my room and write poetry which was fucking awful, but who cares? I was trying to express myself. I look back on my childhood as a very inspired time and I still wake up almost every day feeling like an excited kid.

My mother and I were, and still are, so close. We've always been friends. The mother-child dynamic was definitely there but there was also a real friendship. She would take me to jazz clubs, we would go see movies together. I think I was the only one of my friends who actually enjoyed hanging out with a parent. Our bond was so close that over time, I think she developed this faith that I was going to be okay. Being a school teacher, she realised I sucked at school. She understood that, rather than sit in a fluorescent-lit school room and have someone try to teach me Italian, I'd be better off just going to Italy, living in a squat and having to ask someone 'Where's the nearest pharmacy?' As a parent myself now, it's hard for me to fathom my mother accepting my just disappearing into Europe when I was so young. I didn't have a calling card or money. I would fly standby to Amsterdam and say, 'Okay, I'll see you in two months,' and then send a postcard every three weeks. I'd lose my fucking mind if my child did that. That's a leap of faith, to let your child wander out into the world on their own. But she was right, I was okay. And to this day, my mother and I speak with each other almost every day.

I would probably tell my former self, 'You're gonna make it.' I had this incredible nihilistic fear of war. In the eighties, there was this threat of mutually assured destruction you lived under. And it's such a terrible way to live. I feel like I should have appreciated the world more, rather than living in fear that it would disappear. I still vividly remember the nightmares I had when I was young, of seeing missiles flying over my backyard and mushroom clouds. It just robs you of any hope. I lived with that fear for a long time. I could never imagine myself as an 85-year-old man, watching the sunset. I always imagined, in this dark, pessimistic way, that things weren't going to turn out well. That may have exposed some of my darker tendencies.

If you met the teenage me, first of all, you'd think this person has more energy than any human being I've ever seen.

I was an outrageously hyperactive kid. And from the time I was eight years old, I was a performer. I wanted people to laugh, I wanted people to be happy. I wanted people to dance, to feel good. I would put on shows for my family and friends for no reason. I'd do anything for a laugh. Man, I just had this restless energy – I was like a fucking gnat, I just couldn't stop! But I was also given a good sense of Southern manners by both of my parents. They were both raised in the Midwest in Ohio, but I grew up in Virginia, so my childhood had a tinge of Southern culture to it. So, at an early age I knew there were three things that you don't talk about at the dinner table: politics, religion or money. And I was a good kid, I wasn't gonna steal the stereo out of your car. I was gonna try my best not to offend you in any way. I mean, I'm kind of the antithesis of all of the bands that I loved, Punk Rock bands and fucking satanic Death Metal. But I'd mow your lawn on Sunday for five hours. That's kind of the way it worked.

When I was being raised by a public school teacher, there was never any money. I mean, we just got by. We lived in a little 1,300 square foot house with one bathroom and a small kitchen, just my mother, my sister and I. And we found joy in the simplest things. I never felt like I needed more, a bigger house or a better bike or any of that. For our family trip in the summer, the three of us would pile into our tiny Ford Fiesta and drive to Ohio or Chicago, which is a good 12-hour drive, going through mountain passes and cornfields. And I also learned about rhythm in a funny way on those trips. My mother and I would sit up front in the car and she taught me how to sing harmonies, or we would do these little games – Name That Tune. Or snap our fingers to the song on the radio as we drove through the mountain passes to see if, when we came out of the tunnel, I was still on the beat. Honestly, it taught me about rhythm and metre and still to this day, it's one of my favourite games to play. Those were the days, man!

Both of my parents were musicians – my father was a classically trained flautist and my mother was a singer, though neither of them went professional. I do believe that DNA has something to do with a person's musical capability. It gives you a head start. I think that having been first raised by these two musical people, and having that hyperactive nature, the drums were a pretty obvious choice for me. I mean, I didn't even have a fucking drum set when I was learning how to play drums! I had two drumsticks that were actually marching sticks so they were gigantically fat and I would set up pillows in the formation of a drum set and play along to Ramones records, or Minor Threat records with really fast, 200-beats-per-minute, aggressive drumming. So, when I was 16 and someone gave me an actual normal pair of drumsticks on a normal drum set, I just shattered everything. I was breaking cymbals like they were teacups. That's the reason I've always been such a basher. I've tried to learn the subtleties of dynamic drumming, but it's no use. So, when the rock'n'roll bug hit, I really decided, 'This is who I am.' All the sport went out the window. I was like, 'This is my passion, this is my love.'

Through my life, there have been a lot of moments when I couldn't believe they were happening. I have to say the biggest would probably be getting to meet Paul McCartney and recording a song with him in my own studio in Northridge California, with Krist (Novoselic) and Pat (Smear) from Nirvana, writing and arranging a song from scratch in one day. Just the four of us.

So, Paul starts playing a riff and we all start playing along. And then the stars align and we become connected and the vibe is there and the groove is there. And everyone starts smiling and it becomes that tide that goes back and forth between musicians when they play. So, we record a take and then it's time for the vocals, and I sit and watch Paul McCartney singing lead vocal on something me and my friends just recorded. And then he asks me to go in and sing backup. And I say, 'Okay, what should I do, should I do a harmony?' And he says, 'No, no, just double exactly what I just did. That's what me and John Lennon used to do.' If I could go back and tell my 16-year-old self that someday that would happen, he would say, 'You're fucked up. No way on earth could this possibly ever happen.'

When I first met Kurt (Cobain) and Chris (Novoselic), musically, it was a match made in heaven. But personally, it was a bit off, to be honest. Of course, we loved each other. We were friends. But, you know, there was a dysfunction in Nirvana that a band like Foo Fighters doesn't have. You also have to realise, from the time I joined Nirvana to the time it was over was only about four years. It wasn't a long period of time. Was I close to Kurt, as I am to Taylor Hawkins? No. I did live with Chris and his wife when I first joined the band. I think it lasted a month and then they kicked me out, but we always had this sort of loving connection and it was made even more so after Kurt died. When I see Chris now, I hug him like family. But back then, we were young and the world was just so strange. But that emotional dysfunction in Nirvana was relieved when we put on instruments. If the music hadn't worked, we wouldn't have been there together. I truly believe that there's some people you can only communicate with musically. And sometimes that's an even greater, deeper communication. There are people that I might feel a little awkward talking to, but once we strap on instruments, it's like they're the love of my life.

There was a particular trauma after the end of Nirvana that lasted for a while, but, you know, I think that love of music I had when I was a child eclipsed everything and I realised that music was going to be the thing that would write me out of that depression. For a while there, I wasn't sure if I ever wanted to play music again. But it came back. And thankfully, just as I had hoped, it healed me. To me, music has always been about life. It was the thing I most loved about life, more than anything else. After Nirvana, I needed it to keep me alive and it's the reason why I never stopped.

If I could go back to any time in my life, I remember standing on stage with . . . no, I have another memory. I think of when my 14-year-old daughter Violet played her first show. She's a singer, she's got an incredible voice. Her band was playing at this little club with a lot of bands who were all ten, 12 years old. And my mother came. And I sat there watching my daughter on stage, nervous for her, because I wanted her to do great. And the next day, my mother called and she said, 'Now you know what it feels like to be a parent, watching your child up on stage with that funny haircut, crossing your fingers, hoping they'll make it out of there alive. And with all that pride and happiness and love and joy. Well, that's how I've felt for the last 30 years.'

Dolly Parton

Singer-Songwriter, Actress and Humanitarian

19 October 2020

I actually was a pretty good girl at 16. I was in high school at the time but I had been taking my music very seriously for several years before that, taking trips back and forth to Nashville with my Uncle Bill Owens from my home in East Tennessee, 200 miles away. We'd take some old car and sleep in it, trying to go into different offices in Nashville. We'd stay a few days to try to get a few things going. I didn't have time to run around and mess with boys. And my dad was pretty strict anyway, so I pretty much spent my teenage years just working on my music and hanging out with friends when I had an opportunity.

I was about 13 when I first met Johnny (Cash) and that's when Johnny was all strung out on drugs and everything, but he was so magnetic, so sexy. He was my first male grown-up crush, he just really moved me. That's when I realised what hormones do and what sex appeal really means. He just kind of stirred me somehow. And so I guess that's when I realised I was becoming a little woman. Oh, we laughed about it through the years. I told him, 'You know, you were my very first crush, my first sexy grown-up crush.' He always got a kick out of that.

I knew I wanted to always stay true to my roots. I knew I loved my family – I would never shame them, I was proud of my family. But I just had a feeling inside my gut that I was supposed to do something more. I felt it in my bones early on, it was just like a calling. I wanted to go beyond the Smoky Mountains. My family knew that as well, even though it was a little different for a low mountain girl.

I'm very proud of the fact that I'm so much both of my parents. I can see it so plain in myself. I got my spiritual side and my musical side from my mom's people. Most of them played musical instruments and sang, and we all grew up in the Church. We were the family that played at funerals and weddings and all kinds of shindigs. My dad's people were mainly hard-working people; I got his work ethic and willingness to stick to it until I get the job done. I know what part of me is Daddy and I know what part is Mama and I think it's a good combination. It's why I've lasted so long. Usually, creative musicians are basically kind of physically lazy. They want to stay up all night and write and sing and sleep all day. But like my dad, I get up really early, I work hard and I go to bed fairly early. And I love the fact that I'm not a lazy head, I'm not sluggish. I think that's been a big part of my success – I'm up and at it before most people can get out of bed.

My mom and dad were both very proud of me. My mom was more lenient in the early days, she used to have to cover for me. My dad didn't want me travelling – 'traipsing around' as he called it – he didn't like me going away to Nashville. He and my mom used to have words about that. So, I'd go before he got home from work and Mama had to defend me on that one. She'd say, 'She's alright, and she's gonna leave, whether you like it or not.' Mama understood it because she was a dreamer also. But he was pretty strict – I thought sometimes in the early days he was too strict. It's not that he didn't trust me, he just didn't trust the world. But after I moved to Nashville, he saw that I was serious about it and it was real work and a dream that was actually possible. And he became my biggest fan and biggest supporter.

I always knew my ambition was going to happen, they couldn't preach it out of me. I was going to be a star, I was going to go to Nashville, I was going to sing my songs no matter what. I was never a rebel without a cause, I was not a rebellious child. I did it with grace and style. I wasn't out to cause any grief at all for my mom or dad but I was willing to take whatever punishment I might have got for going against somebody's ruling. I am strong in my beliefs. There is an old saying, 'To thine own self be true'. That has followed me all the days of my life. I know who I am, I know what I'm not. I know what I can and cannot do. I don't get myself involved in things that I know are out of my realm. But if there's something I can do and I want to do, hell or high water ain't gonna stop me! I'm an easy person to work with, but I will not bend to your ways if they go against mine. I have my standards and my principles and if you push me to a point that does not agree with my soul, I will call you on it and I will not compromise. I don't feel like I have to answer to anyone but myself and to God. That's my rule.

It's true I would not compromise with Colonel Tom (Parker, Elvis Presley's manager). Elvis wanted to record 'I Will Always Love You'. They planned the session and told me they were recording the song. I'd been invited down to the studio to meet Elvis and be there when he sang my song. That was the most exciting thing that had ever happened to me. Who doesn't love Elvis? But then the Colonel called me the afternoon before the session and said, 'You do know we have to have at least half the publishing on any song that Elvis records?' And I said, 'No, I did not know that.' He said, 'Well, it's just a rule.' So, I said, 'Well, it's not my rule.' I said, 'I hate this more than you could even imagine but I cannot give you half the publishing. I just can't do it and I won't do it.'

'I Will Always Love You' had been a number one song with me already, it was the most important song in my catalogue. And I cried all night long, 'cause I was so disappointed. It wasn't Elvis, I loved Elvis. And I'm sure he was as disappointed as I was because he had it all worked up and ready to go.

I know he loved the song. Priscilla told me later that he sang that song to her when they were coming down the steps of the courthouse after they divorced. That really touched me and I thought, 'Oh well, I can only imagine.' But it wasn't his fault. I found out later that Colonel Tom had an even bigger demand for any brand new song Elvis recorded: in those cases, 100 per cent of the publishing went to them. Yeah, Tom was a strict manager, he was a good manager and I don't blame him for asking, but I don't blame me for saying no.

When you write songs, you don't know what's going to be a hit. As a songwriter, you know when some songs are better than others and I knew that 'I Will Always Love You' was probably one of the best things that I'd written, because it came from so much heart and soul. But you never know what's going to be a hit or everybody would be rich. I knew it was a good song, but I had no idea that it could ever become what it did, after Whitney recorded it and it went into such a big hit movie (*The Bodyguard*). I'll always be grateful to Kevin Costner and obviously, I'll always be grateful to and always love Whitney Houston.

'Jolene' and 'I Will Always Love You' were on the same album (*Jolene*) around 1972. In fact, they came from the same cassette so it is possible that I wrote those two songs in the same day. 'Jolene' is a song about . . . you know, I've got my pride and I've got my strength. But when I write a song, I'm vulnerable at those moments. I leave my heart out on my sleeve. I've always said I have to leave my heart open in order to receive those kind of songs. I have to feel everything to be a real songwriter. And yes, a lot of my songs are kind of melancholy. Some of them are sad and some of them are pitiful. And I mean for them to be pitiful, those really sad songs like 'Little Sparrow' or 'Jeannie's Afraid of the Dark'. I have a big imagination and I become whoever I'm writing about. It's like starring in a movie – I am that character in that song. So, when I wrote it, I was Jolene.

'Jolene' has been recorded more than any other song that I have ever written. It has been recorded worldwide over 400 times in lots of different languages, by lots of different bands. The White Stripes did a wonderful job of it and many other people too. But nobody's ever had a really big hit record on it. I've always hoped somebody might do someday, someone like Beyoncé.

What I would say to my younger self is, 'All those dreams, they're going to come true. It's not going to be all fun and games, you're going to have to pay the price and do your sacrificing, but it's going to be worth it.' I'd have to tell her about 'I Will Always Love You'. To me, that is really a classic love song. I had a number one on it twice, once in '72, then I did it in the movie *Best Little Whorehouse in Texas* and had another number one. Which is the first time the same song has ever been number one with the same artist. And then Whitney did it and it was considered one of the greatest love songs of all time. Still to this day, I take a lot of pride in that. So, I'd tell my younger self, 'You're going to end up being very proud of your little old self one day so just buckle up and be ready for the ride.'

If I could have one last conversation with anybody, I'd probably talk to Elvis. And I'd probably talk about 'I Will Always Love You' and say, 'Hey, I bet you were as disappointed as I was about all that and I still dream about you singing that song.' Matter of fact, I even wrote a song called 'I Dreamed about Elvis Last Night' and I had an Elvis soundalike sing it with me and we actually sing 'I Will Always Love You' in it. And one day, I'm going to put that track out. So, I think that I'd talk to Elvis and just clear that up with him.

If I could live one moment of my life again, I think it's when I became an official member of the Grand Ole Opry (a weekly country music stage concert in Nashville), back in the late sixties. When I found out it was going to happen, I jumped up and down – I was tickled to bits. I had always wanted to be on the Grand Ole Opry. You would listen to it on the radio back home and hear all those singers and that was where you wanted to be if you were a country singer. I remember that night so well. I remember how proud I felt, thinking of my people listening back home. That memory stands out the most because that was the very first big moment. But I've had many, many special nights since then.

Jarvis Cocker

Musician and Radio Presenter

29 July 2020

I'd wanted to be in a group from being really, really young, probably from around eight. I used to watch The Monkees' TV show and The Beatles films on Boxing Day – they often had them on then – and that just filled my head with the idea of being in a group. I was a fairly shy kid, so the idea that you could have a band who were a gang and they all lived together was very exciting to me. And eventually, by 16, I'd managed to actually persuade some people to be in a band with me.

I recently came across an old school exercise book from when I was 16, so I know exactly what I was focusing on then. It has a plan for the band Pulp – or Arabicas Pulp, as we were called at first – and the first thing I talk about is Pulp fashion. It says, 'Most groups have a certain mode of dress, which is invariably emulated by their followers' – I'd obviously been reading a dictionary. 'The Pulp wardrobe shall consist of duffle coats, preferably blue or black, crew-neck jumpers from C&A' – not sure why, I don't think we had a sponsorship deal – 'garishly coloured T-shirts and sweatshirts, preferably of an abstract design, plain-coloured shirts, thin ties, drainpipe trousers, pointy boots, cheap white baseball boots, Oxfam jackets, preferably with buttonholes, silly socks, hair shortish, no sequins unless for silly purposes'. I don't know how I came up with these ideas, especially the duffle coats. I mean, they'd be too hot to wear on stage, wouldn't they? Maybe I was imagining we'd play a lot of outdoor festivals.

The next thing after fashion is a section called 'The Pulp Masterplan'. The first bit goes 'Category A: Music' – a bit formal for a teenager. Then: 'Being first and foremost a musical unit, it is fitting that Pulp's first conquest should be of the music business. The group shall work its way into the public eye by producing fairly conventional, yet slightly offbeat, pop songs. After gaining a well-known and commercially successful status, the group can then begin to subvert and restructure both the music business and music itself'. So that was the idea. I guess that must have been influenced by being brought up in the Punk years, the idea that music wasn't just a form of entertainment, that it could effect some kind of social change as well. And that's probably why, when we did make it, it went a bit sour. Because I realised we couldn't change the whole world. So, I got a bit of a downer then.

This manifesto idea is the classic thing of locking yourself away in your room and coming up with a way of how you're going to change the world, then when you're out in the world, not being able to actually say any words to anybody, especially girls. I was quite awkward. I think I got my first girlfriend when I was 16. I used to have a Saturday job in the fish market, and it sounds a bit silly, but it was like, our eyes met across a filleted cod. That was exciting to me because she wasn't a girl that went to my school. I did fancy girls at school, but it was just too nerve-wracking to talk to them.

John Peel was my first real musical compass. You read about Punk in the music papers, but you couldn't really get to hear it – not on local radio in Sheffield anyway. There was a Rock show on a commercial station and the DJ made a real point of saying, 'You won't hear any of that Punk music on here, that's not real music.' So, I remember one night when I was about 14, just twisting the dial and I randomly came across the *John Peel Show*. I think he was playing an Elvis Costello song. And once I discovered him, that was it, the gateway was open. It was a musical education. Then when I was 17, Pulp recorded a demo in a friend's house and I knew John Peel was doing a gig at Sheffield Polytechnic so I went along and followed him out to the car park like a stalker and gave him this cassette. A while later, when I was at school, my grandma took a phone call from his producer, John Walters. We were offered a Peel Session. Well, as you can imagine, it just blew my mind.

What I'd tell my younger self is, 'Just chill the fuck out. Calm down.' 'Cause at that age, you think it's just you who doesn't know how to do things. And, of course, what I've learned in the intervening years is that everybody's got that feeling of being an imposter or faking it. Nobody really knows how it all works. Once you realise that, you can start to relax and say, 'We're all just getting through it the best we can.' But I had this very strong feeling when I was young that I was just completely inept. Maybe it was the fact that my dad had left when I was seven, so I'd never really had a male role model, no one to talk to about relationships or any of that stuff from a male perspective. I was a bit all at sea. And I imagine I was some kind of neurotic nightmare to go out with.

Obviously, there are lots of absent fathers and broken homes – that's not a nice way to put it, but single parents. But what was unusual for me was that he just disappeared. He went to Australia and nothing was heard of him. There was no contact. It wasn't like, you know, 'Meet in McDonald's at the weekend,' it was, 'Your dad doesn't exist anymore.' My mum tried to talk about him a bit, but she was not disposed kindly towards him – he never gave her any money, she was just left high and dry, so he wasn't a popular topic of discussion. I was really curious because I had a vague memory of him and you know, he was my dad. And when we had an argument and she was really upset, my mum would occasionally say, 'You're just like your father.' Which was amazing to hear. I kind of grew up with males not getting a good press in our house, let's put it like that. I did meet my dad later, when I was in my mid-thirties, but it was just too late for me and maybe too late for him. It was awkward for both of us. There was nothing to really hold onto, so that was a bit of a letdown.

Both me and my sister (Saskia) took lessons from what happened with my dad when we had children of our own. We both actually ended up splitting up with our spouses but we definitely made sure that we were always in touch with our kids and were with them – we made a big thing about that.

If I wanted to impress the teenage me, given his Beatles obsession, I'd say, 'Listen, in 40 years' time, you'll sit next to Paul McCartney and you'll talk to him for an hour. And you'll get on with him. When Paul McCartney's last album (McCartney III) came out, I hosted a Q&A thing at the LIPA (Liverpool Institute for Performing Arts) Institute he's got up in Liverpool. I was really nervous about doing that because since I was a kid, I'd just thought of him as a mythical figure.

That's happened to me a few times. I got to work with Scott Walker. I interviewed Leonard Cohen, who'd always been such an influence on my songwriting. I don't agree with that thing that people say, 'Don't meet your heroes'. You've got to because then you realise they're just people like you.

When I was 16, I didn't move at all on stage, I was just petrified. Then, at a concert in a pub on 9 October 1980, my exercise book tells me, my guitar amp broke and I just had this big freak-out, basically just a tantrum. I just kind of rolled around on the floor. And people clapped at the end of it. I wrote in my diary, 'freak-out on my part, enjoyable'. And I realised performance isn't just about playing the right notes in the right order, it's actually about acting it out. And gradually over the years, I just kind of evolved. I enjoy being on stage, that's my little kingdom. You have total control, you've got everybody's attention because you're playing over really loud equipment and it's your chance to really do your thing.

Because we had that John Peel Session so early on, we thought, 'This is going to be a piece of piss.' And then it was just a gradual long period of disillusion, which unfortunately coincided with Margaret Thatcher. It was just like 'whoa!' As soon as the eighties really got going, it was like, 'This is really shit now.' Cities were falling apart. It just got to be not fun. There were loads of times I thought, 'What the fuck? I should have gone to university.' I thought I'd made a mistake, taken a wrong turn. Our album from that time, *Freaks*, kind of depresses me because it reminds me of a time when things were not working out. I was coming to the end of my first serious relationship. We had almost no money to make an album. It felt terrible to let that ambition, that I'd cherished from such a young age, die. But I really did think it was over and

I'd have to seek a new career in a new town, as David Bowie said. But I kept going and hoping and eventually, towards the end of the eighties, 'My Legendary Girlfriend' got a good review in the *NME* and we made a breakthrough.

After going through all the Britpop thing, and especially the Brit Awards thing (in 1996, Jarvis ran onstage and flashed his naked backside during a pompous Michael Jackson performance of 'Earth Song'; he was detained by the police but released without charge), people thought I was some kind of shock jock. And that's not at all what Pulp were about. That one moment propelled us into this other world. We had come out of the independent music scene, with roots in Punk from when I was really young. We came from an alternative place. And then we got shoved right slap bang into the middle of the mainstream. And we realised that it's very intense there and you're mixing in a world that doesn't share any of your values. That's what made me feel so uncomfortable.

There are two moments I've been most proud of on a stage. One was playing at Glastonbury in 1995 when everybody sang 'Common People'. That was kind of a crazy moment, when we realised that this fantasy had come true in some way. Then when Pulp got back together in 2011 and we played at Radio City Music Hall in New York, this incredible kind of thirties palace . . . it felt like those formative dreams I'd had as a kid had probably been premiered in a place like that. I think Bowie did a famous concert there where he was lowered onto the stage at the start and it was just amazing. It seemed like I was going back to the source of a lot of my early dreams. And for Pulp, it felt like we'd finally got back to where it all came from.

Lin-Manuel Miranda

Playwright, Composer, Lyricist and Actor

7 August 2019

I am 16 years old and I am obsessed with two things: movies and musicals. I am desperately trying to get myself into a position where I can make these things when I grow up. I am just starting to write my first musical, a 20-minute musical we put on at school, called *Nightmare in D Major*. I've already filmed a couple of two-hour-long movies with my friends with my camcorders. I took it all so much more seriously when I was 16 than I do now. Way more. I remember having a temper tantrum one day when I really wanted to film a scene for my Meatloaf musical (*Bat Out of Hell: The Musical*) and my friends didn't show up. I was like an angry big-wig Hollywood director, trashing my own room. Then I was like, 'Well, who have I hurt here except myself? I'm going to have to clear all this up now!'

My parents both loved musicals – we listened to a lot of musical cast albums: *Camelot*, *The Sound of Music* and my dad's favourite, *The Unsinkable Molly Brown*, with Debbie Reynolds. He was in love with Debbie Reynolds all his life. And I was always interested in Hip-Hop. I grew up just one neighbourhood away from where it all started in the South Bronx. Hip-Hop really was in a great place in the early nineties, with so many different genres. A Tribe Called Quest, Dr. Dre, Biggie... I'm grateful I grew up in that time, when Hip-Hop could be anything and tell so many different stories. Some of the best storytellers I know are people like Biggie. So, it was a no-brainer for me to bring Hip-Hop into theatre because of course it could tell stories as well as musicals could.

I was definitely an anxious kid. I don't think it's an accident that all the protagonists in my shows are grappling with legacy and how much time they have. I think that's hardwired into you as a New Yorker but it's also something I was painfully aware of at a very young age (his best friend in kindergarten drowned in a lake behind her home). I thought, 'We might only get one go around, what am I going to get done in that time?' Cut to me trashing my bedroom because my friends haven't shown up for my video.

I was a very sensitive child, very empathetic. I could watch something bad on the news and that would be me in the foetal position all day because I'd seen something horrible that happened halfway across the world. I think that stressed my parents out a lot, that I would extend my empathy so far that it would cripple me. I mean, it would ruin me for a day. But I also think my mum worked hard to protect that in me. She saw it early and the tools she gave me for dealing with that were . . . 'You want to be a writer, right? It's all grist to the mill. Remember what this feels like. One day, one of your characters will feel like this and you can pull this memory out.'

If you met the teenage Lin now, I think you'd find him pretty funny. He's not without his charms. But he's very self-serious. If you wanted to talk to him about film or theatre he'd talk your ear off about his theories. And probably he'd be a little insufferable with his intensity. Picture your most insufferable record store guy – that would be me at 16 – 'What you really have to underSTAND is . . .' But when you go through making something yourself, you realise how hard it is and you become a lot kinder. Even if you don't respond to something, you just go, 'Well, they tried.' Then you see *Sweeney Todd* or *West Side Story* and you really surrender to it, and then you're transported back to earth at the end of the show and you think, 'What the fuck just happened here? If only I could one day write something as gorgeous or as deep or as complex as that.'

I think the younger me would be very pleasantly and happily surprised that I found someone I love and want to spend my life with, and we'd have kids. Because you're terrified at that age. 'Well, I'm the most hideous, unlovable thing in the world. Will anyone ever kiss me?' and 'Will I ever get to first base?', as it's presented to boys. So that fear that I might never find someone, younger me would be shocked to hear he found someone who is actually just two corridors away in the same high school. But I'd tell him to relax. When I had my first serious girlfriend, around sophomore year, we stayed in the relationship too long because we thought, 'Well, this is it. No one else will ever love me. I've found the one person, so I'm going to hang on for dear life, all through college.' We were terrified to let go. I'd tell the young me, 'It's okay to feel lost and alone for a bit. There's going to be a lot of people in your life.'

I'd tell my younger self to go to therapy a lot sooner. I eventually went when I broke up with my first serious girlfriend. And there were so many giant fallacies that I was holding in my head. Things I thought that only I thought. That's the greatest thing about therapy. You finally confess this huge secret that only resides in your heart and they go, 'Yeah, that's perfectly normal. What else you got?' And that thing that felt so huge in your head looks so tiny once you've laid it on the table. I've gone for intensive periods twice in my life, both around big life changes.

The most nervous I've ever been in my life was in 2009 when I sang the opening number of *Hamilton* to Barack and Michelle Obama in the White House (as part of an evening of music and spoken word). I'd only ever sung that song before to my wife and the guy at the piano. They'd asked for a song from *In the Heights* (his first and at that point, only production). But they also said, 'Unless you have something about the American experience.' And I had 16 bars on Alexander Hamilton. The first vote of confidence I got on it was from Stan Leith, a legend in Hollywood who was producing that evening. I sent him the lyrics – I hadn't even finished the music – and he wrote back, 'Okay, you're closing.' I asked him beforehand, 'Is it cool to sing about a son of a whore?' And he was like, 'Yeah, that's cool.' But the arrogance of youth! I'm appalled at the swagger of the 28-year-old me, to try something untested in an arena like that. I'd only written 16 bars! Me at 39, I'd never do something that risky at the White House. But 28-year-old me, with just one show under my belt, nothing to lose – off I go!

I was nervous at the White House until the moment I started singing the song. If you watch the footage (on YouTube), you can see it. When I'm explaining the set-up to the room, you can see me stutter, and when I explain (why George Washington's Treasury Secretary Hamilton is 'the embodiment of Hip-Hop'), you see them laugh and me scream, 'You laugh but it's true!' My voice breaks. Yeah, the intro was shaky, but as soon as it started, I knew my 16 bars cold and you can see my confidence grow. Yeah, it turned out pretty good.

The biggest thing I've learned since I was a young man is patience. I started writing *In the Heights* when I was 19. We opened on Broadway when I was 28. I was substitute teaching at the time. I was desperate to get it on. As soon as I write a song, I want it in a theatre. I love the applause. And we were offered chances of spots in theatre festivals for *In the Heights*. If I'd been on my own, I'd have been more impatient. I'd have put it up at a festival and it would have come and gone. But my greatest stroke of luck in all of this was finding Tommy Kail as early as I did. Tommy said, 'We can make this better.' And gradually we met all these significant people and the show took a leap, then another. And when we got to Broadway, we were ready.

If I could go back to any time in my life it would be the week we performed the sixth-grade musical. My very ambitious music teacher who directed the sixth graders did a four-hour extravaganza of 20-minute versions of six musicals – that's a lethal dose of musical theatre. I had to play a farmer in *Oklahoma!*, Conrad Birdie in *Bye Bye Birdie*, Captain Hook, backup to Addaperle, in *The Wiz*, a son in *Fiddler* and Bernardo in *West Side Story*. It was hard work, but ah, the joy of all of school being about putting on a musical. And then all our parents and the entire school watching. The sixth-grade show is a big deal. When you're in fourth and fifth grade, you're all going, 'What's the sixth-grade play going to be when we're sixth graders?' So, your whole life is a build-up to it. And the fact that we got to do six of them! It was a wild dream for me. It was the most thrilling week of my life.

Richard Osman

Presenter, Producer, Comedian and Writer

12 August 2020

I don't look back on being 16 with any pleasure, it wasn't my finest hour. I didn't take school very seriously. I didn't have a love of learning, but I understood that you've got to get A-levels and then everyone will leave you alone. So, I did the minimum required. I was just growing into my height then – I was already around 6'4", pretty big. So, I was becoming super-awkward and self-conscious. Being very tall is very othering. I always say to my son, and this is the advice I would give to me if I went back now, 'There's only two ways people are going to see you the first moment you walk into a room. They're going to say, "There's a really tall guy," or they're going to say, "There's a really tall guy who looks really awkward about being tall." So, you have to find a way to love who you are.'

There are some aspects of the 16-year-old which haven't changed much at all. I was obsessed with sport, obsessed with lists. Completely obsessed with television. I thought I loved music but the older I get, especially when I'm around people who really love music, I'm not sure I really like it all that much. My brother (Mat Osman of Suede) was very cool, he was listening to Primal Scream, Jesus and Mary Chain, he truly loved music. I think I just loved reading about it in the music papers. Sport is my love, comedy is my love. And that hasn't changed. So in that sense I haven't matured as much as I might have done. Or perhaps I was just exceptionally mature then. But I don't think I was.

I find it hard when I'm looking back at my childhood to have my dad in it in any form (his father left the family home suddenly when Richard was nine years old). Maybe he's sort of there in my head, I suppose, but he's definitely not in my heart. I remember very clearly when I was nine, and my world was a fairly great place, and I walked into the front room – he was there, my mum was there, my grandmother was there, which was weird, though of course I realised later that was for moral support – and they just said, 'Look, your dad is in love with somebody else and he's leaving.' I just thought, 'Riiight, okay.' And he left and his entire side of the family never spoke to us again.

I'm really, really, really in touch with nine-year-old me, I can really access my brain then. I think it's because I sort of went off in a slightly different direction after my dad left, I went off course. Which is understandable because I had to find a way to fix the pain. And everyone else's pain, which of course I couldn't do. I focused entirely on protecting myself, being overly careful about everything. Listen, we all have trauma and I had a much lesser trauma than a lot of people have. It's our ability to deal with trauma, that's the important thing. And I dealt with it very badly. And this was 1979, when no one talked about such things. You got maybe a couple of days off school and then it was, 'Right, let's get on with things.' Looking back now, I think everything up to age nine, that is the real me. It took me many years, but eventually I found that again and that's how I feel now.

I love all sport. I don't play much 'cause my eyesight isn't great. But I love, love, love watching it. When I think of the companionship it has given me over the years, it's just extraordinary. I remember when I was 15, staying up till after midnight to watch the '85 snooker world final. Then two years ago, I went to do an interview for the BBC and Steve Davis set up the same famous black that he missed, in the final blast of the final frame, to lose that match. And he let me have a go at it. I got down to the shot and I dropped it in. I didn't do any kind of fist bump with him, I just said, 'Steve, you know, that wasn't so hard.' Oh, if I could talk to my 16-year-old self now and say, 'You're gonna put away that shot in front of Steve Davis,' my younger self would say, 'You know what, Richard? You have lived a good life, my friend.'

A few years ago, I went to see my dad. It was one of his brothers' 50th wedding anniversary so I thought, 'I'm going to take the kids, they should really meet the rest of this family.' But it was so cold. There were lots of them standing around, talking about what an extraordinary woman my paternal grandmother was. And they said to me, 'What did you make of her?' I said, 'Honestly, she literally never spoke to me after my dad left, never sent me a Christmas card.' So that's not really a conversation they're gonna join in on. Some families are just like that. The other side of my family fortunately, my mum's side, are completely the opposite. Loving and open. So, I did all right. I think if I was talking to my younger self, I would say, 'You know what? You're a Wright, not an Osman. You'll live like a Wright and you'll have the same sort of career and life and kindness and happiness as a Wright.' And that would be a massive relief to the younger me.

I ran a big TV company (as creative director for Endemol UK) for a long time (he was exec producer on *Deal or No Deal*, *8 Out of 10 Cats*, *Total Wipeout* and other big hits). It was very successful so I was very happy. Then someone said, 'Perhaps you could actually be on this one (*Pointless*).' And I was like, 'I mean, I suppose so. It doesn't appeal to me but you try everything once, right?' I strongly remember being in the make-up chair outside Studio 8 at the BBC and hearing a murmur of audience and thinking, 'This is absolutely mental.' These days, I don't particularly like an audience due to the shyness, I find that quite difficult. But I know how to do it. And I've never done a TV show when I haven't been me. That's so important to me, after all those years of not being me.

Writing a book is the most nervous I've been. That's the one thing that if I told the 16-year-old me, 'You will write a book,' he'd say, 'Yes, of course, that makes total sense.' Because 16-year-old me spent his entire time with a pen and a bit of paper, mainly writing jokes. Younger me would be incredibly proud of writing a book but the first thing he'd say is, 'How many copies have you sold?' I love the book so I want as many people as possible to read it. I think people will enjoy it. I think it will make people happier. It's very dear to me and it comes from my heart.

There's a common idea of me being posh. I'm not posh, I'm just Southern. I grew up in a single-parent, low-income house – very, very happily, by the way, there's absolutely nothing wrong in that. The Cambridge University thing doesn't help. People think you have to be rich to go there. But it was A-levels results that got me there, that's all.

I think if I could go back to any point in my life – and it feels also like the place I'm in now – it would be just before my dad called me into that room and said he was leaving. Because I think I was a deeply happy child. I've spent a lot, a LOT of time, trying to trace my way back there since. And I feel like I have now. So, I would go back to growing up in the 1970s, in that little house, sitting down with a little bit of paper and a pen and writing jokes. I was nine years old and I've never been happier.

The Big Issue was launched in 1991 by John Bird and Gordon Roddick. The aim was clear and simple: to offer the poorest in society – the homeless, the marginalised, the dispossessed, those on the streets or at risk of homelessness – an opportunity to earn a legitimate income. They would work to build their own futures. It was a hand up, not a hand out.

The means to this future was a righteous, dogged, challenging, campaigning, compassionate magazine that would be produced by The Big Issue team then bought for half the cover price by those in need and sold on the street. The difference between the two sums was the income people made.

This identity and means of working has remained hardwired at our core for almost 30 years. The magazine, produced by a team of professional journalists, retains an outsider agenda. We give those ignored or without platform in the regular media a voice. We don't speak FOR those left behind, we invite them to speak for themselves. Then we challenge those in power to do something about it.

Content is key. It is funny, not fusty, pointed, informed, able to access the biggest names and have them reveal things they simply won't to others. They, like readers, trust *The Big Issue*.

The act of selling on the street was revolutionary. Growing out from London, over 210 million copies of *The Big Issue* have been sold in Britain. It has enabled vendors to earn over £115million, money that otherwise would have come from illegal means or handouts. Some 92,000 men and women have worked their way out of poverty selling *The Big Issue*.

It has inspired a global network. There are now over 100 similar street magazines across the world, including Big Issues in Australia, Japan, South Korea, Taiwan and South Africa. *The Big Issue* in Britain now also has a successful social investment arm called Big Issue Invest as well as a shop.

The Big Issue challenges that which is not right. We stand up for what is.

Paul McNamee
UK Editor, The Big Issue